Finding Your Deep Soul

Guidance for

Authentic Living

Through

Shamanic Practices

Paul Francis

Volume 3 in the

"Therapeutic Shamanism" Series.

DEDICATION

As always, to my partner Cat, for groking me and supporting me.
With massive love and gratitude.

To all the Felines and to Eagle Owl.

To Ma'hwen and Lief.

To my Tribe.

TABLE OF CONTENTS

ACKNOWLEDGEMENTS

Again, my thanks to all my wonderful students for your faith in me and for allowing me to develop my ideas. Writing these books would not have been possible without you.

Especially big thanks to Dan Taffler, Joanne Lacey, Kate Adetunji, Lisa Hardi, Maia Weaver, Nathalie Nahai and Sarah Garton for helping with suggestions, proofreading and editing.

My thanks again to Michael Kusz, for the marvellous original "Three Ravens" artwork on the cover. He also makes great sculptures - www.graculus.co.uk

My thanks to Eanna Roberts for professional proofreading. Highly recommended - www.penmanshipediting.com

Most importantly, again, my thanks to my partner Cat for making these books possible; for being a sounding-board whilst I form ideas; for being patient, encouraging, supportive and for having faith in me and my writing. And to Pan, for being such a beautiful and steady presence at my side in the hours, days, weeks and months spent in thinking and writing; for being my companion, familiar, daemon, muse and delight, and my anchor to the more-than-human world.

INTRODUCTION

What This Book Is About

"Finding Your Deeper Soul" is the third volume in the Therapeutic Shamanism series. As such, this book does assume some basic experience and ability in doing shamanic journeys and some knowledge of the different shamanic realms, (the lower-world, middle-world and upper-world). Since that information was covered in the previous books, if you are entirely new to shamanic journeying, then I do suggest at least reading volume one, *"The Shamanic Journey: A Practical Guide to Therapeutic Shamanism"* before reading this book.

Whilst the first book in the series is an introduction to Therapeutic Shamanism and a step-by-step guide to doing shamanic journeys, the second book, *"Rewilding Your Soul: Discovering Your Soul's Deep Roots Through Shamanic Practices"*, begins to explore the shamanic lower-world in detail. This third volume continues this exploration. Taken together, the second and third books form an in-depth description of what the shamanic lower-world is (and what it is not), and an encyclopaedic guide to lower-world practices. To the best of my knowledge, these are the first books to cover the lower-world in such detail, and the first time that the various lower-world practices have been brought together in one place. As such, the knowledge in these two books provides a thorough and in-depth understanding of the lower-world and its vital place in Therapeutic Shamanic practice. Furthermore, the practical exercises in these books help turn this knowledge into direct and personal experience of the lower-world that is deeply rooted and grounded.

There is more to understanding shamanism than simply expanding our repertoire of shamanic practices, though. To really understand what shamanism is means changing how we both experience and think about the world around us. This involves waking up to the reality of the society we live in today. It means de-programming ourselves from the unhealthy stories and ideas of this society, and replacing them with healthier, more shamanic ones. Doing this changes our understanding of the more-than-human world and helps bring us into a right-relationship with the Animal, Plant and Stone People.

In turn, this changes our understanding of what it is to be Human, for as we shall see, from a shamanic perspective, we have lost our ancient, healthy stories about being Human, and replaced them with damaged and unhealthy ones. So, as well as continuing to explore the shamanic lower-world, this book is about reclaiming the healthy stories. Doing this will include exploring something that is profound, precious and life changing, for in our modern time, in cutting off from nature, Mother Earth, and the shamanic lower-world, we lost connection with the truest, deepest and wisest part of us, the thing that we are meant to model and base our lives around. We lost connection with our Human Soul.

This book guides you through the shamanic practices that help you find your Soul. Not the middle-world thing that most people think their soul is, but your true, deep, lower-world Soul. When you find it, you can begin to get to know it, befriend it, fall in love with it and gradually become it, let it mould and re-shape you into what you are meant to be, and take your healthy and rightful place on the Earth.

Ancient Wisdom for Future Solutions

In reclaiming this ancient shamanic knowledge and practices, though, this is not a book about returning to an age long-gone, something that is, in any case, impossible. For we have gone too far to return. We have changed ourselves and the world around us in ways that are so profound as to require radical new solutions. This book is about finding the healthy templates on which these new solutions can be based.

Shamanism holds the key to doing this. This is because, by any sane measure of a society, the principles that hunter-gatherer societies were based upon created the most successful human culture we have ever seen. Contrary to popular misconceptions (the lies of our dominant and dominating colonialist society), for hundreds of thousands of years, as hunter-gatherers, we lived in a way that was ecologically sustainable, largely peaceful, and enjoyed good mental and physical health. What we need to do now is reclaim these healthy principles and use them as templates to find radical new solutions to the challenges we now face.

In this book, we will continue the process of peeling away the layers of our domestication and, in doing so, reveal more of the sacred and ancient knowledge that lies buried beneath. Part of doing this will involve waking up from the spell of the modern world and, quite literally, coming back to our senses. It will involve digging deep down in the shamanic lower-world, to meet our Human Ancestral Tribe and ask them to teach us how best to live on this Earth.

It is not just for the sake of ourselves that we need to find our Soul. As Bill Plotkin reminds us in his wonderful book *"Soulcraft"*:

> *"Your soul is both of you and of the world. The world cannot be full until you become fully yourself. Your soul corresponds to a niche, a distinctive place in nature, like a vibrant space of shimmering potential waiting to be discovered, claimed,...occupied. Your soul is in and of the world, like a whirlpool in a river, a wave in the ocean, or a branch of flame in a fire."*

How to Read this Book

You can approach reading this book in a variety of ways. It is not like a novel that must be read from cover-to-cover in order for it to make sense. Although the chapters do have a sequence, and you can certainly benefit from reading it in order and all the way through, it is also fine to treat this as a reference book and dip in and out, or skip chapters altogether if you like.

How the Book is Laid Out

In **Chapter One**, we begin the journey to find our Soul by exploring, from a shamanic perspective, what it is to be a human being. We look at shedding some of the ideas of the dominant culture that we live in, ideas that keep us apart from the natural world, and we explore how to reconnect with the healing gifts from the other-than-human beings around us.

In **Chapter Two**, we take the techniques and insights from Chapter One and apply them to working with the Animal, Plant and Stone People. Taking each in turn, we look at what we share in common, and the ways in which we differ. We also look at the many different ways in which Animals, Plants and Stones can be worked with in journeys, and how to learn about their specific healing gifts and teachings.

Having looked at the other Peoples, in **Chapter Three**, we explore how this helps us to understand, from a shamanic point of view, what it is to be Human. We explore how we have strayed a long way from what we are meant to be, and what we can do about this. This includes taking an unflinching look at the dominant culture we live in, seeing it for what it really is, and exploring how we can begin to heal from the damage it has done to us.

In **Chapter Four** we look at the practices that help us find and meet our authentic, true and deep Soul. This is the heart (and Soul) of this book. Doing this can, slowly but surely, change us in ways that are profound and deeply healing. To build up to doing this, we first explore what a real Adult human being looks like, how few and far between they are in today's society, and how we can begin to step into our own true Adulthood.

In **Chapter Five**, we look at how to meet our healthy, loving, and healing lower-world Tribe. We examine what truly healthy human groups look like and how different they are to what most of us experience these days. The chapter also includes exercises to deepen your relationship with your lower-world Tribe and the people in it, some of whom may go on to become your greatest shamanic Teachers and Guides.

In **Chapter Six,** we explore the qualities of true Elders and their role and importance to Tribes, how rare real Elders are in the world these days, and how we badly need them. We look at how Elders provide a template for how to grow old in a way that is authentic and of service, and how to cultivate these qualities in our own lives as we grow older.

In **Chapter Seven**, we turn to working with Mother Earth herself. We look at how our personal experience and history of "mother" colours and shapes our experience of the Mother archetype, and why our collective relationship with Mother Earth is so deeply wounded these days. We then look at various shamanic practices to begin healing these wounds.

In **Chapter Eight,** we look at other practices that help us consolidate our relationship with our lower-world Soul. We finish our journey by looking at what the "meaning" or "purpose" of life is, and how knowing our Soul can answer the great question, "How shall I live my life?".

Chapter Eight is followed by short sections about the next books in this series, training courses and workshops, finding a shamanic practitioner, a bibliography, and a glossary of terminology.

Very Important – Mental Health and Shamanic Work

Doing a shamanic journey involves being able to, *at will*, temporarily leave this physical, ordinary reality; go into a trance state; travel in the shamanic realms (the "shamanic journey"); *and then come back to this ordinary reality*. The ability to come back *at will* is essential. The ability to do so is one of the differences between shamanism and psychosis, for being stuck in the shamanic realms and unable to return would indeed be a form of psychosis. Doing shamanic journeys for yourself can often be of great help and benefit if you suffer with things like depression, anxiety, addictions, procrastination, low self-esteem etc., *if* you still have a reasonably good grip on this ordinary reality, too.

But, if you are prone to schizophrenic episodes, paranoid fantasies, moderate to severe dissociation, unstable and unmanaged manic-depression, or anything else that makes it hard to keep a grip on ordinary, everyday reality, then journeying for yourself could make matters worse. Shamanism may still be of great help, done with an experienced shamanic practitioner journeying for you. Ideally, this would be a shamanic practitioner with some understanding and awareness of mental health issues and the appropriateness (or not) of shamanic work (you can find suggestions about finding a Therapeutic Shamanic practitioner towards the end of this book). Given the times in which we now live, being firmly rooted and anchored in this ordinary reality is an essential prerequisite for being able to journey safely for oneself. You need to be able to move between the worlds *at will*, and not become lost in the shamanic realms. If you are not well-rooted and grounded here, in ordinary day-to-day reality, then *that* is what you need to be working on, *before* doing any shamanic journeying for yourself.

Please do take the guidance here seriously. It is important for your own mental wellbeing.

Physical Illness and Shamanic Healing

Also, the exercises in these books are not intended to replace seeking out appropriate help and treatment with physical conditions. Shamanism can indeed sometimes be of great help with physical ailments and can almost always safely be used alongside medical treatments. But shamans are generally pragmatists and fully understand the need for medical treatments. Some things need shamanic medicine, some things need allopathic medicine, and some things need acupuncture, chiropractic, Bowen and other things.

Help with Terminology

When reading the book, if at any point you come across a word or phrase whose meaning you are not sure of, then there is a "Glossary of Shamanic Terms" at the end of this book that you may find helpful.

How to Approach the Exercises

Throughout the book, I will be suggesting lots of exercises. You may want to work through the book slowly, stopping to do each exercise before reading further. Or you may want to read through the whole book first, and then come back to it and work through the exercises. Or a bit of both. Obviously, however you choose to do it is entirely up to you, but to get the most out of this book you really *do* need to do the exercises and not just read them!

On Pronouns and Capitals

We do not, of course, have a gender-neutral pronoun for the third person singular in the English language. However, to keep writing the phrase "he or she" all the time feels clumsy. So, as in the previous books, I have decided to use "they" as a gender-neutral, third person singular pronoun, for want of a better solution.

Also, if you have not already read the first books in the series, you may be wondering about my use of seemingly random capital letters at times. I use capitals and lower-case to differentiate between which of the shamanic realms things belong to. So, I use lower-case to denote middle-world things, and capitals to mark lower-world and upper-world things. For example, "panther" (middle-world) as opposed to "Panther" (lower-world), or "temple" (middle-world) as opposed to "Temple" (upper-world).

Now, let's begin our journey…

CHAPTER ONE

Remembering Our Place in the World

Our Lost Human Soul

A quick reminder:

- The shamanic upper-world is the realm of Father Sky. It is the realm that most people think of as "spiritual", and the home of spiritual teachers, angels, upper-world Gods and Goddesses, and so on. It is a place of wisdom, love and healing.

- The middle-world is everyday reality, both seen and unseen. It is the physical world, and the energies and entities that inhabit everyday reality ("atmospheres" in rooms and buildings, ghosts, spirits of places, and so on). Although it *can* be a place of healing and safety, the middle-world is by no means always so, and can be a place of harm. It is the everyday world we inhabit.

- The shamanic lower-world is the realm of Mother Earth and of wildness. It is the home of the Souls of Animals, Plants and Stones, and the place where we can receive their medicine, gifts and teachings. As such, like the upper-world, it is a place of safety, love and healing.

The lower-world is also the home of Human. Not human, as in our middle-world self, but Human as in our Human Soul. Unlike our middle-world self, which is constructed from the stories we tell ourselves about who we are, our Soul is our truest self, our true nature. It is a part of us that is wild and free, free from the domestication and baggage of the human middle-world. It is part of nature; part of Human, of Animal, a sibling to Plant and Stone, and a child of Mother Earth. It is both who we truly are deep down, and the blueprint for what we are meant to grow into and become in the world. Our middle-world self is meant to be a vehicle through which this authentic part of us can be expressed. All too often, though, it is not. For the sad truth is that most people these days have no knowledge of their lower-world Soul, and so, no knowledge of who they were meant to be.

From a shamanic point of view, living a deep and *fully* authentic life means living in a way that is shaped by, and an expression of, our lower-world Soul. It is how our hunter-gatherer, animist ancestors lived their lives for tens of thousands of years (in fact, for most of human history, for we are 200,000 years-old as a species, and spent around 190,000 of those years living as hunter-gatherers). Through complex initiation rites and ceremonies, and by modelling what it is to be a fully authentic adult human being, our ancestors' ancient animist cultures were designed to help children grow and blossom into what they were meant to be.

It is not how we live our lives today, though. The Neolithic era, which started around 11,000 BC, when we began to abandon hunter-gathering and take up agriculture instead, saw the beginning of our domestication. This accelerates with The Fall, which began around 4,000 BC with the emergence of city-based cultures, kingdoms, nations and empires. Since then, modern-day societies are generally not designed to help us find our Soul, or to grow and blossom into it. Instead, they are designed to turn us into something else—a diminished and domesticated thing, cut off from both nature at large and from our own true and personal nature. Some people are lucky enough to find their authentic Soul (and the purpose of this book is to help you make this discovery), but the reality is that most people live and die never knowing who they really are, the magnificent being that Mother Earth wanted them to be.

This is utterly tragic. The key to turning this around, though, is, in some ways, simple. It lies in rediscovering the wisdom of our animist and shamanic ancestors, and then finding ways to apply this to the times in which we now live.

All beings have a template, like a seed within them—a blueprint of what they could become—and all beings, deep down, have a drive to grow into this. The founder of counselling, Carl Rogers, called this drive the "actualising tendency". It is the drive each being has to reach their full potential, to be the best they can be. For animals and plants (stones are different, as we shall see later), whether a being succeeds in growing into what it is meant to be depends, not only on this drive, but upon the environment around it. Think of a plant. Given the right environmental conditions, a healthy seed will grow into a healthy plant and thrive. However, if it has not enough light, or is missing essential nutrients, it will grow into a sickly plant, trying to be the best it can be, given the environment in which it lives.

As an environment to grow in, whilst not *everything* in modern human culture is bad, there is much that makes us sickly. And yet, like a plant trying to grow as well as we can in a poor environment, we still try our best.

Sometimes it is easy to look around at modern humans, and despair. There is so much cruelty, bigotry, indifference and misery in our world. And yet, looked at in another way, it is amazing how well we are doing given the society in which we live. For amidst all that is wrong with the ways in which we are living, we still strive to look after each other and the world around us. We know much of what we are doing is wrong, that we have somehow lost our way, and yet our actualising tendency keeps us striving to be what we are meant to be. For our true nature is not to be aggressive, selfish and greedy (despite the lies fed to us by the dominant culture). Our true nature is to be cooperative and compassionate, and to live respectfully with each other and with the other beings who we share this beautiful world with. Like a sickly plant given healthier conditions in which to grow, we will thrive if we change the society we live in.

From Despair to Empowerment

I know the idea of changing society can feel overwhelming, or even hopeless. I completely understand that. However, if we sink into that despair and let it overwhelm us, then it is indeed hopeless, both for society as a whole and our own individual life, our *one and precious life*. That is no way to live. Instead, as the great eco-therapist and environmental activist Joanna Macy shows us in her life-affirming (and even, life-saving) book *"Active Hope: How to Face the Mess We're in without Going Crazy"*, we can turn this despair around. To do this, we first need to stand and face things as they really are, and feel our feelings about the situation we find ourselves in. We need to be the shamans, the people in the tribe who are prepared to see the things that most other people prefer to avoid.

When we do this, we can transform the energy of despair into empowerment, and into an implacable motivation and determination to act. What does this involve? In terms of following a shamanic path, it means working on your inner world, and on your relationship with the outer world. In terms of the latter, this means not withdrawing from the world, but taking your place in it and actively being of service.

Wanting to withdraw from the pain of the world is understandable. Such is the pain of the modern world that, as our dominant culture arose, alongside it (indeed, *intrinsic* to it) emerged the idea that withdrawing from the world is "spiritual", a more "highly evolved" thing to do.

Literally nobody in shamanic cultures did this, however. Telling yourself that the world does not matter and withdrawing from it to concentrate on your own "spiritual" development is, from a shamanic point of view, not spiritual at all. Rather than being spiritual, it is a psychologically unhealthy avoidance strategy, and a narcissistic avoidance of responsibility. For, in shamanism, the *world itself* is spiritual and sacred, and it was the role of the shaman to honour that, and to help the rest of the tribe to do so, too. Withdrawing from the world is simply not the way of the shaman.

From Despair to Empowerment

Joanna Macy calls her method of turning despair into empowerment "The Work That Reconnects". This is a very shamanic name, because, from a shamanic perspective, a healthy human is an *inter-connected* human. The sickness in modern society, the madness that has led to the social and environmental crisis we now face, is caused by our being *disconnected* (and that includes Earth-rejecting disconnection dressed up as "spirituality"). This is precisely why there is no tradition in shamanism of renouncing the world. Instead, shamanism is a path of spirituality through being of service in, and to, the world. Rather than withdrawing from it, the role of the shaman is to be in the world and to hold the sacred balance between the beings that live within it; to *actively* be the intermediary and advocate. In short, it is a path of embodied spiritual activism.

The Shaman and the Outer World

There are many ways of being an activist in the world, of course, and not all of them are obviously spiritual—they can include everything from life-style choices to campaigning and volunteering. Whether obviously "spiritual" or not, all these things matter. It is a nonsense to ask for help from animals and plants in journeys, and then ignore their plight in this physical world and do nothing to help.

Shamanism and animism can bring a lot to activism, for they have something unique they can offer. Think of it this way. If someone has a life-threatening bacterial infection, then antibiotics may be needed to save their life. However, if the infection is a symptom of a deeper problem, then antibiotics will only serve as an emergency measure to stabilise the situation until the underlying cause can be addressed. The general practitioner may prescribe antibiotics, but the patient may then need to be referred to a specialist, to diagnose and treat the deeper issue.

In terms of the social and environmental crisis we are in now, things like campaigning, legislating, lifestyle changes, protecting habitats and so on, are vital emergency measures. However, when it comes to diagnosing the underlying issues and causes, and coming up with a treatment plan, who do we consult? Who is the specialist we can refer to?

As the author and cultural critic Daniel Quinn points out in his writing, the answer is obvious really. We need to look to societies that were healthy and learn from them; to the people who knew how to live in right-relationship, both with each other, and with the natural world around them. In short, hunter-gatherer people. In those cultures, we can find knowledge and wisdom that we desperately need today.

Specifically, we can find this knowledge and wisdom in the shamanism practiced by our hunter-gatherer ancestors. More than anyone else in a tribe, it was the role of the shaman to be the wisdom keeper; to be the person who could keep the tribe on the right path and in right-relationship and advise and guide the tribe when it had strayed from what was healthy. It really is no coincidence that when we killed off all our shamans, we lost our way.

In rediscovering shamanism and making it relevant for the times in which we now live, if, as shamanic practitioners, we only think of shamanism in terms of journeying and doing shamanic healing, then we are practicing a stunted, diminished and domesticated version of it. We are missing out on the most important thing that shamanism can contribute, and the very thing that our society most needs: the knowledge of how to live in right-relationship. That is why discovering this deep and ancient knowledge, the maps and templates that show us how to live, is a key focus of these books.

The Shaman and the Inner World

Shamanically, helping to heal society is not just important in human terms, for we are in the Anthropocene (or Holocene) extinction event. Mass extinction events are a natural phenomenon, of course, as there have been five previous ones in the history of life on earth. The sixth, however, the one that we are in right now, is not natural. It is *human*-created. I went into this in detail in the last book, so just a quick reminder here. As a result of human activity, extinction rates across species are anywhere between 1,000 and 10,000 times higher than the natural rate. Between 10,000 and 100,000 species are becoming extinct each year because of human activity. That is somewhere between 30 to 300 unique species that we humans are wiping out *every single day*.

I sometimes come across some "spiritual" people, life-avoiding spiritually-bypassed people, who say that none of this matters because the world is just an illusion. Other times, people say the Anthropocene extinction does not matter because life will always survive and recover and evolve again, as it always has done (as if that makes it alright for us to carry on wiping out hundreds of species a day). Such views are the *antithesis* of shamanism. From a shamanic point of view, they are profoundly wrong, and symptomatic of our wounded relationship with Mother Earth.

My main Power Animal is Black Panther. It is entirely possible that within my lifetime there will be no panthers left in the wild. Something similar is probably true of your Power Animal, for most animal species on the planet are in severe decline. And if it is not true of your own Power Animal, then it will nevertheless be true of most of the other Animal species you will encounter in your shamanic journeying.

This is just *wrong*.

To put this right, we need to change the way in which we are living. However, outer work alone, such as political and social activism and making changes in our personal lifestyles, will not be enough to do this, *even if* we add in what shamanism can teach us about living in right-relationship. For you cannot have a healthy society if it is full of sick people. A healthy society is made up of healthy individuals. The outer work needs to go hand-in-hand with inner work. This means each of us taking personal responsibility, not just for how we are in the outer world, but for healing our inner world too.

For I would say that the way we are destroying other species is not only a sickness, but a *spiritual* sickness, a sickness of the soul. It shows not only that our relationship with nature is profoundly wrong, but that there is something deeply wrong with our relationship with our lower-world Soul, too.

In terms of healing our inner world, there are many different approaches we can take, of course. Psychotherapy in all its many and varied forms, meditation practices, acupuncture, EFT, and a host of other things can all be useful and play their part. Some can help with things that traditional shamanic healing cannot. As a therapist, I know this to be especially true of psychotherapy, which is why I teach that shamanism and psychotherapy have much they can learn from each other (something I began exploring in the first two books, and will continue to explore in more depth later, for it is at the heart of the Therapeutic Shamanism approach). Each healing modality has its strengths and its limitations. In terms of healing our personal wounds, though, there is something shamanism offers that is almost entirely unique. For shamanism shows us how to find and connect to the lower-world and, in doing so, most importantly, how to find our lower-world Soul.

How we Lost our Souls

When we turned away from shamanism, we adopted hierarchical thinking. We fell into the sickness of thinking that "up is good and down is bad". Consequently, we turned away from the lower-world, seeing it as lesser, tainted and corrupt, and even as being evil. We did this in order to justify abandoning hunter-gathering, with its respectful and non-hierarchical relationship with nature, and replacing it with totalitarian agriculture, which is based on dominating, plundering and exploiting the natural world.

There is another reason we turned away from shamanism and the lower-world, though, a reason that is central to what this book is about. The lower-world is the home of our Soul. This part of us is a wild, untamed, free and undomesticated being. As our dominant culture emerged (and while emerging), it needed to subjugate, tame and domesticate not just animals and plants but, most importantly, humans.

Modern-day culture does not just dominate and exploit other animals, plants and mineral resources. What makes all of that possible is the subjugation and exploitation of the majority of human beings. Our wild and free lower-world Soul is a threat to this. It was not a threat to our animist ancestors, though, because they were not trying to dominate nature. Quite the reverse. They lived lives that were in balance with nature—sustainable and respectful. This was because their lives were shaped by their lower-world Souls and modelled on healthy stories of what it is to be Human.

Our modern-day, domesticated, middle-world versions of being human is a long way from what our authentic Human Soul truly is. Indeed, our domesticated and distorted ideas of human are what keep us apart from our true nature. If we are to find our true Soul, and who we are really meant to be, then we need to begin deprogramming ourselves from the stories of the dominant culture that we live in.

One of the stories we need to free ourselves from is the idea that our true nature is bad. That, without the benefits of "civilisation", we would be savage, selfish and violent brutes. This is simply nonsense. We know from anthropology that hunter-gatherer people were not at all like that. In fact, the history of our dealings with tribal cultures show that it is us, the so-called "civilised" people, who are the most brutal, selfish and savage.

The message our Fallen culture gives us about our inner nature is that it cannot be trusted; that we must not trust our instincts, but instead submit to the will of "God" or suchlike (though in reality, this often means submitting to the will of a hierarchical, patriarchal protection racket).

Take the concept of original sin, for example. This doctrine not only says that our nature is to be sinful, but goes so far as to say that everyone is *born* sinful. New-born babies are sinful! They are born with a built-in urge to do bad things and to disobey God (of course, what this really means is that we are born without an in-built urge to obey the priests, which is true, but they say it as if it is a bad thing). Original sin is seen as the normal, spiritual and psychological condition of human beings. Rather than blaming our psychopathic culture (enabled by organised religions) for causing things like poverty, mass exploitation, inequality, genocide, totalitarian warfare, wholescale environmental destruction and the Anthropocene extinction, instead it is all the fault of original sin—a story which conveniently ignores the fact that prior to Christianity and other organised-religions, we lived in a sustainable and largely peaceful and cooperative way for *tens of thousands of years.*

Another wonky idea that you will often hear is that without religion we would have no ethics: the moral and ethical values of organised religions are what keep us in check and, without them, the world would be a terrible place. Again, even a brief examination of the time before the Fall (the rise of what we absurdly call "civilisation", beginning about 6,000 years ago with the emergence of the first city-state cultures, and the first organised religions) shows this to be unfounded. Pre-Fallen cultures had no notion of us being in a state of sin and having to submit to the will of some external God.

If we look even further back, to the time before we started to adopt agriculture (so, before 11,000 BC), we find that our hunter-gatherer ancestors had no notion of not being able to trust their inner nature. We know this from studying hunter-gatherer animist cultures that survived until recent times. No matter what part of the world they were from, and how different their cultures were to each other, one thing all these animist cultures had in common was that there was no concept of human beings being inherently bad. There was no concept of not being able to trust one's inner instincts and nature. Quite the opposite, in fact: they no more distrusted their inner nature, their Soul, than wolves distrust their ability to be wolves, or oak trees distrust their ability to be oak trees. This created cultures that were, in many ways, *far* more moral and ethical than today, because, as we shall see, the truth about our inner nature is much more beautiful and positive than we have been led to believe.

We Can Trust Our Nature

Just to be clear, I am not saying that *everything* about organised religion is bad. In some ways, religions have kept the flame of spirituality alive through what have been some very dark times over the last few thousand years. What I am saying, though, is that, like the dominant culture as a whole, they are a mixed bag, and that some aspects of their teachings can be distinctly at odds with the shamanic and animist way of seeing the world. Plus, it is not just in organised religion that you see this idea that our inner nature is not to be trusted. It runs through our dominant culture at all levels.

For example, traditional psychoanalysis tells us that our psyche has three main parts—the id, the ego, and the super-ego. According to Freud, the id is a primitive and instinctual part of the mind that contains sexual and aggressive drives and hidden memories. The super-ego operates as a moral conscience. These morals initially come from outside of us and need to be imposed upon us and then internalised (forming the super-ego), to rein in the otherwise monstrous id. Eventually, the ego emerges to mediate between the desires of the id and the demands of the super-ego.

At first, this may seem true. Children need to learn morals and the values of the society in which they are being raised, and need boundaries placed on their behaviour and impulses. Without that, children would grow up to be narcissistic, selfish and greedy. To many people, that seems patently obvious. The thing is that while there is a *degree* of truth to this, both anthropology and humanistic psychotherapy show that it is far less true than it might first appear.

Let's consider anthropology first. Most cross-cultural studies of animist tribes show that the children were usually raised in a much more laid-back way than we raise our children. As we shall see later in the book, physical punishment of children was almost unheard of in animist tribes. Children's needs were usually quickly and attentively responded to (babies were never left to cry). Far from making the children spoilt brats who grew up to be selfish adults, the children raised in this way became well-adjusted and cooperative adults (and often much better members of their society than most adults are these days).

Next, let's consider humanistic psychotherapy, which emerged some fifty years or so after the birth of psychoanalysis. One of its founders was Carl Rogers. Unlike Freud, who believed that people were inherently selfish until socialised, Rogers believed that people were inherently good. In contrast to traditional psychoanalysis, where the therapist analyses, direct and interprets the client (essentially, a power-over model), Rogers helped people listen to their own inner-knowing. He developed what became known as the Person-Centred approach. This puts the client in charge of the sessions, with the therapist acting as a compassionate and attentive facilitator, listening without judgement and with empathy. The result is that the client learns to go inwards and trust their own feelings, intuition and inner knowing, and discover their own solutions.

When Person-Centred therapy began to take off, one of the criticisms levelled at it was that it was self-indulgent, and that it would make people selfish. Given that the dominant culture believes it is our inner nature to be selfish and sinful (and therefore should not be trusted), this is not surprising, of course. Again though, the criticism proved not to be true. Rogers and others did extensive research on the changes in people who went through Person-Centred counselling. What happened is that, far from becoming more selfish, in being treated with compassion and respect, and in learning to trust their inner-nature, people became more compassionate, less judgemental, more co-operative and empathic. They became more ethical and moral, not from an externally-imposed set of rules, but because being ethical and moral was innate to them.

The point I am trying to make here is this: the central theme of this book is how to meet your true nature, your lower-world Soul, and begin the process of letting that part of you guide and shape your life. Despite what you have been told, that part of you is good. It is kind and compassionate, empathic, considerate, and naturally ethical. It is also brave, authentic, wild, untamed, undomesticated and free. And these are *good* things.

It Was Not Always Like This

The ironic thing about the notion of original sin is that there is some truth in the story of how it came about, but it is the opposite of what people usually think. We are told that original sin started with Adam and Eve defying God and being cast out of the garden of Eden. The truth is that you find stories in many places other than the bible. Most Fallen cultures have a version of a story where once we were living in a golden age. In these stories, we are living in a paradise of sorts, with bountiful food. In many versions, it is a time when we can talk to the other animals and plants, and they talk to us. In all these stories, we are living how we should be, in harmony with the world around us, feeling good about ourselves. We are living how we are meant to live, just as every other creature does the same. What these stories describe is a memory of our hunter-gatherer lifestyle, for these stories all date from around the time we turned our back on that lifestyle and began to adopt agriculture. They are stories about how we lost our way and now feel bad about ourselves and the way in which we are living. They are stories of disconnection and loss, and about feeling sick in our souls. If there is any "sin", it is in having turned our backs on living in right-relationship. It is about living in a way that, deep down, our Souls know is wrong.

The truth is that *it is the dominant culture* and the organisations within it—including the organised religions, but also political ideologies, notions of patriotism, empires and so on—that have brought us genocide, totalitarian warfare, inequality, mass exploitation, wholescale environmental destruction and the Anthropocene extinction. In terms of human history, these are all recent things. They are a recent sickness, and not something innate to being human. Because of this, the answer to the problems we face is not more shaming, more messages about sin and the handing over of power to priests and politicians. The answer is to begin listening to our Souls again, and shamanism can teach us how to do this.

Takers and Leavers

In my previous books, I discussed how Daniel Quinn calls the dominant culture the "Taker" culture. It is the society that arose at the beginning of the Neolithic age, with our adoption of totalitarian agriculture and our own domestication. Quinn names it the *Taker society* because it takes everything and leaves nothing. This contrasts with the Leaver culture that preceded it—the animist and shamanic hunter-gatherer people who took only as much as they needed and left the rest. This is the culture the Takers destroyed and replaced.

If we are to *really* understand shamanism, then as well as unlearning a lot of Taker thinking, we need to replace that thinking with a healthier way of seeing the world. This healthier thinking includes understanding, from a shamanic point-of-view, what it is to be a human being. Shamanically, a human is an interconnected being, part of a larger family of beings. From a shamanic perspective, then, it is only possible to make sense of what it is to be human by understanding the other beings around us and what our relationship to them should be. In other words, to understand ourselves as humans, we need to understand what it is to be animal, plant and stone, too. In this chapter, we are going to look how to begin reconnecting to the Stone, Plant, Standing and Animal People, and explore how to work with them shamanically.

The Myth of Human Supremacy

In order to do this, we need to free ourselves from a spell that most of us are under, one that is enormously powerful and damaging. Yet, like many cunning spells, it is one we do not realise we are captive to. It is the idea that, as humans, we are superior. It is the *myth* of human supremacy.

This myth is one of the central stories of Taker society. It is at the heart of our modern-day separation from nature. It is *so* fundamental to Taker thinking that we cannot truly heal our disconnection if we continue buying into it. Freeing ourselves from the spell of this story involves clearly identifying and naming it, seeing it for what it really is, dismantling it and instead, *thinking like an animist*. Until we do that, then we cannot be in a healthy, animist, right-relationship with the other beings we share this world with.

The author Derrick Jensen has been called the philosopher-poet of the environmental movement. In his powerful, compelling and paradigm-shifting book, *"The Myth of Human Supremacy"*, like a shaman waking their apprentices, Jensen demolishes this notion that humans are superior to other beings; the story that, because we are the "highest" life form, we have the right to use the earth and all other life forms to our benefit.

Taker society people are human supremacists. They (we) have been indoctrinated into believing that humans are the only species that are self-aware and sentient to any great degree, intelligent, able to make tools and capable of complex communication.

In his book, Jensen exposes the logical fallacy behind this myth. By defining what we regard as intelligence in essentially human terms, then of course when we do experiments to measure intelligence in other beings, humans will emerge with the most favourable results. If we only recognise self-awareness in its specifically human variety, then obviously we will appear to be the most self-aware species. If we define communication in essentially human terms, then inevitably we will find that we are the best species when it comes to communication.

This is "garbage in, garbage out". It is blinkered and nonsensical because the tests are biased.

Jensen also makes the point that much of what we humans do is not at all intelligent or rational. There is nothing intelligent about what we are doing to the environment on which we depend. You could argue (and Jensen does), that what we are doing marks our species out not as intelligent, but as uniquely stupid and irrational.

Jensen devotes much of his book to exploring the wealth of scientific evidence that is now emerging, which shows the intelligence and sentience of other beings, and the degrees to which they cooperate and communicate, in ways that are just *different* to us but not *inferior* to us. Another marvellous book that does this is Peter Wohlleben's *"The Hidden Life of Trees: What They Feel, How They Communicate"*. In the book, Wohllenben examines ground-breaking scientific research that show how tree parents live together with their children, communicate with them, support them as they grow, share nutrients with those who are sick or struggling, and even warn each other of impending dangers. Similarly, the primatologist and ethologist Frans de Waal, in his book *"Are We Smart Enough to Know How Smart Animals Are?"*, explores how we have grossly underestimated the scope and the depth of animal intelligence. He points out that people usually assume that intelligence is a kind of "cognitive ladder", from lower to higher, with human intelligence at the top. Instead, de Wall says that a more accurate way of thinking of intelligence is to see it more like a bush, with cognition taking different forms on different branches.

We are Surrounded by Wise Beings

Our animist ancestors knew this already, of course. With the arrival of the Taker culture, though, such knowledge became suppressed. The historian Yuval Noah Harari, in his best-selling book *"Sapiens: A Brief History of Humankin"*, says that hunter-gatherers saw animals and plants as equal in status to humans.

Exercise 1: Non-Hierarchical Thinking

Try this thought experiment.

Take a moment to feel how it would be to see all animals and plants as having equal status to humans. See if you can really think like that.

Everything equal. Not just animals like eagles and lynx, but beetles and ants, too. Not just great old trees, but all plants. And not just animals and plants either, but the land, too. The rivers and rocks, mountains and lakes, seas and clouds.

What would that *feel* like, to live with that awareness?

How would that awareness change the food that you eat, the products that you use, the job that you do?

The truth is that most of us Taker society humans find thinking in these terms to be a hard thing to do. This is because we are so deeply indoctrinated into the myth that life is a hierarchy and that we are superior and at the top.

In *"Sapiens"*, Harari points out that for hunter-gatherers, just because humans hunted sheep, it did not make sheep inferior to humans, in the same way that tigers hunting humans did not make humans inferior to tigers. Instead, all beings were part of an interactive community which, Harari says, "communicated with one another directly and negotiated the rules governing their shared habitat". This is the very essence of animism as a way of being. By contrast, when farming emerged, farmers saw themselves as *owning* plants and animals. Other beings became possessions and things to be manipulated and used. To justify this, other beings were "downgraded" in terms of their sentience, or even denied sentience altogether. And as "property" other beings had no rights. Human desires and needs overruled everything and were supreme. Some species even became the "enemy"; things to be hunted or rooted out—the wolves who might eat "our" sheep, the plants who might try and grow in "our" wheat fields. And so, we began to wage war on the Earth.

Exercise 2: Being a Hunter-Gatherer Animist

Another thought experiment.

Take a moment to try and imagine what it would have been like to be one of your animist hunter-gatherer ancestors. See if you can temporarily "shapeshift" into them, by imagining the following:

As a hunter-gatherer animist, you have almost no possessions other than a few clothes and some bone or stone tools (and even those you do not think of in terms of ownership, so much as working with them).

You do not own the land but are a part of the land.

You live surrounded by other alive and conscious beings—the more-than-human world.

Everything around you is sentient and has its own wisdom. Everything has its place and is part of a whole.

There is no separation, only inter-connection and communication.

You are part of a whole, a larger family of beings.

Animists know that not only is everything around us sentient, but everything around us is a teacher. Wolf can teach us about healthy relationships; about how to keep the balance between independence and being with others; how to balance honouring our own needs with honouring the needs of others. It can teach about loyalty without losing personal integrity, about faithfulness, about being at ease both in a group and when alone, about working as a team when needed, and about stamina and determination. That is a lot of wisdom.

Deer can teach us about gentleness and sensitivity, kindness, peacefulness and empathy. It can teach us how to live together as a community. It can teach us how to be alert to danger and be able to move silently and disappear when needed.

Raven can help us wake up to the other realms. It can help us to notice and understand the signs, signals, synchronicities and significance of the things around us. It can help us See through the illusion of surface appearances and make the darkness conscious. It can teach us about death and rebirth.

Heron can teach us about patience and maintaining balance and focus. It can show us the value of moving with slow, deliberate actions, about persisting when others would give up, and about knowing the right time to act.

It is not just animals. Every plant also has teaching. Even the things that modern-day humans mistakenly regard as non-living things are in fact alive and great teachers: the freedom and power of the wind, the persistence of water and its ability to change, the joyfulness and cleansing of a waterfall, the stillness, silence and patience of stone.

Showing Some Humility

In fact, for hunter-gatherers, the other Peoples were the beings that showed us how to live and how to be Human. For every animal, plant and stone just knows what it is meant to be. Once they have learnt from their mother, bears just get on with being bears. Turtles hatch just knowing how to be turtles. Oak trees just get on with being oak trees, and rivers get on with being rivers. The exception to this is humans. We have a unique ability to not know who we are or how we are meant to be; a unique ability to become lost. As such, our animist ancestors knew that we need almost constant guidance from the wise non-human beings around us.

Part of the reason we get so lost is that, in terms of the Peoples, we are children. The myth of human supremacy tells us that we are the wisest and most intelligent species on the planet, whereas the truth is entirely the opposite. Hunter-gatherers say that the oldest and wisest of the Peoples by far are the Stone People. Next oldest and wisest (but still vastly younger than the Stone People) are the Plant People. Then come the Animal People, and *then* us Human People.

This is not about hierarchy, but about family. It means that we are the children. We are the youngest and *least* wise of the Peoples, and like children, we need regular guidance and have a lot to learn. Knowing this, our animist ancestors lived with humility, respect and gratitude—one of the many things we need to remember and learn from them.

How the Healing Gifts came about

Most tribal cultures have stories about how particular animals and plants, and even things like waterfalls or lakes, acquired their teaching and healing gifts. In the first book in this series, I recounted a story that is found in different versions throughout many shamanic cultures.

In the story, the Animal People were furious with us humans because of our lack of respect for Mother Earth. So, they formed a plan. They decided that they would get together and wipe us Humans out. Off they went to get ready. The Stone People and the Plant People heard about the Animal Peoples' plan, and so they called a great council of all the Peoples. At the council, the Stone and Plant People told the Animal People that they understood their anger but that what they planned to do was forbidden, for it was not in accordance with Great Spirit. It was also against the wishes of Mother Earth herself, as Humans are her children. The Stone People and the Plant People explained that, as children, Human People need help and teaching. So, at the council, every type of Plant, Animal and Stone agreed to take on a healing gift and teaching, and to give this freely to any human who asked for it.

Another similar story goes like this:

A long time ago, there was a young man who was a great hunter. Before hunting, he always asked the spirits for their permission and blessing. When hunting, he always did so with great respect and gratitude. He always killed as quickly and kindly as possible. He always took time to do a ceremony and give thanks to the spirit of the animal he had killed. He always used all parts of the animal's body, and never wasted anything. When he was not hunting, if he had food to spare then he would leave a share for the other animals. When gathering plants, he would always give thanks and gratitude to them, and never take more than needed. He lived on the Earth with respect. He honoured the water that he drank, the air that he breathed, the fire that warmed him and the ground that he walked on. Of all the humans, he was the favourite of the animals, the plants, and the stones, for they saw in him the beauty of what a human can be.

One day, he was attacked by another human and left for dead. When his animal, plant and stone friends saw this, they were stricken with grief, and resolved to help him. They each took on a healing gift, derived from their own true natures, and worked together to use these gifts to create a powerful medicine to heal him.

This medicine is so powerful that it exists to this day, and in memory of this human who lived in such a right way, and to honour him, the animals, plants and stones still offer their gifts to those humans in need.

I do love these stories. They are, of course, not *literally* true; they are mythos, not logos. But like all good mythos, they convey important ideas and knowledge. What they tell us is that everything around us, *every* animal, from a lion through to something seemingly as insignificant as a worm, *every* plant, and *every* stone (not just gemstones) have a healing gift and things to teach us.

Just think about that for a moment. When in nature, we are surrounded by *thousands* of things with healing gifts, knowledge and wisdom, and all given freely to us. All we have to do is ask. That is immense. We are *surrounded* by powerful medicines and profound wisdom, and yet as modern humans we generally go about our business entirely unaware of this. We have cut ourselves off from all the love, healing and other help that is literally just there for the asking. This is what Taker society does, and it is quite insane!

These stories can help us with the process of reconnecting. They remind us that we are *not* alone. Far from it. Rather, we are the children of a larger family that cares about us; a family that wants to help us, teach us, and guide us. Our animist and shamanic ancestors understood this. It was, and is, the role of the shaman or shamanic practitioner to go to the Plants, Animals and Stones and ask them for their healing gifts and teaching, in order to help heal the humans in a tribe, and to help us live as humans in harmony with nature.

The Medicine Bundle

How do we discover what healing and teaching each particular animal, plant or stone has, though? In indigenous cultures, a shaman would teach their apprentice about the healing properties of each individual being and the best way of working with them. The apprentice's shamanic guides would directly teach them this knowledge. Through this process, a student would acquire a body of knowledge that is sometimes referred to as a shaman's "Medicine Bundle" (or, "Medicine Bag").

Sometimes this would be a physical bag or bundle. In it would be things like stones or crystals, animal bones or teeth, seashells, beaks, claws, feathers, bags of herbs, tree bark or mosses. Unlike herbalists, however, who would use plants and other things to make medicinal teas, poultices, ointments and so on, the things in the shaman's medicine bag would be used in a different way. Shamanic healing is largely done in the shamanic realms. When physical objects are used, their purpose is usually to help the shaman connect to that object's healing power in *shamanic* reality. For example, holding a bone or other part of an animal would help the shaman tune into that animal in the shamanic realms. Likewise, a shaman may use smoke to smudge someone in physical reality, but what they are doing is acting out something that is happening at a much more profound level in shamanic reality. Similarly, after doing a shamanic healing for a "patient", if a particular stone featured prominently in the journey, the patient may then be given a physical piece of the relevant stone, with the idea of strengthening the patient's connection to what happened in the shamanic healing.

Because of the shaman's Medicine Bundle, I have sometimes seen shamanism described as the "path of paraphernalia". In Fallen shamanic cultures, shamans may accrue a great many ritual objects, not just bones and suchlike, but also magical clothing, fans, masks, amulets, knives, bowls, bells, whistles, combs and more. By contrast, some shamans may not use any physical objects other than the drum or rattle. Such shamans still have a Medicine Bundle, in that they have an extensive knowledge of the healing properties of particular plants, animals, and stones, but they do not bother with having physical representations of these things, and instead just work with them directly in shamanic reality.

How many physical objects a shaman has tends to reflect how much their work involves ritual and ceremony; the more ritual and ceremonial their work, the more physical objects they will have. Personally, I do very little ceremonial-style work. I use very few physical objects aside from my drum, my rattles, and some cleansing and protective sprays and feathers. Other practitioners I know of do mostly ritual and ceremonial work, and use a number of physical objects in doing so. There are even practitioners who are insistent that the physical tools in shamanism are essential to doing the work, and that without them the work is impossible. The reality is that there are practitioners who work effectively *without* using physical tools or representations. In the end, whether you want physical representations of things is a matter of personal preference and what works for you. What is important is not the physical representation itself, but knowing about its teaching and healing properties, and how to work with it shamanically—for it is this *knowledge* that the Medicine Bundle really refers to. In other words, it is the lower-world Medicine Bundle that is important and what is needed, not a middle-world medicine bundle. So, how to gather our Medicine Bundle is what we are going to explore next.

Lost Knowledge and Lost Connections

In a hunter-gatherer animist tribe, a shaman would be taught the healing gifts of the more-than-human Peoples as part of their apprenticeship and, in that way, they would acquire their Medicine Bundle. In learning shamanism in modern times, we also need to acquire our own Medicine Bundle, but in doing so it is important to remember that we are living in different times to our animist ancestors, and be mindful of the consequences. For one thing, unless you are living in a place that still has an authentic shamanic tradition that has survived right up till the present day, then most of the knowledge that would have been taught to you has been lost. Where I live in Wales, for example, the last hunter-gatherers were wiped out around 6,000 years ago. The shamanic knowledge of how to work with the animals, plants and stones in this area was lost long ago. Some *aspects* of it did survive, in folklore, or was kept alive and passed on in secret by hedge witches, herbalists and suchlike. But no specifically *shamanic* knowledge survived into the present day.

Journey, then Research

For those of us living in a broken shamanic lineage, and in the absence of shamanic teachers, the knowledge that makes up our medicine bundle (as with many other aspects of shamanism) is something that mostly we will have to discover for ourselves. How then do we go about discovering the healing properties of particular Animals, Plants and Stones?

One way, of course, is through shamanic journeying. Sometimes the healing gift of a particular Animal, Plant or Stone is obvious from what happens in a journey. For example, in journeying, we may learn that Ivy is useful for binding recently returned soul parts back into the body. Or that Wren can teach us that we do not have to be big to find our voice. Given the symbolic nature of shamanic work, though, often things in a journey will have to be "unpacked" afterwards, in order to really understand them and learn about them. As I discussed in the last couple of books, if you encounter an Animal, Plant or Stone in a journey that you are not familiar with, then after the journey you can research it. In this way, you can build up your Medicine Bundle. Doing this can have the added advantage of building up your confidence, both in your abilities, and in the validity of shamanic journeys. For nothing quite shuts up the rational and sceptical left-hemisphere of our brains than looking up something that appeared in a journey, something that you did not know anything about beforehand, and finding that its healing medicine is exactly what was needed.

As well as helping build your confidence, and helping gather your Medicine Bundle, researching things after journeys can be important for another reason, too. Often something will appear in your journey because you need to work with it for your own personal healing. This is especially true if the journey was for you (i.e. not one that you did for someone else). Sometimes, though, things appear in journeys not because you need whatever it is for your own personal healing, but because your guides are trying to teach you something new as part of your shamanic development (remember, you are an apprentice to them). In effect, they are saying, "You need to learn about this thing now." The reason I am saying this is it might not be obvious this is what they are trying to do. This is because they are trying to communicate not with words, but by showing you things.

In everyday life, we are so used to paying attention to words in communication, that we may miss the other ways that communication happens in journeys. Because of this, it is important to learn to pay attention to what your Guides *do* in journeys, and to try and understand its significance and the deeper layers of meaning and teaching. For, as I explored in the last book, if you are journeying deeply in the lower-world, then your journeys will be mostly beyond words, for human language is largely a middle-world thing.

Think about looking up the healing uses of a particular crystal, for example. The description of its medicine may run into several pages of writing—hundreds of words in all. If your guides were to describe the healing properties of a crystal to you in that level of detail, using words to do so, then that is channelling, not lower-world journeying. Lower-world shamanic journeys are more metaphorical, and full of symbolism and imagery rather than words. Channelling has its uses. However, it is much more of a middle-world practice (as is anything that is that wordy), and like most middle-world things, it means there is usually some erroneous thinking mixed in with whatever useful information there may be. There is usually a certain amount of discernment needed in order to "sort the wheat from the chaff". This does not mean there is anything *wrong* with channelling. It is just that, like all middle-world work, it needs to be approached differently to lower and upper-world work, and with a more critical eye (and it is, in any case, not what we are about here, as this is a book about *lower-world* work).

Remember, in shamanic journeying we are trying to go *beyond* language, into a deeper reality that can only be experienced through sensations, imagery and metaphor. My lower-world Guides rarely speak to me in journeys, and if they do, it is usually only single words or simple sentences. They may say things like "Pay close attention", "Do this", "Be this", and so on. Consequently, if they want me to work with something for my own healing, or to learn about a particular thing to develop my shamanic work, then all they can do is try and bring it to my attention. It is then up to me to *pay* attention, realise what they mean, and explore further.

The Teachings of Dandelion

One day, in a shamanic journey, I found myself sitting in front of

Dandelion. I sensed my Guides wanting me to become Dandelion, so, I shapeshifted into it. In doing so, the first thing that I experienced was how long and deep its taproot is. It is much longer than the above ground part of the plant. In some ways this surprised me, because although I knew Dandelions had long taproots, the bit of them that had previously always drawn my attention had been their flowers and seed-heads. But in becoming Dandelion, the "heart" of the plant seemed to be the taproot and its deeply grounded connection to the Earth. I then became aware of the bright yellow flowers and the way they face straight upwards towards the Sun. I sensed how the flowers are tiny microcosm of the Sun. I sensed how the plant gathers the warm, cheerful Solar energy, and draws it down through itself and releases it into the Earth. I then became both Dandelion and Human at the same time, each superimposed on each other. I sensed Dandelion's healing medicine. I sensed its strong downward and outward motion and the way it releases any blockages of heat and tension as it moves down through the body. I felt my body relax. I tried to pay attention to exactly where this was happening most. In doing so, I sensed my shoulders relax and let go. I sensed my jaw relax. I sensed the downward motion through the organs in my abdomen, my stomach, liver and gallbladder, intestines, and my kidneys, too—everything relaxing and releasing downwards. I also sensed its strong grounding energy and the way that connects us to Mother Earth. I became aware of its strong ability to pull energy, sustenance and strength up from the Earth. As well as the strong connection to the Earth, I sensed its strong connection to Father Sky. I felt my body fill with vitality and light. I sensed its cheerfulness, its sunny disposition and ease, and a sense of irrepressible optimism and the ability to thrive in any environment. I felt full of life.

In researching Dandelion after the journey, I found as a flower essence it is for people who do not "flow" in life but who push too hard and become rigid and tense. They develop tight muscles, particularly around the shoulders and the jaw, liver problems and fluid retention. Dandelion's medicine can help release the mental and emotional issues that create this tension, helping people to relax and let go. It helps people to stop pushing and thrusting their way through life and, instead, to accept nurture and support. It is also helpful for such people when they (almost inevitably) burn out and become exhausted. In such cases, it restores energy and enthusiasm. It brings a sunny disposition, optimism, and ease with oneself and with life. As a herb, it is indeed good for liver and gall-bladder problems, indigestion, intestinal gas and constipation. It is a diuretic and so is good for releasing fluid retention (hence its French name, *pissenlit*—piss the bed). It is rich in nutrients, including trace minerals, antioxidants and soluble fibre. In volume 2 of the fantastic books *"The Energetics of Western Herbs"* by Peter Holmes, Dandelion is described as a herb that dredges and stimulates the liver and kidneys, clears heat, including "liver fire" and "liver energy stagnation", and promotes bile flow and bowel movement. It restores connective tissue and is helpful in chronic degenerative conditions, lack of appetite and lethargy. As a physical plant, Dandelion can thrive in a huge variety of environments, being happy in rich, loose soil, but growing just as easily in compacted or rocky ground, and even in sand dunes and dry soils. It can grow anywhere from sea level to altitudes of up to 10,500 feet. It can grow in lawns and cracks between paving stones. It is irrepressible. Its deep roots loosen up compacted and stagnant soil, drawing in earthworms who gradually help transform the soil into something more alive and vibrant. Its bright yellow flowers open with the morning sun and close in the evening, showing its strong solar affinity.

All this confirmed what I had sensed in the journey, of course. As I have said, when this happens it is great for building confidence, and for most people this is an important part of the process of learning shamanism. More than that, though, as a teacher I know that having *both* the experience of a journey *together with* the knowledge from re-searching consolidates and deepens learning. This is because the em-bodied and visceral right-brain experiences what happens in jour-neys, and the more factual information of left-brain researches—each has their place and together, they complement and reinforce one another.

Research, then Journey

Central to shamanic practice is bringing both hemispheres of the brain into balance, so that neither has dominance. This then allows the shaman to move between these two ways of being, and ways of knowing, at will. Journeys themselves are about right-brain, largely non-verbal knowledge. But whilst an enormous amount of the Med-icine Bundle knowledge can be gained through journeying, in a sha-manic culture, not everything that an apprentice shaman would learn would be gained this way. The physical, flesh-and-blood shamans in the tribe would also teach the apprentice, using words. This verbal, left-brained knowledge has an essential place and importance. So, in the absence of a physical teacher to tell us the left-brained knowledge, when something appears in a journey, your Guides are essentially saying, "You need to Google this."

Instead of researching things after journeys, though, what if you were to do extensive research on something *before* journeying? There are some compelling reasons for doing things this way round. How-ever, when teaching people who are new to shamanism, if I suggest doing research on something before journeying on it, then students often ask, "But how will I know that what happens in the journey is real, and that I am not just making it up because of my preconcep-tions?" To which, the answer is, "You won't." Looking things up af-ter journeys and discovering how pertinent they are does indeed build confidence when you are new to journeying. After a while, though, you learn to trust the process. You do not need proof any-more and can relax into the journeys and trust what comes up. This does not in any way mean that it becomes mundane or unsurprising. Even if you have been journeying for years, it can still be astonishing when you look things up after a journey and discover just how spot-on they are. *However*, lovely though those confirmatory experiences are, after a while, as you learn to trust the process, they are no longer *necessary*.

Another objection to journeying with prior knowledge that I some-times hear from shamanic practitioners is that it is "cheating", or that it is not "trusting your guides". Whilst it can be impressive when someone journeys without prior knowledge and then comes up with things that are accurate and relevant, *that is not the point of journeying!* It is not about being impressive—that would be to reduce journey-ing down to a cheap parlour trick. Rather, the point is to be as helpful as possible, and if prior information helps with that, then so be it.

Another objection people sometimes have about journeying with prior knowledge is that they just "want to experience what is there". In answer to this, it is important to remember that shamanic jour-neys are not an objective experience, but something that is co-cre-ated between us and Spirit. What we are experiencing is real, yet to make sense of it we need to give it some form and imagery that we can comprehend. Journeys are never objectively true. They are my-thos, not logos. In that sense, journeys are like great paintings, music or poems that attempt to describe and convey something that is mys-terious, intangible and ineffable. They are an *interpretation* of what we experienced. As such, like a painting, they are an interpretation that is inevitably shaped and informed by our own frameworks, beliefs, experiences and (this is the important point) by our prior knowledge and preconceptions.

If I suggested that you journey to find out about streaked tenrecs, unless you already know what they are (they are a real, physical thing), then you would be extremely unlikely to come up with anything accurate when you journeyed. In fact, given how bizarre looking they are, I very much doubt you would even get an accurate image of them. If, however, I gave you a picture of a streaked tenrec to look at *before* you journeyed, then your journey would be much more likely to be accurate and revealing.

This is because we usually need *something* to help us to initially tune in. Some prior knowledge, however little. Even shamanic practitioners, who do journeys for people without much background information, usually want to know the person's sex and age at the very least. Often, they want a photograph too, or a lock of hair, or one of the person's belongings, to help them tune in.

Lessons from Bird

The fact is that although you can discover things in journeys that you did not already know about, when it comes to journeying, prior knowledge really helps. This is in part because our modern-day disconnection from nature affects and limits what we experience in journeys.

Take birds, for example. Except for large birds that have lost their ability to fly (ostriches, emus and alike), all birds have light-weight, mostly hollow bones. This is probably not surprising, and wouldn't be very remarkable if you experienced it in a journey. What *is* remarkable, however, is that birds breathe in more air than their lungs can hold. This is possible because a birds' bones are connected to their lungs. When birds breathe in, only 25% of the fresh air they inhale goes directly into the lungs. The other 75% bypasses the lungs and flows into a posterior air-sac, which connects to the bird's bones and fills them with air. When the bird exhales, the used air flows out of its lungs, and the fresh air stored in its bones flows back through the air-sac and into its lungs. In this way, birds' lungs receive a constant supply of fresh air during both inhalation and exhalation. It also means that they are full of fresh air, all the time.

Any ornithologist would know this, of course. However, most people do not. I have taught that fact to hundreds of shamanic students over the years, and everybody is always amazed. And yet, we live our lives surrounded by birds. Even our cities have pigeons and starlings. As a society, we eat vast quantities of chicken, and yet most people do not know that quite remarkable fact about the bird they are eating (nor probably anything much else about chickens).

Exercise 3: Being Bird

Take a moment to sit and close your eyes.

Imagine your bones are hollow and light.

When you breathe in, as well as your lungs filling with air, feel the air filling your hollow bones, so that your whole skeleton fills with air.

When you breathe out, feel the air leave your lungs, and the air from your bones flow into your lungs, filling them with fresh air again.

Keep experiencing this with each inbreath and outbreath.

Experience yourself as constantly full of fresh air.

Experience the inside of your bones themselves being constantly swept clean by this cycle of air.

Experience what it is like to be a creature that is at home in the air.

When you are ready, experience having no teeth. Instead, you have a solid beak.

You can bite, but you cannot chew.

Instead of chewing, you have a gizzard; a part of your digestive tract that is full of small stones that you have eaten, so that you can use the stones to grind up the food that you bite and swallow. Experience what that would be like.

Experience having wings instead of arms.

You have no hands, so unlike being a human. The only way you can manipulate physical objects is with your beak and feet (claws).

Imagine being covered in feathers.

Imagine being able to fly, with your hollow bones, full of air.

It is possible in a journey that you could have experienced that birds' bones are hollow and connected to their lungs, and then researched it after the journey and been blown away to discover that it was true. However, I have taught an awful lot of people over the years and, to the best of my knowledge, none of my students have done that. This is not surprising, for the idea of bones breathing is just out of our experience. We think of bones as being solid, dense, almost stone-like things. Unless we know otherwise, we are likely to bring our own, human experience of bones to our journeys.

There are all sorts of things about birds that most people do not already know. For instance, although there are some exceptions, the norm across bird species is co-parenting. That is, both parents will be actively involved in raising young. It is probably true that most people do know this, but most people do not understand the significance of it. This is because (again, with some exceptions), shared parenting is the norm for us humans, and so it might not seem that remarkable. However, we are mammals, and across mammalian species as a whole, shared parenting is not the norm. In the other vertebrate groups—reptiles, amphibians, and fish—whilst some examples of co-parenting exist, it is extremely rare. With bird species, though, it is very much the norm, and this makes shared parenting a stand-out characteristic of Bird. It makes co-operation in parenting part of Bird's medicine. In particular, it also makes healthy fathering part of Bird's medicine.

In the majority of human tribal cultures, good fathering was very much the norm. Although men and women often had different roles, both were actively and intensively involved in raising the children in a tribe. We know that men in tribal cultures spent *far* more time actively engaged with the children than most modern-day fathers. Since we turned our backs on tribal living (and on living according to our healthy Human nature), we have lost this balance. In recent times, we have seen a breakdown of nuclear families, with the result that around one in five men now lose touch with their children altogether. In addition, of those fathers who do maintain contact, the majority spend little if any quality time with their children. Given these statistics, it may look like the crisis in healthy fatherhood is a relatively recent thing. However, the crisis is much older. It is as old as patriarchy itself. It goes back to the Fall and is a characteristic of Taker society.

Before going any further, I just want to clarify that I am in no way saying that all healthy parenting must involve both a man and a woman. I completely know and understand that single parents can raise children healthily, as can same sex couples. What I am saying is that when men are involved in raising children, their parenting must be healthy and not toxic. The unhealthy fathering that has been endemic to the last few thousand years of human history is both a symptom of Taker culture, and one of its maintaining causes.

This is beginning to change, though. Earlier in the book I mentioned the psychologist and author Steve Taylor. Taylor says that in the last few hundred years, in what he calls the "post-Fallen" era, we have seen signs that we are beginning to recover our sanity and regain our empathy. He points out that in this era we have seen things like the abolition of slavery, universal suffrage for both men and women, the move towards equal rights for women, child protection laws, the right to free education, access to healthcare for all, care of the elderly, the more humane treatment of prisoners, animal rights legislation and more humane farming practices, increasing tolerance of people's gender choices and sexual orientation, awareness about environmental issues, conservation and rewilding movements, and this includes changing attitudes towards fatherhood. Whilst many fathers do indeed lose contact with their children, of those that do not, more are choosing to spend more time with their children; are choosing to play an active part in their children's lives and finding ways to be good fathers, even if they did not have good fathers themselves. It has become fairly normal for fathers-to-be to attend pre-natal classes with the mothers-to-be, mother-and-toddler groups are changing their names to parent-and-toddler groups, as growing numbers of fathers attend them. And whilst the uptake is still slow, growing numbers of men are choosing to take paternity leave (indeed, even the fact that paternity leave exists these days is a sign of how things are changing).

In helping with this, remember that our wise animist ancestors knew that it was human nature to stray and lose our way in terms of living in right-relationship. This is why they turned to the other Peoples—Animal, Plant and Stone—for teaching and healing. Bird's teaching about healthy fatherhood is a part of its medicine and healing gift. This is something our ancestors would have known and understood about Bird (along with its other healing gifts). It is also a medicine that is so appropriate and needed for the times in which we live now. However, I doubt that it is something you would have thought of.

Indeed, in my many years of teaching, I know this is not something most people know about Bird—not until they are taught and have had it pointed out to them.

Prior Knowledge Helps us Grok

The word "grok" is from a science-fiction novel, "*Stranger in a Strange Land*", written by Robert Heinlein in 1961. In the story, "grok" is a Martian word (as in the planet Mars) there is no exact equivalent of in English. A professor and literary critic, Istvan Csicsery-Ronay Jr., said that Heinlein's book is an extended definition of the word. Hard though it is to define (translate?!) precisely, "grok" means things like: "to understand profoundly, with intuition and empathy", "to communicate empathically with something", to understand something "so thoroughly that you merge with it and it merges with you", and that "the observer becomes a part of the observed". Sometime after the novel was published, the word entered common usage, ending up in English dictionaries. So, in Chapter One, we will explore the process of shamanic groking and see how it allows us to understand things deeply from the inside-out, by moving beyond our human consciousness (and, even animal consciousness) and "becoming" something quite different, thereby understanding its knowledge and its powerful medicine.

Knowing that birds have hollow bones they can fill with air, no teeth, and gravel in their gizzards can help us to tune into being Bird, shapeshifting into it and groking it from the inside out. It helps take us out of being Human, beyond our limited human knowledge and preconceptions, and into being Bird. Knowing that Bird models good co-operative parenting helps us grok Bird further, and knowing that Bird also teaches us about the healthy role men can play in raising children, helps further still.

Basically, knowledge helps us grok.

It is the same process in psychotherapy. As a psychotherapist, over the weeks, months and even years I listen to a client, the more I begin to know what they will be feeling about something, or what thoughts will be going on in their head. So, too, they begin to anticipate what I am about to say to them, or what I am thinking. A kind of shorthand develops between us. In shamanic terms, we grok each other. This does not happen just in therapy, of course. It can happen with anyone you know really well, from the "inside out", and not just with other humans, either. It can happen between you and your cat, dog, horse and so on. In most cases, the more you know about someone or something, the more you understand, and the more you grok them.

In any case, the idea that groking in shamanic journeys without prior knowledge is somehow a "purer" way of journeying is a modern conceit. It is not found in hunter-gatherer cultures. Our shamanic ancestors did not go into journeys about Animal with no prior knowledge. Given that they butchered their own meat, made tools and instruments from bird bones, and so on, they would have known the inside of birds intimately. They probably would not have known about the 25%-75% ratio of air flow between a bird's lungs and its bones, as they would have had no way of measuring those percentages (and would not have cared about numerical ratios in any case). But they would absolutely have known about the posterior air sack and the connection between birds' lungs and their bones. They would also have known that birds' bones were hollow and full of air. This, and their gift of flight, makes them one of the primary links between the physical world and the upper-world. Knowing that, shamans understood birds as messengers of the gods.

Tuning-In

In consciously setting out to learn about something's healing gifts, doing prior research on it can include factual information, but also researching any already known uses and healing properties, any mythology or folklore, its magical uses, and so on. Doing all this can be of great help prior to doing a journey. Gathering all that knowledge and information is mostly a factual process. However, it is possible to do more intuitive research, too. There are various ways of doing this. Essentially, they start with giving our full attention to whatever it is that we wish to learn about; really noticing it, noticing the details of it, and almost meditating on it.

Exercise 4: Intuitive Research

Pick an Animal, Plant or Stone that you wish to know about. As well as doing some research, try the following exercise.

This is not a shamanic journey, but is done in this physical reality.

As you go through each part of the exercise, you might write down what you experience before you forget it, before moving on to the next part.

Visual

Really look at whatever it is. Examine it up close and in detail. It may help to speak out loud when doing this, speaking to whatever it is, and describing it. As I am writing this, Pan, my cat familiar, is curled up next to me. So, for example: "Your fur appears black most of the time, but when I look closely, I can see that you are really different shades of very dark chocolate brown, and stripy like a tabby cat. Your fur is in two layers, a short and dense layer next to your skin, and longer guard hairs that sometimes make you look like a shaggy little black bear. Underneath your fur, your skin is alabaster-white. You have big paws like a panther, each with five toes and needle-sharp retractable claws. When you want us to know that you are coming, you allow your claws to make clickety-clack noises on the wooden floors when you walk. At other times, you can move in complete and utter silence, without giving away your presence …"

Environment

Notice the environment it is from. With stones, this can be about knowing the environmental conditions that formed them. Understanding this can help with groking. For example, sedimentary rocks are formed through the solidification of sediment. They can be formed by organic remains, such as the remains of ancient forests or bogs, or by the skeletal remains of plankton falling to the seafloor, or by mud cementing together other rocks. Over vast periods of time, these layers build up and the huge pressure created compresses the layers into sedimentary rock. Igneous rocks, on the other hand, are formed by the cooling of magma deep inside the earth, or as the lava from volcanoes cools and solidifies. Unlike most sedimentary rocks, igneous rocks are usually hard. Metamorphic rocks are formed from igneous and sedimentary rocks being exposed to heat or great pressure, which then transforms them into something new.

With animals and plants, notice their chosen habitat. Different environments have different medicines and significances. Are they creatures of the sea, with all its symbolism and meaning? And if so, are they creatures of the deep sea, or do they choose to live by the shoreline, a place of transition between different realms. Or are they creatures of the high mountain tops? Do they prefer to be hidden in the undergrowth or seek open spaces and bright sunlight?

Sensation

If appropriate (and possible), hold whatever it is and feel the texture of it. Close your eyes and notice how your body reacts to touching it. Allow any images, thoughts, sensations and impressions to emerge.

Smell

Again, if appropriate and possible, smell whatever it is. Close your eyes and notice how your body reacts to the smell and allow any images, thoughts, sensations and impressions to emerge.

Taste

N.B. *Only do this if you are 100% sure that it is safe to do so!* Some gemstones are toxic, some plants are poisonous or skin irritants, and tasting animals risks infection. If you are sure that it is safe, however, taste whatever it is and again notice how your body reacts, and be aware of any images, thoughts, sensations or impressions that emerge. Pay attention to any physical sensation in your mouth (astringent, mucilaginous, warming, cooling etc.).

Hearing

As well as listening to any physical sounds that an animal makes, you can also listen to things with your "inner" ear. Tune in to whatever it is and see if it has anything to "say" to you.

Shamanic "Dieting" and "Groking"

As well as the methods above, if a shaman wanted to discover the healing properties of something new, they would sometimes use a technique known as "dieting". Different shamanic cultures had different ways of going about this, but the basic principles behind it are quite simple. Essentially, the shaman would take some time to prepare themselves. In some cultures, this may be elaborate—a period of fasting, or a prolonged ritual, for example. In other cultures, it would be a much simpler process. Once the shaman was ready, though, they would take a tiny piece of whatever it is they were wishing to learn about and ingest it. Over the next few hours, days, or possibly even weeks, the shaman would carefully notice any changes they experienced in themselves, whether physical, emotional or mental, and any dreams they had.

In doing a shamanic dieting, a shaman is "groking" the thing they wish to learn about. As well as shamanic dieting, another way of groking something is to become that thing in a shamanic journey by shapeshifting, and experience what it is like from the inside out. Another version is (as in the previous exercise) to hold a piece of whatever it is you want to learn about, hollow-out, and then tune into the thing you are holding and closely noticing what happens to you physically, mentally and emotionally.

This latter process can be especially powerful when done not just on your own, but with a group of people all tuning-in together. On the Three Ravens training courses, if we wish to learn more about a particular stone or plant, one person will act as a scribe to record what people say. All the other people then sit or lie down close to each other, holding a piece of the stone or plant. They then hollow-out and tune into the plant or stone. Then, as people start to notice things, whether physical, mental or emotional, they voice them out loud, and the scribe notes down what people are saying. What is interesting in doing this is that very often it turns out that several people are experiencing the same thing at the same time; somebody will voice something, and several other people will nod or voice agreement.

On the courses, if I introduce and explain this process to a new group of students, I often see them looking somewhat underwhelmed or sceptical at first. The process does not sound like there is much to it, or that much is going to happen. However, after having done the group groking and experienced it, students are usually amazed by it. For when doing a groking, people often drop into a surprisingly deep altered state of consciousness. Indeed, people often do not realise how deep they have been until they come out of the groking. What blows people away, though, is more than just that. Some definitions of the word "grok" include the experience of understanding something deeply from the inside-out is a joyous one, and this is often what people experience.

To make that kind of deep connection, to open yourself up to that degree, is another way of healing our disconnectedness and isolation. It helps take us out of our insular, human-centric way of being and reconnects us to the other-than-human Peoples and the interconnected web of life. It is profoundly healing, and it just feels *good*. Plus, most importantly, it helps us to *experience* the world more like an animist—a world that is alive and conscious and full non-human and yet sentient beings; beings with healing gifts and wise teachings for us.

CHAPTER TWO

Animals, Plants and Stones

"Provings"

If homeopaths want to find out the healing property of something they do not already know about, they do what is known as a homeopathic "proving". The term "proving" comes from the German word, "prufung", which means to "test" or "examine". There are different ways of doing this, but in many ways, it is similar to a shamanic dieting. In essence, the process involves a group of people taking a miniscule amount (an extreme dilution) of the substance they want to find out about. Over the next few weeks, the provers are not allowed to discuss with each other what they are experiencing. Instead, they write down anything unusual they notice in themselves (mental, emotional or physical). At the end of the proving, all the information from the provers is then collated and analysed. Now, obviously, people doing homeopathic provings are generally not shamans—people skilled in hollowing-out and being able to communicate with other beings. In fact, they are not necessarily even trying to communicate with the sentience of whatever it is they are proving, but just noticing symptoms and changes in themselves over a period of a few weeks. I mean this as no disrespect for homeopaths, I hasten to add. Many of my best friends are homeopaths! I worked as a homeopath for many years, have overseen numerous homeopathic provings, and still use homeopathic medicines on an almost daily basis myself.

As such, though, I *do* know that in the initial information collected in homeopathic provings there is inevitably an element of subjectivity. Many of the symptoms that people record will be nothing to do with the healing properties of whatever it is they are doing the proving on, but just random things, or things that are peculiar to them individually. So, in collating the information and writing up the healing properties, what makes it into the final edit are symptoms that *several* people experienced and reported.

There are differences between grokings and provings, but a lot of overlap, too. In many ways, homeopathic provings are a modern reinvention or interpretation of the ancient practice of dieting. Amazingly, in the absence of skilled shamans who can clearly and objectively tune into the healing properties of plants, stones and animals, we have still managed to come up with an ingenious collective version of dieting that, as much as we can, filters out much of our modern middle-world subjectivity and lack of individual skill. As such, and in other ways I am about to come to, homeopathic provings have an enormous amount to contribute to the process of rediscovering and reinventing shamanism, and making it practical and relevant to the reality of the times we now live in.

Energy, not Chemistry

Just a quick aside here before moving on. It has become fairly common knowledge these days that homeopathic remedies are usually diluted to the extent there is no physical trace left of the original substance. Consequently, for many people this means homeopathy simply cannot work. As a result, homeopathy has become the subject of a fair amount of ridicule and hostility in popular culture over the last few years. This is because most people think of medicines as needing to have a physical, biochemical mechanism and are dismissive of any talk of "energy". I am guessing though that, since you are reading a book on shamanism, you are not so reductionist in your thinking. Clearly, homeopathy (like shamanic healing, Reiki, chi gong, therapeutic touch, acupuncture, and many other healing modalities) is energy medicine. Whilst there may be no *physical* trace of a substance left in a homeopathic medicine, what *is* there is the substance's healing gift.

New Insights

Whilst both (traditional) shamanic dieting and (modern) homeopathic provings involve essentially the same practice—that of ingesting a tiny amount of something and then noticing its effects in order to learn its healing properties—there is an important difference, too. That difference is writing. Traditional hunter-gatherer shamans lived in cultures with no writing. In doing a dieting, they would have had to remember all the teachings that came out of it. Research shows that people in cultures without writing usually have much better memories than we do, because writing makes us lazy. There is no need for us to discipline ourselves to remember things or learn things by rote most of the time, as we can always just write things down and look them up again if needed. What writing does is allow us to record far more information than it is possible to remember. Consequently, homeopathic provings usually contain *vastly* more information about something's healing properties than traditional shamanic grokings could do. Take the homeopathic remedy Pulsatilla, for example, a remedy made from a plant commonly known as wind flower, pasque flower, or meadow anemone. The known healing properties that have come out of the homeopathic provings of this plant run into thousands of things that it can be an effective medicine for. Then put that into the context that there are now thousands of different things that have had homeopathic provings done on them. That adds up to millions of known healing properties of various animals, plants, stones, and other things. Were it not for the invention of writing, this would have been impossible.

Several thousand years after the invention of writing, along come computers. This now allows us to start analysing this massive amount of written information and start to discover patterns. You can run analyses and see if there are any common healing properties within the various plant families, for example. You can look at all the known healing properties of Pulsatilla, and see if it has any healing properties in common with other members of the Ranunculaceae family to which it belongs (this includes plants such as Aconites, Buttercups, Delphiniums, Hellebores, and more, in case you were wondering). It turns out that there are. You can do the same thing with other groups of things, of course. You can see if there are healing properties that all of the various sodium salts have in common, or all of the potassium salts, or all conifers, all fungi, even all spiders or all frogs. Again, you find out that each group has its own distinct healing properties.

Before going further and exploring the relevance this can have to shamanism and to thinking like an animist, there is something that I need to point out. Homeopathic provings are usually done blind. What this means is that the provers have no knowledge of what it is they are ingesting and doing the proving on. The only person who knows what the provers have taken is the person who set the proving up. If this were not the case, then it would be no great surprise to see at least some similarities between remedies within the same groups. For example, if all the people doing provings of the various bird remedies had known what it was they were proving, then if you did a comparative analysis between the provings, it would be no great surprise to find common symptoms between the remedies. For in writing down what they noticed was happening to them during the proving, people would have inevitably allowed their own ideas of "bird" to influence what they experienced and reported.

However, the provers do not know what they are proving (and, remember, are not even allowed to talk to each other about their symptoms during the proving and compare notes). What is remarkable then, *really* remarkable, is that "being able to rise above things and see the bigger picture" or "a sensation of floating", and other things you might expect to find, do indeed emerge from the various bird remedy provings. Similarly, all the blind provings done of conifers show similar themes, and these themes are different to the themes of the cactus family, for example. Likewise, the snake remedies show common themes, and these are different to the common themes of the insect remedies, and so on.

The Nature of Animals, Plants and Stones

The more you look at the coherence of information that emerges from blind provings, the more it becomes clear that the proving process works. What emerges is clearly not just subjective and random, but is actually tapping into the things being proved and revealing their healing qualities. The modern proving process developed by homeopaths is a form of groking. It is shamanic in its nature, provides us with reliable and detailed information about the healing gifts all around us, and yet does not require years of training in shamanism to do.

Because provings are (relatively) easy to do, and so many of them have now been done, the information from them (alongside other ways of groking), can be immensely useful in helping us gather together our Medicine Bundle. Given how many of us live in places of broken shamanic lineage, where most (or even all) of the shamanic Medicine Bundle knowledge has been lost, this makes provings a rich treasure trove of knowledge. Treasures that can help us grok the other Peoples—understanding them from the inside out—rather than perceiving them through the lens of our limited, modern-day human perception. As we shall see next.

The Animal People

When you search for the common themes in the provings of the animal remedies, the following themes emerge (in other words, this is what the provings tell us is the nature of Animal):

- Predator/prey
- Dominant/dominated
- Strong/weak
- Competition/cooperation
- Aggressive/affectionate
- Stressed
- Caring
- Bonding
- Mischievous
- Deceitful
- Playful
- Communicative
- Emotional
- Social
- Colourful
- Expressive
- Noisy
- Animated
- Hiding
- Subterfuge
- Mobile
- Restless
- Proactive
- Excited
- Fast-paced
- Changeable
- Curious
- Inventive

Let's make sense of these. [In doing this, when I use a word from the list above, or its related form, then I will underline it, to highlight how what I am saying relates to the themes that have come out of the Animal provings.]

Unlike plants who can manufacture their own food through photosynthesis, no animals can produce their own food. Because of this, all animals are <u>predators</u>. They predate on plants, either directly or indirectly. They either eat plants themselves, or eat other animals that eat plants, or eat both plants and other animals. Then, on top of that, within the animal kingdom itself, all animals are either predators, <u>prey</u>, or both. Given this, the predator-prey dynamic is intrinsic to Animal.

The predator-prey dynamic means that there is <u>competition</u>. Stones do not compete. Plants compete to a degree, for space and resources. But the level of competition in Animal is there to a much greater degree. It is one of Animal's fundamental driving forces. It leads to <u>stronger</u>, more <u>aggressive</u> animals taking advantage of weakness in others, and often to hierarchical structures where some animals are <u>dominant</u> and others are <u>dominated</u>. Think about the way hunting animals prey on the elderly, the young, or the <u>weak</u> and injured. Think about the hierarchical way beehives or ant colonies are organised, or the pecking order and hierarchies in things like herds of horses or deer, prides of lions, wolf packs, and troops of monkeys.

Interestingly, as well as competition, the predator-prey dynamic gives rise to its opposite—<u>cooperation</u> between individuals. We know that plants can cooperate to a degree. There is a growing body of scientific research showing this. Plants can warn each other about insect or fungal attacks, for example. They can send nutrients along their roots and along the interconnecting mycelium fungal network, to help neighbouring plants who are struggling. In some cases, if they know they are dying, they will begin to break down their own bodies and send the nutrients to their neighbours to help strengthen them. But, characteristic of many animals is an extremely complex degree of cooperation between individuals. Being able to cooperate to this degree requires highly-developed communication and social structures. To do this, social animals evolved to become expressive. This led them to become (compared to plants), noisy and animated. It led them to develop things like complex mating rituals, including physical displays, giving gifts, displays of colour, scents, vocalisations and even complex language (we are by no means the only animal with language, of course). Likewise, to form the bonds necessary to be social, and to manage intricate social structures, animals developed things like playfulness, mischievousness, mimicry, seduction, displays of affection, caring, and the ability to form deep interpersonal bonds. It also led to developing the ability to be deceitful, form alliances and pacts, and play politics.

The stresses of navigating these (potentially dangerous) interactions and dynamics led to many social animals developing a complex range of ever-changing emotional states. These range from terror, fear, anxiety, apprehension, annoyance, anger, rage, disapproval, antipathy, disgust, loathing, forgiveness, regret, sadness, remorse, guilt, shame, grief, jealousy, boredom, acceptance, anticipation, longing, hope, optimism, trust, surprise, amazement, excitement, contentment, love, passion, empathy, joy, ecstasy and awe. Essentially, many animals are highly emotional beings.

Of course, not all animals are social and cooperative. In these animals, rather than seeking to be noticed, they may deliberately hide and try to avoid drawing attention to themselves. This may include using camouflage or mimicry as forms of subterfuge, to hide from predators or in order to catch their own prey.

Giving up the ability to synthesise their own food meant that animals had to become proactive, restless and mobile in order to seek food out. This need to find food, coupled with the need to find a mate in order to procreate, led most animals to become inquisitive and <u>curious</u>, <u>changeable</u>, inventive, <u>innovative</u> and adaptable, in order to make the most of every opportunity.

All this makes Animal driven and <u>restless</u>. Plant has some drives, of course. But compared to Plant, the sheer restlessness and drive of Animal is off the scale. The thing is, being animals ourselves, we are used to this. So used to it, in fact, that we may not even realise it. For it is how we habitually experience and interact with the world around us. It is how we go about our everyday business. When it comes to shamanic journeying, what this means is that, unless we are consciously aware of this, then we will unwittingly take this Animal way of being with us into journeys. Indeed, in teaching, this is what I usually observe in new students. Their journeys are very "Animal-like"; very busy and restless, and full of Animal concerns and motivations. Whilst there is nothing wrong with this, it does have its limitations. Journeying like this can only get us so far, as it gets in the way of being able to really grok the oldest and wisest of the Peoples—and Stone.

As we shall see, knowing what Animal is like and how it differs from Plant and Stone helps us to know what to step away from, and what we need to step into, when it comes to understanding and working with the non-Animal Peoples. Before turning to the other Peoples, though, I want to look at working with Animal in journeys.

The Animal People and the Medicine Bundle

I know from teaching that, no matter how clearly I say to people that their Power Animal should always be with them in journeys, I usually have to say it over and over again before it really sinks in. So, a quick reminder here—your Power Animal should be with you *all of the time*. There are *no* exceptions to this. They should be with you right now as you are reading this. They are your primary and most important link to the more-than-human world. Without them, you are suffering from Power Loss, leaving you vulnerable to intrusions, unhealthy entanglements, and entity possessions. Plus, when it comes to journeying, journeys should be Spirit-led. Your Power Animal should be leading your journeys, not you. As a lower-world being, they are a transcendent being that exists outside of (middle-world) space and time. This means that they are not subject to ego and the other limitations of the middle-world. As such, no matter how skilful and experienced you become in shamanic work, they will always be more skilled and infinitely wiser than you. Because of that, there are *no* journeys when they should not be with you.

That being said, you will probably have noticed all sorts of Animals other than your Power Animal crop up in journeys at different times. Indeed, the lower-world is full of Animals. Some will just make fleeting appearances, whilst others may be regular companions. Some may appear only once, whilst others may be with you for months or even years. Some you may come to associate with specific aspects of journeying work, such as extractions, disentanglements, psychopomping, or so on.

In terms of gathering your Medicine Bundle, when a new Animal makes an appearance in a journey, then as I discussed earlier, it is good to reflect on it and do some research to learn about its healing gifts and teaching. So, too, as discussed earlier, as well as learning about Animals that spontaneously appear in journeys, a good Medicine Bundle practice is to choose an Animal without waiting for it to crop up in a journey first. Do some research on it, and then journey to meet it and find out more about it. Over the years, at a rough estimate I have probably done this with well over two-hundred different Animals. For example, when I wanted to understand more about the Sea in shamanism, I spent time doing journeys to meet and grok everything from Dolphin, Limpet, Crab, Octopus, Jellyfish,

Turtle, Coral, Shark, Seahorse, Sea Anemone and more. Not to forget the Plant and Stone People too; as well as Phytoplankton, Seaweed, Sand, Seawater itself, I even journeyed to see if I could find out what Waves are and what they teach (something that turned out to be unexpectedly profound and quite life-changing for me).

Another idea is to journey to meet the Animals that live in specific landscapes. This teaches you not just about the individual species, but about how they interact with each other and the land, and their place in the whole. For example, I am drawn to northern landscapes, and so I have done journeys to Animals like Artic Fox, Arctic Hare, Elk, Reindeer, Ptarmigan, Canada Goose, Musk Ox and Snowy Owl.

Another idea is to journey on the animals that are native to the environment that your Power Animal is from. This helps you better understand your Power Animal and their place in the whole. My main Power Animal is Black Panther, and so I have journeyed to meet Panther's prey Animals, to get a better understanding of their relationship. This has included doing journeys to grok Armadillo, Peccary, Capybara, Tapir and Caiman, amongst others.

It is also good to journey to grok the Animals of the land you live on and are a part of. This can be a powerful re-wilding practice, helping you connect to the land more. It can help you notice the animals and the web of life around you, and begin to heal any disconnection from it you may suffer from. For me, over many years, this has included meeting Hedgehog, Mole, Vole, Barn Owl, Osprey, Wild Pony, Blackbird, Woodpecker, Sparrow, Raven, Crow, Jackdaw, Heron, Robin, Swan, Frog, Newt, Bumblebee, Honeybee, Wren, Ladybird, Mouse, Badger, Butterfly, Adder, Otter, and more.

Another way is to explore different Animal groups that you feel drawn to. My partner, who is appropriately named Cat (she was christened as Catriona) is very drawn to the Cat family (interestingly, she was frightened of cats as a child—but given her childhood, it would have been dangerous for her, and not an option, to step into her full Power as a child, so wisely she kept Cat away until she left home). As an adult now, she has Panther and Snow Leopard as her Power Animals, and also has worked with Lynx, Lion, Tiger, Mountain Lion, Ocelot, Caracal, Bob Cat and more. Plus, Cat itself, of course.

I do not mean for any of this to feel overwhelming! Quite the contrary. It is a joyous and richly-rewarding thing to do. There is a lifetime of endlessly fascinating exploration to be had in meeting other animals. Several lifetimes worth, even (I might say, *if* I believed in reincarnation).

Exercise 5: Animals you Would Like to Meet

If you have not already got one, get a notebook (or open a new document on your phone or computer, if that is more your style), for making a list of journeys you would like to do one day.

Make a list of the Animals that you would like to journey on. This could be any that pop into your head. Or you could base it around themes such as Animals from particular environments, including Animals that live in the same ecosystem as your Power Animal, or Animals that are local to you, or environments that you want to explore, such as the sea, mountains, deserts, rainforests, the arctic, and so on. Or you could base it around exploring family groups (Felines, Birds, Cetaceans, and so on).

At your leisure, or when you want to journey but are stuck for ideas, gradually work your way through this list.

Mythical and Prehistoric Animals

Sometimes people ask if it is alright to work with mythical Animals in journeys. It is fine. My only comment would be that *some* of them, particularly the flying ones, such as Pegasus, Griffin, Thunderbird, Hippogriff and so on, can have a more rarefied, upper-world quality to them. This is not always the case, as some can indeed be of the lower-world.

Whilst mythical Animals are fine to work with in journeys, they do not always make good Power Animals. There are no hard-and-fast rules about this (one of the things I love about shamanism is that there are no rules, only guidelines), and I do know one or two great practitioners who work with mythical Power Animals. Generally, though, an important quality of a Power Animal is that they connect you both to the lower-world and to nature. The connection to the lower-world means that the more upper-worldly mythical Animals are generally not a good choice as a Power Animal. And in terms of connecting to nature, what I have seen usually works best is to have a Power Animal that exists both in the lower-world *and* as a real, flesh and blood animal in this physical reality too. This is because your Power Animal is your link between this reality and the shamanic realms. So, it helps if it is something that bridges the different realities; both something of the shamanic realms, and something that is physically manifest here, too.

As I said, though, there are no rules—I am only (ever) offering my observations and suggestions.

It is fine to work with prehistoric or extinct Animals, too. This includes not just Dinosaurs, but animals that have become extinct more recently; animals that became extinct in human times and that we still have an ancestral memory of. So, animals like Mammoth, Giant Sloth, Cave Bear, Cave Lion, Auroch, Woolly Rhinoceros, and so on are all good to work with. I have found these Animals seem to make good Power Animals because they once were physical, flesh-and-blood animals and, in the scale of things, it is not that long ago since they lived on the Earth. Besides, their physical remains are still all around us—bones, teeth, antlers, and bodies in the permafrost. They are even remembered through cave paintings done by our human ancestors not so long ago.

Oversouls

In working with Animal in the lower-world, it is important to understand the difference between (for example) lower-world Fox and an individual fox. In doing lower-world work, if we are *truly* in the lowerworld, then when working with Animals, we are working with their Oversouls. Think of the Peoples as being like a great tree that is rooted in Mother Earth and grows up and out of her. The Stone People are like the roots, and then the main trunk emerging from the Earth is Plant (the second of the People). The trunk then divides, one trunk carrying on to form the various different types of Plant (Conifer, Liverwort, Flowering Plant, and so on), whilst the other trunk forms Animal, diverging from Plant, and itself then branching to form Invertebrate and Vertebrate, then Reptile, Amphibian, Mammal and other branches. The Mammal branch then divides to form Cat, Horse, Bear, Fox, and so on. These are the Oversouls—branches of Mother Earth in the lower-world that represent the whole of a species (or, with the thicker branches nearer the trunk, the whole of a genus, order, family, class, or phylum). So, Fox Oversoul in the lower-world is all of Fox, the whole of the species. It is the archetype of Fox, the Great Fox that all individual foxes come from. All of the *individual* foxes in the middle-world are protrusions from this branch, twigs projecting into the middle-world from the Fox Oversoul.

Individuality then is a characteristic of the middle-world, and wholeness is a characteristic of the lower-world. Because of this, if you work with individuals in journeys, the work will *inevitably* have a middle-world energy to it to some degree. If, then, your intent is to do truly lower-world work, then in working with an Animal your aim needs to be to connect with its Oversoul, not with an individual (the same goes for working with Plant and Stone too).

In doing this, it is important to remember that shamanism is a co-created process. How you think about things, and the language you use, will shape and affect what it is that you encounter. So, try to think in terms like "Next, Bear appeared" rather than "Next, a bear appeared", or "And then Raven swallowed my eyeball" rather than "And then the raven swallowed my eyeball". Or even, "Next, Panther licked my face" rather than "Next, my panther licked my face". Using "a", "the" or "my" reduces Animal to animal; it makes it less lower-world and more middle-world. It is a small change to make in terms of thinking and language, and yet it has a profound and immense effect on what happens in journeys and on the authenticity of them.

Exercise 6: Journeying to Meet an Animal Oversoul

Decide which Animal you want to meet in a journey.

Optional (but recommended): before the journey, do research on the Animal in order to help you really grok it.

[You are going to need a recording of a shamanic drumming session for this exercise (and for many other exercises in this book). Since this is not a beginner's book, I am assuming you already have one. But if not, then these are easily available to buy online as CDs or digital downloads. You will also find them on YouTube. Alternatively, you may use the free downloads from the Three Ravens College website on this page:

www.therapeutic-shamanism.co.uk/downloads.html

Prepare for doing a journey in whatever way works for you.

When ready, start the recording of the drumming.

Go to your axis mundi and hollow-out. That is to say, at your axis mundi, before setting off to the lower-world, as much as you can, put aside your middle-world concerns, agendas, preoccupations, and identity, and become a hollow vessel for Spirit to work through (as discussed in detail in the second book in this series). Then, with your Power Animal as always, go down to the shamanic lower-world.

In the lower-world, either ask the Animal that you want to meet to come to you or ask your Power Animal to take you to them. Remember that the intent in the lower-world is to meet not an individual but the Oversoul of the Animal—something that represents the whole of the species.

Once the Animal has appeared then you can:

Examine it in detail.

Notice what it is like to be in its presence.

Ask it for healing. Remember that, as well as healing you, it is also trying to teach you. Pay attention to what it does and learn from it.

Shapeshift into it and experience what it is like to be it.

On the call-back, thank the Animal—always work with gratitude. Return back to your physical body.

After the journey, it is good to write down what happened in as much detail as you can remember before your left-brain starts to erase bits from your memory.

You might also want to consider doing something to help that animal here in the middle-world too, as a way of showing gratitude towards them, such as donating to a charity that works with them, or anything else that feels appropriate.

The Plant People

Turning now to the Plant People, here are some of the common themes that come out of the many provings that have been done on plants:

- Calm
- Grounded
- Slow
- Passive
- Gentle
- Little competitiveness
- Receptive
- Sensitive to
- Reactive
- Adaptive
- Affected by
- Influenced by
- Immobile
- At the mercy of

[As with Animal, in discussing these themes, when I use a word from the list above, or its related form, then I will underline it to highlight how what I am saying relates to the themes from the provings].

In making sense of these differences between Animal, Plant and Stone, it is important to keep in mind that they are relative. For example, compared to a stationary rock, plants are not at all slow or immobile. However, relative to most animals, plants are slow and immobile as a rule. Likewise, rocks are not at all competitive, whereas plants do compete for space and resources, but are far less competitive and territorial than most animals are.

The first thing to notice about the Plant list is that it is much shorter than the Animal one, about half the length. This is because being Plant is much simpler and less complicated than being Animal. This is not about "better" or "worse"—it just is what it is. Being Animal is *complicated*. There is so much stress involved in being Animal, so much to do, so many places to be, so many drives, so many complex relationships to navigate. By contrast, Plant is chilled and relaxed. So, it is no surprise that the themes calm, slow and grounded feature so prominently in the hundreds (even thousands) of plant species that have had provings done on them. For remember, the predator-prey dynamic, the need to seek out food whilst avoiding becoming food yourself, the need to find a mate, the stresses of navigating complex and potentially dangerous social interactions, all lead Animal to be characterised by an ever-changing range of emotions ranging from fear to elation. Plant has none of this. It is true that plants can get stressed by environmental factors. If resources such as water or sunlight are in short supply, plants will exhibit stresses in that they adopt strategies in order to try and survive. Remember, though, that everything that we are looking at here is relative. Compared to Animal, Plant really is supremely relaxed and unstressed. Think about how you feel when spending time around plants. Think about lying down in a meadow, or spending time in a quiet forest, or sitting with your back resting against the trunk of a tree. And in groking Plants in journeys, you can experience this calmness of Plant in a visceral way for yourself. It is a great feeling and can be a temporary but welcome relief from being Animal (and, even more so, from being Human) for a while.

The words <u>passive</u> and <u>gentle</u> appear prominently in the Plant provings. Plants are not *entirely* passive, of course. If a plant is under attack from insects, for example, it will take steps to defend itself by producing chemicals to try and fight off the attack. However, in this case, the plant is still essentially being <u>reactive</u> rather than proactive. It is being <u>affected by</u> something and responding and <u>adapting</u>, rather than instigating. It is being <u>receptive</u> rather than being the protagonist.

Some plants can be somewhat more proactive than others. Allelopathic plants deliberately produce chemicals that inhibit the growth of nearby plants. This is an active step to protect their own space, and thereby reduce competition. Likewise, carnivorous plants may take active steps to lure insects to them, to trap them and "digest" them as an added source of nutrients. Plus, most flowering plants, a huge group representing well over 350,000 known species, actively use scent and colour to attract pollinating animals to them—not just bees and butterflies, but also pollen wasps, ants, hoverflies beetles, and even birds and bats.

Compared to most animal strategies, though, these are all still essentially <u>passive</u>. They involve being <u>immobile</u> and defending yourself and your space, or trying to attract what you need to you, rather than going out and actively hunting for it in the way that most animals do. This is, of course, because plants are, quite literally, rooted to the spot. There are some animals, the sessile animals such as corals, sponges and barnacles, that spend most of their life rooted to the spot too. But even sessile animals are mobile (motile) in their larval stages and either move actively by swimming (nektonic) or just go with the flow (planktonic). It is only when they reach the adult stage of their lives when they attach themselves to something and spend the rest of their lives rooted to the spot like a plant. And interestingly, the provings of sessile animals show many plant-like qualities.

Most animals though are motile. Indeed, gaining mobility was the great trade-off that us motile animals made in giving up the ability to photosynthesise. Plants immobility means that, although they can defend themselves (to some extent) when attacked, they are otherwise <u>at the mercy of</u> whatever it is attacking them. Mobility gave animals the option of much more actively fighting back when attacked, plus it opened the option of fleeing predators, or simply avoiding them in the first place.

Gaining movement also opened new options and strategies when it came to reproduction. Being immobile, to reproduce, plants rely on strategies such as attracting pollinating insects, or even just releasing vast quantities of pollen into the air and hoping that the wind will carry some of it to a receptive plant. Gaining mobility, however, meant that animals could be proactive and seek out a mate, and actively fight off any competition if needed.

If you really want to grok Plant in journeys, then you have to feel yourself into a very different way of being and approaching the world. You have to give up on a whole range of strategies, options, drives and responses that are familiar and habitual to you as an Animal. In a journey, to become a Plant, you need to give up movement; certainly, movement as you know it and understand it as an Animal. You need to let go of the restless and relentless drive to find the things that you need in order to survive. You need to stop *doing*, and just *be*. As a Plant, you do not need to find food. If you have enough water, trace nutrients, air and sunlight, you can literally make everything you need. And if you do not have those things, there is nothing you can do about it in any case, so there is literally no point worrying.

That last point is an important one. For motile animals, if they are hungry then, if they are to survive, they must *do* something about it. There is a drive to act. If that action is unsuccessful, there is an imperative to keep trying. This becomes more and more urgent until the hunt is successful. Similarly, if an animal is being hunted or under attack, there is a need to try and hide, flee, or fight back. All this produces levels of stress and anxiety. This is the background noise and reality of being Animal. It is the need to *do* things. If you work shamanically with Plant, though, if you can step out of being Animal and grok Plant, one of the really striking things is how this drive to do things just falls away. Anxiety is a frantic attempt to think of *what to do*. That is an *Animal* thing, though—an Animal way of being. For Plant, worrying is just not in its nature. This is why, compared to us Animals, for Plants, life is much less about doing and more about just being. Plants do not worry about the future. They do not worry about where their next meal will come from, or about finding shelter for the night. They do not worry about whether anyone will ever love them, or whether they will ever find a mate. They do not worry about who will take care of them in old age.

Plants have no agendas, either. They do not deceive, seduce, manipulate or keep secrets. Simply put, Plants never play politics. This is because they do not have individual middle-world egos, and because it is simply not in their nature to become driven by emotions such as anger or disappointment. It is crucial to understand this if you are to really grok Plants, and not project Animal qualities onto them. As an example, many years ago I was approached by someone who produces and sells a set of flower essences. She said that a particular Plant had approached her and revealed itself to be one of the most useful Plants to use in doing soul retrievals. She wanted my help, as a shamanic practitioner, to work with the Plant and explore this more. I was intrigued and asked which Plant it was. She said that she would tell me, but that I must keep it secret and not tell anyone else, as the Plant had told her that it was not ready to reveal its healing gift to the public yet but would do so in six months' time. Now, I do not know what the flower essence producer had been talking to, but whatever it was, it was not the Plant. She may have been talking to a middle-world being, mistaking it for the Plant. Many people talk to elemental beings that live in and around plants in the middle-world, thinking that they are talking to the plant itself. Such beings are notoriously tricky to work with and are full of their own agendas. Or she may have been dialoguing with a part-of-self from her own unconscious drives and agendas. Who knows? But I do know that, whatever it was she had been talking to, it definitely was not the Plant itself. For no Plant has agendas like that. None would swear people to secrecy, nor withhold its healing gift until it was "ready". Those kinds of things are simply not in Plants nature.

By the way, in case you were wondering, the Plant was Selfheal. I already knew it as a Plant that is indeed helpful in soul retrieval. For remember, every Plant has a healing gift and teaching that it will give freely when asked, and without any agenda attached, and I had asked Selfheal about its medicine long ago.

This lack of worry, freedom from the restless need to be doing things, and lack of agendas means that plants can relax and slow down. They operate at a *much* slower pace to animals. This is essential to grasp in trying to grok Plant. There is a Star Trek episode in which the Enterprise is boarded by aliens who move so fast the crew of the Enterprise cannot see them. For the aliens, the Enterprise's crew seem like inert matter, not living beings. The point is that we are the aliens, moving too fast most of the time to realise the sentience of plants. It is a point being made by some scientists now, who are studying plant intelligence; that the reason we had not realised before just how intelligent plants are is that we had not slowed down enough. To really understand Plants, to get inside them and grok them, you need to slow right down. I mean, *really* slow down. As Stefano Mancuso, one of the leading scientists studying plant intelligence says in the book *"Brilliant Green: The Surprising History and Science of Plant Intelligence"*, "Plant lives unfold in another dimension of time".

Or, as Spock might have said, "It is intelligence Jim, just not as we know it."

A Different Kind of Consciousness

This difference is not because Plants are any less conscious than we are. Far from it. Rather, it is because they have a different *kind* of consciousness. Understanding this difference is crucial in being able to really understand Plant from the inside out, and not letting our human and animal way of seeing things get in the way. To get this, it is important to realise that most people associate consciousness with self-awareness. For example, in experiments, scientists may place a sticker on an animal's forehead, and then show the animal a mirror. Humans, of course, can recognise themselves in a mirror, and so will identify the sticker on their head. Chimpanzees will do the same, as will gorillas. No great surprise there, as those are species very closely related to us, and so are likely to have a similar kind of consciousness and self-awareness. Some other species can also identify themselves in the mirror, maybe more surprisingly as they are not closely related to us and are "bird brained"—corvids, such as ravens and crows, and some species of parrot. Slugs, on the other hand, cannot do this. Plants do not do it either. Slugs and plants are seemingly incapable of recognising themselves in a mirror. From this, scientists conclude they are not sentient, whereas humans, great apes, corvids and some parrots are.

One of the problems with this experiment is that it is not measuring consciousness but *self*-awareness. This is part of our arrogance as humans and the myth of our supremacy. We think that our kind of consciousness—self-awareness—is the "highest" form of consciousness. In fact, self-awareness is the *only* kind of consciousness that most people even recognise. So, we design experiments that have this bias built in, and which then seemingly prove to ourselves that we are right.

There is, though, another kind of consciousness—*collective*-awareness. Think of a continuum with self-awareness at one end and collective-awareness at the other. We are, indeed, it would seem, the most self-aware species on the planet; we are right at the end of the self-awareness side of the spectrum. That also makes us the least collectively-aware species. Indeed, as modern humans, we are so far away from collective-awareness, so cut-off and isolated in our narcissistic awareness of self, that we cannot even recognise collective-awareness as being a form of consciousness and sentience. Well, we *kind* of get it with some animals. Whilst recognising that insects that live in colonies do not have individual consciousness, we do recognise that the colony as a whole may have a kind of collective intelligence—what we call a "hive-mind". But that is usually as far as we go. Understanding collective-awareness, collective-consciousness, is at the heart of beginning to understand plant sentience, though.

Think about the individual cells in your body. The average human body contains an estimated 37.2 *trillion* cells (37,000,000,000,000 individual cells). Although each individual cell generally wants to survive and stay alive, in the end, what is important is the survival of your body as a whole. The individual cells of your body have little or no *self*-awareness, instead they form a collective, that, in your physical life here, allows you to experience yourself as a self-aware and individually-conscious being. Similarly, the individual ants in a colony may have little self-awareness, but the colony as a whole has an awareness and can act like an individually-aware being. It is the same for plants, but on a much bigger scale. An individual plant of grass has no self-awareness. Instead, like one of the 37 trillion cells in your body, it is a minuscule part of a vastly bigger whole. All the individual grass plants on the planet are part of one single consciousness. Think about that. Grass is an almost planetary-wide *single* consciousness. This is why shamans say the Plant species are vast interdimensional beings. Vast because of the huge areas of the planet they cover, and interdimensional because, no matter where they are geographically located, each individual specimen of a plant is connected to the whole of its species.

Plant can Heal our Deepest Wound

In the last chapter, we looked at how humans have a tendency to lose their way, and how our animist ancestors knew this, and knew to turn to the other Peoples for healing and wisdom, to help keep us on the right path. Like individual Animal species, each individual Plant species has its own healing gifts for us (so, Daffodil has its healing gifts, Dandelion has other healing gifts, and so on). On top of each species' individual gifts, taken as a whole, Plant has a great gift, one of the most important gifts of all. It is a gift and teaching that can heal one of the most fundamental wounds of our modern times—the Taker society idea that "up is good and down is bad".

In case you have not read the first two books in the series, or in case you have but need a quick reminder, the idea that "up is good and down is bad" is the idea that Heaven is good and the Earth is bad. It is a foundation stone of Taker society. It is what both allowed and created our domestication and the Fall. It is the idea that the physical world is not sacred but corrupt, and that "spirituality" lies in "ascension" and in "transcending" the world. It is, of course, at the heart of the sky religions—the organised religions that promote, maintain and police this deeply wounded (and wounding) story. For, from this story flows patriarchy—the distorted and unbalanced idea that the upper-world and Father Sky is good, and that the lower-world and Mother Earth are bad. It tells us the lower-world is hell, and the Earth is corruption, that God is good and Goddess is bad and so, that men are good and women are bad. It is also hierarchical thinking. In adopting it, we move away from what Yuval Noah Harari describes as a "spiritual round table", the way in which our animist ancestors saw all life as equal, and instead adopt the idea of a spiritual hierarchy, and of human spiritual supremacy. Adopting this hierarchical thinking then also allows (and justifies) things like mass social inequality, the oppression of sections of society, and the Anthropocene extinction itself—indeed, all the ills of Taker society and the Fall.

In *"The Shamanic Journey"* I discussed the idea of "spiritual bypassing". It is a term coined by the psychologist John Wellwood to describe the way in which some people use "spiritual" practices and beliefs to avoid dealing with painful feelings and unresolved psychological wounds. Amongst its symptoms, Wellwood includes such things as: an unhealthy degree of detachment, being ungrounded, emotional repression, projecting one's repressed emotions onto others, and thinking that one is full of compassion whereas in fact one is full of judgements. However, in looking at this again, notice how the things that Wellwood lists are all human, psychological issues. This is not surprising, as he is a psychologist. I absolutely agree with Wellwood's analysis on a psychological level. And though, his thinking shows the characteristic limitations of Fallen-thinking, in that it is entirely focused on, and limited to, *human* concerns.

Psychotherapists and psychologists tend to reduce everything down to the human. Transpersonal psychotherapies do reach beyond the human in that they bring in what is, from a shamanic perspective, the upper-world. What is almost always missing from these therapies, however, is nature: the other Peoples, the lower-world, and Mother Earth herself (ecotherapy and eco-psychology are the exceptions to this rule, but unfortunately, they only make up a tiny fraction of psychology and psychotherapy at the moment.).

Hence Wellwood sees spiritual bypassing as avoiding dealing with painful feelings and unresolved *psychological* wounds. On a human psychological level, this is indeed true. However, in a larger context, if we step outside of our narcissistic obsession with human, spiritual bypassing is a symptom of something that is, in fact, much bigger. It is a *symptom* of our narcissistic obsession with human and, as such, it can never be properly healed by addressing it only on a psychological level. For addressing it only on that level is to treat the symptoms but not the underlying cause—that underlying cause being our disconnection from nature.

So, too, Wellwood sees the costs of spiritual bypassing only in human psychological terms. Whereas, again, if we lift our heads up from our self-obsessed human navel gazing and look around us, the cost of our spiritual bypassing has been (and still is) utterly devastating to far more than just us humans.

Just to be clear here, I am not having a go at Wellwood. I love his work! In particular, I think spiritual bypassing is such an important and useful concept. It is not just Wellwood, but almost the whole of psychotherapy, psychiatry and psychology to date that has had problems when it comes to thinking outside of human concerns. As the Jungian psychologist James Hillman once said:

> "Sometimes I wonder…how psychology ever got so off base. How did it cut itself off from reality? Where else in the world would a human soul be so divorced from the spirits of its surroundings? Psychology, so dedicated to awakening the human consciousness, needs to wake itself up to one of the most ancient human truths: We cannot be studied or cured apart from the planet".

And it is not just psychotherapy, psychiatry and psychology that are guilty of this either. Not by a long way. Not all, but *most* of our thoughts and actions in Taker society are human-centric and have been since we stopped thinking like animists; *since we started to tell ourselves the story that "up is good, and down is bad".*

But what has all this got to do with Plant and its great healing gift? If a plant bought into "up is good and down is bad" then it would die. It would have shallow roots and instead pour all its energy into reaching upwards and growing taller. It would be top-heavy and prone to being blown over in storms and become sickly due to a lack of water and nutrients from the earth. However, plants do not subscribe to "up is bad and down is good" either, for plants know they must keep a balance between their connection to Mother Earth and Father Sky. This is how they live and how they thrive—by keeping this balance.

The story that "up is good and down is bad" is a sickness. It leads to death. Plant teaches us that if we continue to think like this, the inevitable outcome is that, as a species, we will die too. That is a great and powerful teaching from Plant, and one that our animist ancestors listened to and understood. Listening to the teachings of Plant can save us as a species. Now, obviously, not everyone is going to start listening to plants! If that is what had to happen, then we would indeed be doomed. But that is not how this needs to work (and has never been how this works). For remember, in hunter-gatherer societies, not everyone was a shaman, nor did they need to be for the tribe to be healthy. Rather, it was the specific role of the shaman to communicate with the other-than-human and then bring their wisdom and teachings back to the tribe.

We need to start really listening to Plant again, one of the oldest and wisest of the Peoples. In terms of shamanism, when we do listen to Plant, when we slow down and step out of being Human and Animal enough to grok Plant, we find that Plant teaches us how to hold this balance between Father Sky (Sun) and Mother Earth. Plant shows you what this feels like. *What* this is like is not something that can be easily put into words. If I tried to describe it, it would not mean much. Through shamanic journeying, though, it is something you can begin to experience for yourself. For it is a *somatic* thing, an *energetic* thing. It is something you feel in your body, and which changes your centre of gravity. It changes your relationship with the world around you. It changes your sense of who you are. It is not an idea, but a *feeling* of inter-connectedness and openness, a deep and certain knowing that you belong and are a part of the Earth. The message that comes from this experience is that we must honour the Earth as much as the Sky. That hierarchical thinking is a sickness.

That descent is as valuable, as *essential*, as ascent. That to cut off from the Earth is to die. That healthy beings and cultures are ones that are deeply rooted. These messages (along with other messages, like the value of slowing down, being less aggressive, and being more content with what we have) are the messages from Plant we need to bring back to our modern-day tribe. I know of nothing that teaches these things more than Plant. It is why shamans all over the world often revere Plants as the greatest of teachers.

The Plant People and the Medicine Bundle

In a shamanic journey, there are lots of different way to work with Plants. Here are a few of them:

- In the journey, the Plant Spirit may take on an appearance that is different from the Plant itself, something you can more readily interact and work with. The Spirit may emerge from the Plant to work with you, appearing in humanoid (or even animal) form, such as a woman with skin made of tree bark, or a winged fairy-like creature, for example. Or it may simply appear as a ball of "energy", or any number of different things. In this case, it may either direct the shamanic healing, or conduct it itself. Either way, this may involve using any number of shamanic methods (extraction, depossession, burial, burning, smoking, singing etc.).

- You may be told to shapeshift into the Plant. This can be both a groking, and a way of receiving the Plant's healing.

- The plant may grow around and into you.

- An energy from the Plant may flow into you (if so, pay attention to where it goes in your body, and what you experience).

- You may be placed inside the Plant (this often happens when working with Trees).

- You may bathe in an infusion of the Plant.

- You may be buried, burnt, dissolved or cocooned with it (the transformations journeys, including burnings, burials, dissolvings and cocoonings were covered in book two in this series).

- You may smoke the plant, or the smoke from burning the Plant may be used to cleanse you.

- The plant may be blown up your nose as a snuff or powder.

- The Plant may be applied directly to your skin as a poultice, or in the form of a paste or ointment.

- The Plant may be bound around you (this often happens as a form of protection when needed, or to bind recently returned soul parts back into the body).

- The Plant may be eaten or drank in the form of a tea.

Exercise 7: Journeying to Meet a Plant Oversoul

Decide on a Plant Oversoul you want to meet in a journey.

Optional (but recommended): before the journey, do research on the Plant in order to help you really grok it.

As usual, prepare for doing a journey in whatever way works for you.

When ready, start the recording of the drumming.

Go to your axis mundi and hollow-out. Then, with your Power Animal, go down to the shamanic lower-world. Ask your Power Animal to take you to the Plant Oversoul. Once there, ask the Plant for healing and/or shapeshift into it.

On the call-back, thank the Plant—always work with gratitude. Then return to your physical body.

Write down what happened.

The Standing People

Interestingly, hunter-gatherers saw trees as slightly different to other plants. They referred to them as the Standing People. In terms of biological taxonomy, trees are not a distinct group. What defines a plant as being a tree is its size and structure. Precise definitions vary, but they are along the following lines: a tree is a perennial woody plant that has many secondary branches supported clear of the ground on a single main stem or trunk, and a minimum height at maturity of at least three meters (some definitions also stipulate a minimum 10-centimeter trunk diameter too). As such, trees have evolved separately in unrelated classes of plants in response to similar environmental conditions (a classic example of what is known as parallel evolution). The earliest tree-forms to evolve were seen in ferns (and the related lycophytes—fern-like plants), and horsetails. Later, conifers, ginkos, cacti, cycads and then flowering plants all developed tree-forms too. Flowering plants and conifers form the majority of trees that most people are familiar with these days.

Shamanically, Trees (the Standing People) share all the characteristics of Plant. As members of Plant, they have a highly collective awareness. One of the things that makes them different to other Plants, though, is that they generally live far longer. Many of the Standing people can live for hundreds, or even thousands, of years. This, combined with their size, means that over the years, individual trees acquire middle-world stories. They gradually develop a history and middle-world personality. Think about great, old trees. Each is unique. Palpably, each has its own character and stories to tell. Because of this, as well as being *collectively* conscious, the older a tree is the more it acquires an individual-consciousness. This is why shamans say the Standing People are more like us than the other Plants (which generally means we find them easier to communicate with).

Another characteristic of trees is their height. Some species can even grow up to 400 feet (120 meters) tall. To do this, trees must be deeply rooted into the earth. In this, trees epitomise both being deeply connected to Mother Earth, and reaching upwards to Father Sky (Sun). This is why they are seen as spanning the realms. They connect all realms together and help us move between them. For this reason, the axis mundi is often depicted as a great tree, the "World Tree", with its roots in the lower-world, its trunk in the middle-world, and its branches in the upper-world.

This gives the Standing People a more upper-world connection than other Plants, and more than most Animals (other than Bird), too. So, they are great teachers of upper-world themes such as ethics ("right action", "right speech", "right living", and so on), acting for the greater good, objectivity and healthy detachment, compassion, and so on.

As well as their upper-world connection, their huge root systems make them great teachers of grounding and connecting to the Earth. They have great medicine for those who find it hard to be in the physical world, for those who see the world as dangerous or unwelcoming, and for those with a top-heavy "spirituality" who reject worldly things and want to escape to the Sky. Their medicine brings a deep, rooted connection to Mother Earth—a knowing that one belongs, and that one is loved, supported and welcome here.

Trees are almost unique in the extent to which they provide habitats for other plants and animals. They provide shade, shelter, food, places to hide, nesting sites, and all sorts of other things. An individual mature tree can provide a home for dozens, or even hundreds, of other species. In this way, each tree creates a miniature ecosystem, a community. As such, the Standing People are teachers of generosity, selfless giving, cooperation, and how to create and protect communities. Trees are gentle giants, and yet the pillars of a community. They teach about the correct use of power. As such, they can teach us not to avoid our power but how to embrace it and use it well. This makes them powerful medicine for depression (as what is usually being de-pressed in depression is our own power).

Their long lives mean they are wisdom keepers. Their long memories mean they are the historians of the community. They can help teach us how to connect to the ancestors and to ancestral knowledge and wisdom. Because of their age, they are also great teachers of Eldership (Eldership being a vital role in a healthy community—something we will explore later in this book).

They are an utter joy to work with. If you work with them, some can become close allies and Guides. Like with Animals, you can have a Power Tree, who you have a deep and special relationship with. Alongside them, as with Animals, you can have other species who are regular Guides, and others still who you may only work with now and then. For example, Yew Tree is my Power Tree and I have a close and personal bond with it. I also regularly work with Hawthorn, Giant Redwood, Pine and Cedar. As well as these regulars, I know and work with the medicines of Beech, Holly, Apple, Olive, Oak, Chestnut, and have got to know many more of the Standing People over the years.

Next, let's look at the Stone People.

The Stone People are not just Stones

The Stone People are not just rocks, stones and crystals. They are physical matter. In their simplest form, they are the chemical elements—the building blocks of the physical universe. This means they are not just solids, like iron, tin and copper, but liquids in the form of bromine and mercury (the only two chemical elements that are liquid at room temperature), and gases, such as oxygen, nitrogen and argon. The Stone People are all the things made from chemical elements. This includes all the things that, in Taker society, are mistakenly thought of as non-living—rocks and stones, of course, but also water, the air, sand, soil, and so on. It also includes things like your mobile phone, computer, television, fridge, car, and so on. These are all Stone People too.

You may have already realised that the Stone People are also the things that we modern humans do deign to recognise as living things. Plants, Animals and Humans, we are all the Stone People too, as on a physical level we are composed of chemical elements. *All* physical things are Stone People, temporarily experiencing a particular form. They may be other things *as well*—Plant, Animal or Human—but they are nonetheless Stone People too. As such, someone once beautifully said that Animals and Humans are "the Stone People dancing". As well as being Human, at another level, your physical body is the Stone People having the experience of being you, a self-propelled, mobile, restless human animal. When you die, the Stone People who made up your physical body will continue their journey for billions more years, going on to experience other things (for the Stone People are *immensely* long-lived).

The Stone People are the oldest of all the People, by a very long way. They are literally as old as the universe itself. When the Big Bang brought this universe into existence around 13.8 billion years ago, it created vast amounts of hydrogen and helium gasses. Most of the physical matter in the universe, somewhere between 98% and 99.9% of it, still consists of these ancient gasses, drifting in enormous clouds through the universe. Some millions of years after the Big Bang, some of these clouds became so dense they collapsed under their own gravitational weight. This smashed the individual hydrogen and helium atoms together, creating nuclear fusion reactions, and giving birth to the first stars. In these stars, the other chemical elements were formed. When these stars eventually burnt out, they created great dust clouds of chemical elements, some of which, over millions of years, coalesced into planets. Literally everything in and on this planet, including your own body, is made from chemical elements that were forged in an ancient star; you are literally made from stardust that was itself made from hydrogen and helium created in the Big Bang.

The Stone People are the closest thing to Mother Earth herself. I do not mean just in the sense of the planet that we live on, but in the vastly bigger sense of the Great Mother, the Creator Goddess, the Spider Grandmother, Shakti, Durga, Parvati, Panchajani, Neith, Kuaket, Izanami, A'akuluujjusi, Eingana, and all her countless other names and guises. For the sake of simplicity here, let's just call her "Yin", and Father Sky "Yang". In terms of creation, Yin is like a primordial "clay" that everything else is formed from. The clay is seemingly undifferentiated, and yet within holds the patterns and forms and the potentiality of all things that can come into existence. Yang is the polar opposite. Yang is pure consciousness, pure oneness with no patterns within. Creation happens when these two fundamental energies, Yin and Yang, Creator God and Creator Goddess, come together and then Yin gives birth. The Stone People are the first of Yin's children. Or looked at another way, they are Mother Earth manifest and made physical. In turn, the Stone People go on to form everything else in the physical universe, including the stars, the planets, the Plant People, the Animal People, and us Humans.

The Stone People are, of course, themselves conscious and alive, just in a way that is very, *very* different to us. *Way* more different to us than Plant is. Off the scale different. So much so, that these days, most modern humans do not even perceive them as being alive at all. This is simply a sign of how much we have fallen, as our animist ancestors knew they were alive. They knew the mountain was alive and had to be treated with honour and respect. So too the rivers, the rocks and the waterfalls. And when they encountered western "civilisation", they knew the machete had a soul, too, as did the outboard motor, because everything is alive and conscious.

Exercise 8: Everything Is Conscious and Sacred

It is interesting to do the following exercise in natural environments, and in human-made environments, and notice the difference between the two.

Take a moment to look around you.

As you look at each thing, allow the possibility that it is conscious. Remember, this does not mean conscious in the same way as humans. It does not necessarily mean self-aware. Whatever it is may instead be part of a more collective-awareness. Remember, too, that consciousness operates at different speeds. What may not seem conscious to us at our speed, if we slow down enough, then consciousness becomes apparent.

As you look around, notice how easy or difficult you find it to accept that what you are looking at is alive and conscious. You may have no trouble accepting this with some things, but find it harder with others. Usually people find it easy with animals, and often with plants, too, but harder with other things. Simply notice where your edges lie with accepting consciousness.

With things that you do struggle to see as conscious, try to just allow yourself to be open to the idea, even if you cannot experience it.

Even if you cannot genuinely feel it as yet, just allow yourself to accept the possibility that:

- everything around you is alive and conscious.

- everything around you has a spirit and is part of Great Spirit.

- spirituality is not separate from matter.

- everything is sacred.

Done regularly, this is a great animist practice for gradually overcoming our modern-day separation and alienation from the living world around us. Done alongside journeying and other shamanic work, you will almost certainly notice that the more you do it, the more you begin to *experience* that all of the world around you is alive, rather than just thinking that it could be. Bit-by-bit, you begin to experience the world as you were meant to. You begin to become what you were meant to be—an animist.

Stone People Characteristics

These are some of the common themes that emerge from the mineral remedy provings:

- Still

- Immobile

- Passive

- Unhurried

- Non-competitive

- Structured

- Organised

- Systematic

- Regular

- Predictable

- Practical

- Detached

[Again, in discussing these themes, when I use a word from the list above, or its related form, I will underline it to highlight how what I am saying relates to the themes from the provings].

Remember, being able to grok something means being able to resonate with it. It means being able to match its frequency, mirror it, and almost become it. When it comes to groking Plants, I pointed out how much you need to step out of the fast pace of being Animal and really slow down. When it comes to groking a rock, just think about how much more you need to slow down to match its pace.

We usually think of Stone as being still – immobile, even. Or of them moving at an incredibly slow pace, too slow for us to see (tectonic plates may move only a centimetre or so a year). This is not always the case, though. Remember, the sea is one of the Stone People, and is in visible and constant motion, as are rivers and waterfalls. As molten lava, Stone can move quickly, even up to 40 miles (60 kilometres) an hour, and the rocks ejected from volcanic explosions can move at anything up to an astonishing 900 miles (1,440 kilometres) per hour. In earthquakes, too, we can experience Stone as moving quickly. Winds can be fast compared to us, of course. The highest wind speed ever recorded on Earth is 231 miles (372 kilometres) an hour, whilst the fastest winds recorded on any planet in our solar system are on Neptune, and can reach a staggering 1,500 miles (2,400 kilometres) per hour. This pales into insignificance compared to the solar winds that come from our sun. These can reach anything up to 1,600,000 miles (around 2,500,000 kilometres) an hour. Not as fast, but still an impressive thought to contemplate, is that right now we are riding on a planet that is orbiting the Sun at around 67,000 miles (107,000 kilometres) per hour.

Although Stone can move astonishingly fast, far faster than any of the other People, most of the time we experience Stone as slow to the point of appearing immobile to us. The fact is that Stone can be both vastly faster than any of the other People, and far slower. So, when it comes to speed, when groking the Stone People, that means matching and resonating with whatever speed it is moving at. Sometimes that means speeding up, and sometimes that means slowing down. It means matching the constant restlessness of the Sea, the endless flow and tumble of Waterfall, the speed of Wind, and the stillness of solid Rock.

In addition to matching speed, the real key to groking Stone is to match its sense of time. I said earlier that the Stone People are around 13.8 billion years old. In numerical long-hand, that looks like this: 13,800,000,000 years. And as if that figure alone is not hard enough to comprehend, the age to which they will live is something else again. For instance, in what is known as the "heat death" of the universe model, the universe will effectively end in 10^{100} years. In numerical long-hand, that looks like this:

10,000,000,000,000,000,000,000,000,000,000,000,000,000,000,0
00,000,000,000,000,000,000,000,000,000,000,000,000,000,000,0
00,000 years.

So, you see, the Stone People are <u>not in a hurry</u>. They really do have all the time in the world; literally, all the time in the universe. They really have seen it all, because they have actually *been* it all. They have <u>nothing to compete with</u>, and nothing to worry about. They have no Human, Animal or even Plant-like drives or agendas whatsoever. They can sit back (be *passive*) and enjoy the ride as it unfolds. This also means they are unflappable. They never get flustered, or lose the plot, or swept up in emotions. They follow the laws of physics, not feelings and agendas. In working with them, this means they are always <u>practical</u>, <u>predictable</u>, <u>regular</u> and <u>reliable</u>, <u>structured</u>, <u>systematic</u>, <u>and organised</u>.

In terms of the spectrum between self-awareness and collective-awareness, the Stone People are the ultimate in collective-awareness; at the opposite end of the spectrum to us. This is why most modern humans, trapped as they are in their human-centric world view, struggle to even recognise the Stone People as conscious at all, as their consciousness is so far away from Human.

One last thing before we turn to how to work with them in journeys. Because of things like their time-scale and their calm and unemotional nature, they can come across as supremely <u>detached</u> to us. And in a way, they are, and this is part of their teaching. They do show us that, in the great scale of things, a lot of the middle-world stuff that we get caught up in and agitated about really does not matter. When needed, they can help us step back from our human middle-world stories, entanglements, agendas and emotional responses.

The Stone People and the Medicine Bundle

As always with lower-world journeying, remember that when working with any of the Peoples, we are aiming to work with their Oversouls.

Here are a few ways to work with Stone in journeys:

- In the lower-world, if you go underground (usually by following a cave) you can come to different underground chambers, each one made from a particular kind of Rock or Crystal. So, there is an underground chamber made of Carnelian, another of Rose Quartz, and so on. These are powerful places to go if you want to work with Rocks and Crystals, as just by being in them you can soak up and absorb their specific healing medicine. They are also a great place to go to meet particular Stone People's Oversouls.

- As with Plant, the Stone's Oversoul may take on an appearance to make it easier for you to relate to them and work with them. This may be something humanoid, (or even something animal or plant-like) in appearance. More commonly, though, the Stone's Oversoul appears just as some kind of "energy". Whatever form it takes, it may either direct the healing, or do the healing itself (including the usual things, such as extraction, depossession, disentanglements etc.).

- You may shapeshift into the Stone and become it, or sink inside it and become enveloped by it, groking it from the inside out.

- The Stone may be placed inside of you, in a particular part of your body.

- You may drink an infusion of it, or bathe in water with it.

- You may be buried, burnt, cocooned or dissolved with it.

- You may inhale it as a snuff.

- You may swallow it.

- It may be used as an ointment or applied as a paste to your body.

- You may be given a piece to wear, or a blade or staff made from it (in this case, remember that there is no metalwork in the lower-world—every constructed item will be made of stone, leather, wood, bone, antler, teeth, tusk etc.).

Exercise 9: Groking a Crystal Oversoul

Choose a Crystal (or other kind of Rock) that you want to work with. Do some research on it, to give you enough of a starting point for the groking.

To do the groking, you will need either a physical piece of the crystal, or an essence made from it [there are instructions for preparing essences below]. The size of the crystal is not important, as it is simply a way of connecting to the Oversoul.

You will also need a means of recording your voice.

If using a physical crystal, because of some crystals ability to pick up and store energies, it can be wise to cleanse it first. There are all sorts of different ways to do this. These include:

- Rinsing the crystal in running water. This can damage some soluble crystals, such as selenite, calcite, halite and so on, so do some research first.

- Soaking it in saltwater for a while (this will damage some crystals, so do some research first).

- Using smoke from a cleansing herb, such as sage or mugwort.

- Leaving the crystal for a time in sunlight (or moonlight—whatever feels right).

- Leaving it packed for a time in organic brown rice.

- Blowing your breath on it.

- Holding it whilst you go into a journey, and then asking your Guides to cleanse it in the lower-world.

Whatever means you choose, the thing that is most important is your intent to cleanse it. The method itself is not that important, and not something to get hung up on, as it is really just a vehicle for your intent.

When ready, sit or lie down, and start the recording device. Then, holding the crystal, and/or taking a few drops of the essence (how many drops really does not matter), close your eyes.

Take a few moments to centre yourself, bringing your attention to your breath for a while. Then notice any tension in your body and let your body relax with each out-breath.

When you are ready, tune into the crystal that you are holding, or the essence that you have taken, and use it as a way of connecting to its Oversoul (remember, this is about working with Oversouls, not the individual middle-world crystal).

Tune into the Crystal's Oversoul.

Pay attention to what happens to you. Notice any physical sensations, and any changes to how you feel mentally or emotionally, too. As you notice things, speak them out loud so they can be picked up by your voice recorder.

Keep doing this for as long as you want. Usually somewhere between 15 and 30 minutes works well.

When you feel finished, thank the Oversoul, and then gently come back to your body and your physical surroundings. Take your time doing this, as you have probably gone deeper into trance than you realise. Make sure you are fully back in your body and take time and care to ground yourself if needed.

When you are ready, listen back to the recording and what you have learnt and experienced, and take notes.

You can do this without the use of a recording device, of course, just writing down what you can remember after the groking. In practice, though, I have found that people tend to forget things that happened in the groking (often you really are in a deeper trance than you realise). Plus, using a voice recorder means that you do not need to worry about remembering things, and so most people find that it helps them to relax deeper into the experience. In addition, listening back to what you recorded does help bring the experience back into this reality, and helps form a bridge between the worlds. As always, though, it is about whatever you find works for you!

Bottling It

Before moving on to look at the Human People, I want to discuss another way of working with Oversouls. As well as journeying, a powerful way to connect with the medicine of a Plant or a Stone is to make an essence of it. Essentially, this involves transferring the healing properties of a Plant or Stone into water (or some other liquid). This "essence" (or "elixir") can then be ingested, or used in some other way, such as adding it to baths, using it in healing lotions, and so on.

In modern times, the essences that people are usually familiar with these days are the Bach Flower Essences. These were originally made and developed by Dr. Edward Bach (1886 - 1936), an English Harley Street medical specialist in immunology. Through intuition, research, groking and experimentation, Bach developed a set of 38 flower remedies that have become well-known all over the world, the most well-known probably being Rescue Remedy, a combination of five essences from the original set.

Although Bach helped make the knowledge of essences widespread, the practice of making essences is ancient and goes back to shamanic times. For example, Australian Aborigine hunter-gatherers drank flower water for healing, and used flower water in sauna-like healing techniques. Many other cultures collected the dew from plants to use its healing properties. In places like Mongolia, Nepal and Tibet, shamans drank water that had been prepared in special ceremonial metal bowls and empowered with healing rituals. In more Fallen times, Ayurvedic medical practitioners and ancient Egyptians used water infused with the healing energies of metals and stones for healing. The Benedictine abbess, composer, visionary and writer, Hildegard von Bingham (1098 - 1179), taught about the connection between the "green" health of the natural world and the holistic health of the human person. She would wrap muslin cloths around flowering plants and leave them overnight to collect dew, then use the cloths to wrap patients in. Paracelsus (1493-1541), a Swiss German physician, botanist, and alchemist, also believed that the healing properties of plants were transferred to the dew that collected on them.

Since Bach popularised the use of essences, many people have taken up and developed his work. The result is there are probably hundreds, maybe even thousands, of different sets of essences available worldwide these days. One thing that has come out of this that I really like is that the whole process of making essences has become simplified, demystified, and made accessible to all. For essentially, making essences is a very simple process, and one that can be useful as part of one's shamanic toolkit.

Making an Essence

Making an essence simply involves transferring the healing properties of a Plant or Stone to water. There are lots of different ways to do this, and no right or wrong way. Like most things, though, people can get precious about the process and invent all sorts of rules and rituals about it. As with all my shamanic work, though, I like to keep things relatively simple and uncluttered. So, here is one straightforward way of making a Plant or Stone People essence:

Exercise 10: Making a Plant or Stone Essence

Disclaimer! Before doing this, it is important to check whether the plant or stone that you are using is poisonous or not, and whether it is safe to handle. If you are using something that is poisonous in any way, then take appropriate precautions in handling it and carefully follow the instructions below. And use your common sense!

To make the essence you will need:

1. Whatever plant or crystal you are choosing to work with.

2. A clean and empty dropper bottle.

3. A sticky label for the bottle.

4. A clear glass bowl. You want something clear so that sunlight can shine through it, and not patterned or coloured (unless you specifically want that colour in the essence).

5. Clean water. People can get very hung up on this, insisting on purified water, or water that has undergone various healing rituals, but honestly, I have found that filtered water is fine, and in the absence of that, I have found that even tap water can work fine if you use your intent to cleanse it in some way.

6. Vodka to act as a preservative if you wish to keep the essence for any length of time. You can use brandy, tequila or any other spirit instead if you wish. Or if you want to avoid using alcohol, then you can use vinegar or vegetable glycerol, or even a small amount of pure vitamin C powder (ascorbic acid). The point is simply to use something to act as a preservative (after all, you are trying to make a healing essence, not something that will end up giving you food poisoning).

Making the Essence

1. Clearly set your intent to make an essence from the Oversoul of the Plant or Stone. The individual plant or stone that you are using is just a means of connecting to the Oversoul. *Your intent matters*. It can make the difference between whether you end up making an Oversoul essence, or the essence of an individual middle-world plant or stone.

2. Ask permission from the Plant/Crystal. This is really just about good manners. Remember, all lower-world beings have healing and teaching that they will give freely on being asked, without any strings attached, but it is still good to be polite! If you ask and then get the answer, "No", then that is a middle-world response.

3. Cleanse the bowl (see the previous exercise for ideas as to how to do that). Half fill the bowl with the water.

4. Check whether the plant or stone are poisonous. If they are not, then put the plant or stone into the water (with a plant, you can use leaves, flowers, twigs or a mixture—it really is about what feels right). If the plant or stone is poisonous (or if it is a crystal that you do not want to be damaged by water), then use the double-bowl method. Put the plant or stone into a smaller bowl without any water, and then sit this smaller bowl inside the larger one, making sure that no water from the larger bowl touches the plant or stone in the smaller one.

5. Put the bowl of water in sunlight (or moonlight). Ask the Oversoul of the Plant or Stone to flow its healing into the water.

6. Leave for a period of time, until it feels ready. This can be as little as a couple of hours, or up to a day—whatever feels right.

7. Fill a dropper bottle 2/3^{rds} full of your chosen preservative (vodka, glycerol etc), then top it up with the water from the glass bowl.

8. Give the bottle a good, vigorous shake to energise it. Then label it.

9. Thank the Plant or Stone.

How to Use your Essence.

1. You can take a drop or squirt of it directly into your mouth. Or put a drop or so into some water, and then sip the water.

The quantity that you take does not matter. What matters is how often you take it, not how much. Generally, take it two-four times a day (but you can take it much more frequently if needed in acute situations).

2. It can also be added to baths, made into ointments, etc.

3. The bottle can be topped up as often as needed, just add more preservative and/or water. The healing information will copy itself into the fresh preservative/water. It will not be any weaker or more dilute, though. Essentially, you are copying digital information. Each copy is the same as the original.

4. Further bottles can be made simply by filling a bottle with 2/3^{rds} preservative and 1/3rd water, and then putting a few drops from the original bottle into the new bottle and then then shaking it vigorously. Again, the essence in the new bottle will not be any weaker than the essence in the original bottle.

This is, of course, an adaptable and flexible process. Feel free to experiment with it. If you are tempted to make Animal essences in this way, say by using a feather or bone, then all animal parts should be treated as potential sources of infections and the essence made by the double-bowl method as outlined for poisonous plants or stones, and good hygiene observed.

Being, Not Doing

Before moving on to us Human People in the next chapter, there is one last thing I want to say about working with Plant and Stone. Sometimes I see people filling their journeys up with different Plants and Stones. For example:

"My guide then took you out of the Oak Tree and blew some pow-dered Quartz all over you. She then made you drink a tea made from Burdock, Mugwort, Pine Needles and Meadowsweet. After that, she made a paste of Red Ochre and Seawater. Gorilla spat into the paste and mixed their saliva into the paste, too. Gorilla then massaged the paste into your shoulders."

This is far too cluttered. It is using the Stones and Plants more like ingredients in a spell (a "pinch of Dandelion and the eye of a Newt" kind-of-thing) rather than working with them as the great sentient and wise teachers they are. It is more Harry Potter than shamanism. Instead, keep it simple, unhurried and uncluttered. Slow down and let each thing take its time to properly work its medicine. Really ex-perience what is happening and how it feels, and pay attention to the details. This way, you will learn the most about its healing medicine.

CHAPTER THREE

The Human Story

The Long, Slow Fall

Having got a sense of the other-than-human Peoples and how to work with them, we are ready now to begin looking at what it is to be one of the Human People. The first thing I want to start with is to look at what our place is in relation to the other People, and then go on to look at the qualities of Human, and how to grok what it is to be Human (that is, Human as opposed to the domesticated, middle-world human that we are familiar with).

To do this, let us go back to the Stone People. Remember, in many ways, they are Mother Earth made physical; the result of the union of Father Sky and Mother Earth. They have no need to keep a balance between Yin and Yang. They exist in perfect balance already. They have no need to do anything. They just "exist", and the vast majority of the universe is them doing exactly that.

Some 12.8 million years after the Stone People came into existence, around a billion years or so ago on this tiny planet, a few of them went on to become Plant, second of the Peoples. To be Plant requires actively keeping a balance between the Sun and the Earth and opens up something that had never existed before—the possibility of getting the balance between Sun and Earth wrong. Then, about 200,000 million years later, Animal begins to appear. Animal does something extraordinary. It largely cuts off from having a direct connection with the Sun and the Earth. It uproots itself to gain mobility and, although still dependent on sunlight for warmth, loses the ability to take sunlight into its own body to make food. Instead, directly or indirectly, it relies on predating on Plant to survive. As Animal evolves, and social Animals begin to emerge, something else happens. Rather than just being molded by the physical environment as Stone and Plant are, these new Animals are now shaped by social structures. In learning to submit or dominate, rebel or cooperate, seduce and deceive, form bonds and love, these Animals slowly but surely open a gap between their true nature and what they need to be, or choose to be, in order to fit in.

Most things are just true to themselves and their true nature. Their middle-world self reflects their lower-world Self (or Soul, if you like). With social animals, though, in order to fit in, sometimes they need to conceal their true nature, and so the gap that begins to open is between the lower-world Self/Soul and the middle-world self. This starts imperceptibly at first, but gradually becomes wider as Animals with more complex social structures begin to evolve. This is the very beginning of domestication, the initial seeds of it. It is not domestication as we know it, as these are still wild animals. However, it is the embryonic beginning of the taming of the Self in order to fit into a social structure.

And eventually, into that gap strides Human, saying, "You call *that* not being true to your Self? Hold my beer".

We start off slowly at first. Our early human ancestors—Australopithecus, Homo habilis, and Homo erectus—would have been much the same as our nearest living relatives—orangutans, gorillas, chimpanzees and bonobos—all of whom have complex interactions and social structures they must manage. Like any great ape, our ancestors would have formed pacts and alliances, toppled leaders, told lies and practiced deception, cajoled and bargained, seduced and bonded, submitted and dominated, kept their heads down or shown off, made enemies and formed friendships, and so on. Then us modern humans, Homo sapiens, evolved, and we start off in much the same way. Somewhere along the way, though, something else happened. We developed complex language. Exactly when we developed complex language is far from settled, and there are wildly different estimates in academic circles. It seems likely that our early hominid ancestor had some form of proto-language, but as to what we would recognize as a complex, modern language, the estimates range from around 150,000 years ago to as recently as around 50,000 years ago. Whenever it happened, though, the emergence of complex language began to separate us further from simply experiencing things as they are, and living in a way that is true to Self. Instead, we increasingly began to live in a more socially and mentally constructed world.

Whatever the advantages complex language brought us, it also came with a cost. It meant that we could think abstract thoughts, thoughts that are removed from the facts of the here and now. It gave us the ability to think new ideas, create stories and myths, and invent belief systems. However, it also meant that we could begin to think and believe things that were not necessarily true. This meant that we could lose our way. Our animist ancestors knew this. This is precisely why animist tribes looked to the things that do not do this, the things that do not lose their way but which remain true to their true nature, to guide and teach humans—the other-than-human Peoples. It is also, of course, why the tribes needed shamans. They needed people who could really communicate with the other Peoples and share the other Peoples' wisdom with their tribe. And they needed people who did not fully buy into the tribe's stories, but who could be wisdom-keepers, the keepers of the good and true stories, and who could help the tribe if they began to become lost in bad stories. In this way, the shamans kept our animist ancestors living in right-relationship with each other and with the more-than-human.

And then we go and kill all our shamans.

You know the rest—the bad stories that we begin to tell ourselves and believe. Stories about "human supremacy" and "up is good and down is bad"; and then everything else that unfolds—things like totalitarian agriculture, our full-blown domestication, our cutting off from the lower-world (and losing contact with our own Souls in the process), the Fall, the Great Forgetting, patriarchy, colonialism, social inequality and, the crowning glory, the Anthropocene extinction.

Looking back like this, we can see we are the culmination of a long, slow fall. It started off slowly, way back in time, then gathered pace, almost imperceptibly at first, but gradually accelerating. Then, in just the last few thousand years, it has moved with great speed.

Remember, though, that our story is not yet over. Remember that if you look back over the last few hundred years, there are clear signs we have begun to enter a post-Fallen recovery. We are (or at least some of us are) beginning to regain our sanity, our balance and our compassion. This is also a process that started off slowly, but it is one that has picked up pace rapidly, and is speeding up still more. The signs of our recovery, of us regaining our sanity, are all over the place these days.

Remember, too, that we are surrounded by wise beings who love us and want to help us. We just need to begin listening to them again and ask them for their healing and teaching. It does not need everyone to do that. That has never been the way. It is the role of the shaman. It just needs a few of us to be willing to step into that ancient role of communicating with the more-than-human world, and bring its knowledge and healing, and its healthy stories, back to our tribe.

Humans are Animals

Within that context then, let's look at the nature of Human in more detail. As well as being Human, we are still very much Animal, and so all the themes of Animal that we looked at earlier apply to us— predator-prey, dominant-dominated, competition-cooperation, aggressive-affectionate, stressed, caring and bonding, mischievous and playful, deceitful, fast-paced, communicative, emotional, colourful, noisy, restless, curious, innovative, inventive, adaptable, and so on.

In fact, some Animal characteristics *especially* apply to us [again, I will underline words here from the Animal qualities, to highlight them]. Looking at our linguistic, technological, scientific and artistic achievements, we are undoubtably the most innovative, adaptable and *inventive* species on the planet (whether we have put these talents and abilities to good use is another matter). This inventiveness is not just a modern phenomenon, either (although the pace of it in modern times has become breath-taking). Our ancestors learnt how to prepare animal hides and weave plant fibres, and invented needles, sewing and clothing. They learnt how to knap flints and make glue, and how to make tools from stones, bones, antlers, sinews and wood. They learnt how to harness and use fire, and cook, and how fire could be used to harden spear tips. They learnt how to heat water, and how to smoke, ferment, salt and dry foods. They learnt how to prepare and use poisons, and invented spears and spear throwers, bolas, catapults, boomerangs, blow-darts, throwing axes, slings, bows and arrows, and ingenious hunting methods. They invented jewellery and body paint, painting, sculpture, and made musical instruments.

Developing complex language, and then writing and now computing, has also made us the most communicative Animal. We are without doubt the most dominant species on the planet, the most competitive, the most predatory, and arguably the most aggressive, and yet, we are also capable of quite extraordinary acts of caring and empathy. We are also quite astonishingly restless as a species, curious, and rarely satisfied with what we have or what we already know. Modern humans like to think of themselves as better than the other animals, as having risen above our "animal nature". But when you look at the these defining themes of Animal, the opposite is true. Far from having transcended Animal, we are the very definition of Animal, the *epitome* of it.

In fact, in some ways, you could say that we are the qualities of Animal taken to an extreme.

We are Something Else too

On top of these Animal characteristics, though, as we have explored already, we do have things that set us apart. They are not necessarily unique to us, but the extent to which we can do them is what makes us unusual. We may be the most animal of Animals, yet hunter-gatherers knew we were not only Animal, but something else, too. These key qualities are:

1. being the most self-aware of the Peoples, and so the least collectively-aware (i.e. the most separate of the Peoples).

2. the ability to be something other than our true, authentic Soul.

3. the ability to think abstract thoughts and imagine being something else.

Understanding these things and their consequences can help us to understand the true nature of Human.

Because they understood the extent to which, as Humans, we can be strangers to our true, authentic Soul, all hunter-gatherer cultures had initiation ceremonies. Performed around the time of adolescence, these ceremonies were designed to shock the initiate out of childhood thinking and help them step up to become a true Adult. In these animist cultures, being an Adult meant far more than just taking on middle-world adult responsibilities in the tribe. For being an

Adult (rather than just an adult), meant being connected to your true Soul. It meant knowing your true Human nature. It meant stepping up to take your place on the Earth as an interconnected-being, a part of the web of life and a member of the great tribe of *all* the Peoples. It was only once you had done this that the tribe considered you to be a fully Human Being.

These days, we no longer perform these initiation ceremonies, of course. The result is that true Adults are extremely rare in our society. For as we shall see later on in this book, the truth is that, in our culture, most people never really grow up to become truly Adult. Instead, we live in a society not of Adults but of adults; a society of children in adult-sized bodies. A culture made up of people who do not know their true authentic nature, but who are lost instead in human middle-world concerns. People who never step up to take their true place in the more-than-human world, and so, people who never take on the responsibilities that go with that.

Consequently, many years ago, my Guides told me that I needed to do an initiation into Adulthood. Getting ready for this took months of preparation. Eventually, when it came to the initiation journey itself, it was a remarkably intense and visceral experience, quite unlike any journey I had ever done up to that point. It was, as it should be, life-changing. In the journey, there were a series of tests and challenges to overcome, before I could find my lower-world Soul and step into my rightful place in the World and accept the responsibilities that come with that. After doing that, things calmed down in the journey and I found myself in an ancient forest. Bear appeared, and I was instructed to become Bear. No sooner had I done that, then Eagle Owl appeared, and I was instructed to become Eagle Owl. As soon as I had done that, Stag appeared, and I was told to be Stag. This went on and on, Animal after Animal appearing, and my shapeshifting into them one after another. I began to wonder what was going on and what on earth my Guides were trying to teach me.

And then I got it. One of the key things the initiation ceremonies are about is to teach you what it is to be Human. What my Guides were showing me was that Humans are *shapeshifters*.

It is hard to convey the impact this realisation had on me in the journey. As soon as I realised it, from the bottom of my Soul, I knew it to be true. It felt like I had finally come home. It was as if previously I had been a lost jigsaw piece, alone and isolated, a puzzle that did not make sense, and then I was placed in my rightful place in the rest of the picture. In being placed where I belonged, I made sense. I was still an individual, but now part of a whole. Being part of this bigger picture made sense of me. It was not that everything suddenly fitted into place and made sense, but that *I* fitted into place. Everything else already made sense; everything was already in its rightful place and helped make up the bigger picture. It was me who had been missing. Once I took my place, my *rightful* place, I finally understood, really groked, what animists mean when they say that to understand what it is to be Human, you have to understand our place in the bigger picture. Without that larger context, without being in right-relationship with the other pieces (the other-than-human), we are individual jigsaw pieces that have no context or meaning.

Realising this, I also understood, at a much deeper level, the truth that the World itself cannot be whole until we take our rightful place in it. Taking our place in the World not only helps make us whole, but also helps make the World whole too, for we really are a part of the whole.

Embracing our Gift

Every Animal, Plant and Stone has its unique properties and abilities, so it would be bizarre if we did not. So, what is it about us that makes our gift shapeshifting, and what does this mean for us?

Think back to the three qualities of human that I picked out earlier.

Our being the most self-aware and least collectively-aware species means that we have an ability to separate our consciousness off from the things around us that would otherwise define us. This includes separating ourselves from even being Human. And then we have this amazing ability to imagine things, to think abstract thought, coupled with an enormous curiosity, restlessness and desire for new experiences.

I am blessed to share my life with a remarkable cat called Pan. We have a very close bond, and so it was no great surprise when he started turning up in my shamanic journeys. It turns out that he is exceptionally gifted shamanically, and I have seen him do shamanic healings that are way beyond anything I can do, and my Guides treat him with great respect. Usually in journeys he is in Cat form. Sometimes he appears as a Cat-like Human, too, and if we are flying in a journey then he is in Cat form but with Raven wings (Raven being my other Power Animal). I think his taking Human-like and Raven-like forms is an expression of the closeness between the three of us—the more you work with your Power Animal(s) the more you become like them and the more you become merged. Otherwise, though, I have hardly ever seen him shapeshift, unless it is necessary to do particular things. By contrast, I am constantly shapeshifting in journeys. I am constantly wondering what it would be like to be *that* Tree, or *that* Rock or *that* Animal. I spend my time in journeys experiencing being things like Waterfalls, Mountains, Clouds, Waves or the Wind. Because it is my Human nature to be curious, and because of the unique extent to which, as a Human, I can take my awareness and separate it off from my own nature and use my imagination to think outside of myself, I can shapeshift into being something else. By contrast, Pan has no desire to do this. Most of the time he is perfectly content to be Cat. In the same way, Oak Tree does not spend its time wondering what it is like to be Waterfall, nor does Hematite wonder what it is to be Hedgehog. With our ever restless, malleable, curious, adaptable, and inventive Human nature, though, we wonder all the time.

Think about talents. Whether you have a gift for painting, photography, playing a musical instrument, writing, cooking, teaching, being a good manager, playing a sport, listening to people well, knitting, dancing or singing, whatever it is, discovering you have a talent for something is one thing, but getting good at it is another. Becoming good at something usually involves hard work and practice. Sometimes this process is enjoyable, but often it can be repetitive and boring, can involve a struggle at times, and sometimes can even be torturous. Given that, what keeps us going? Because doing something well that we have a talent for makes us feel good. It is our Soul finding a way to express itself in the world; it is us being able to be what we were meant to be. This makes us feel alive.

Whatever individual talents you may have, a talent we all have as Humans is this ability to shapeshift. Once you embrace that, if you truly take it on board and practice it and get good at it … well, honestly, I have spent ages pondering what to write next. I could say that it is exhilarating and fascinating. I could say that it is both liberating and at the same time gives life a purpose and direction. I could say that it is deeply rewarding and satisfying, or that it feels profoundly healing. Or that it feels like coming home. Or that it is like being "in the zone"; surfing the crest of a wave, scaling great heights, scoring that winning goal or achieving a personal best. That it feels like having survived against all the odds, triumphing against adversity—the Hero's journey. And it is all these things. However, written down, they are just words. To really grok what I am talking about here, though, like most things, you must experience it for yourself.

Working with the Human People

This talent that we have, of being able to step outside of what we are and become an awareness that we can put into something else, and in doing so imagine what it is to be that thing, is of course what we do in a shamanic journey. In hollowing-out, we are stepping away from our familiar middle-world identity and becoming an "awareness" that can then travel the shamanic realms and which we can place into something else, becoming it and experiencing it. What shamans know, though, is that it is essential to be able to come back at will. We need an anchor-point to return to. Without this, we would become lost in the shamanic realms, and in that direction lies madness. In this sense, our ability to shapeshift is a gift, but it does come with dangers so needs to be used wisely.

The best anchor-point, the thing that we can most reliably return to and trust to keep us sane and grounded, is our own true lower-world Soul and the way in which it is rooted in a larger, interconnected whole. With Taker society, in abandoning the lower-world and our connection with it, we also lost connection with our authentic, interconnected, rooted and grounded Souls. In doing this, we set ourselves adrift and became lost in our own imaginations and in increasingly wonky and distorted middle-world stories—the route to madness. When present-day indigenous animists and shamans look at us Taker society people and say that we are mad, they are not joking or using a figure of speech. They really mean it.

This has consequences when it comes to shamanic work. For it might seem that working with the Human People should be easy because we are already familiar with being a human. However, what we are familiar with is human, not Human. Moreover, what we are familiar with, indeed the only kind of humans that most of us know, are Taker society humans. Because of this, when it comes to meeting lower-world Humans and Tribes, our middle-world experiences and ideas about human tend to get in the way.

This is also true when it comes to meeting our own lower-world Human Soul and taking our place in the World. Meeting our lower-world Soul is what we will explore in Chapter Four of this book.

Like doing an initiation ceremony (for, after all, meeting and beginning the process of becoming our true Human Soul is indeed an initiation), we need to do some preparation. For, just like getting to the authentic lower-world, we have to get past layers of distorted middle-world Taker society thinking that gets in the way; our lower-world Soul lies buried beneath layers of distorted thinking about what it is to be Human. To get down to our true Soul, we need get past these layers, and so this is what we are going to turn to in the next chapter. This is not going to be light and fluffy. It does mean facing things that most people do not want to face. It is the "road less traveled". Like all true initiations, there are things that we must do first.

Shamanism is Part of Animism

Shamanism is part of a wider spiritual practice known as animism. Animists believe that everything is alive and conscious. This includes things that most modern humans do not even consider to be alive, let alone conscious—rocks, rivers, mountains, the wind—literally everything. This is far more than *just* a belief, though, for animists actually *experience* the world in this way. They also experience themselves as being part of nature, not in any way separate from it. Nor do they feel themselves to be above or better than other animals we share this planet with, nor even above plants or stones. For in animism, there is no hierarchy. Everything is equal and part of one big family of beings. For animists, we humans are one of the Animal People, cousins of the Plant People and Stone People, and part of an interconnected and inter-dependent web of life. As such, we humans are not *apart* from Mother Earth but literally a *part* of Mother Earth.

In addition to experiencing the world in this way, shamans are people who have the ability to go into trance-states at will, leave their bodies and travel the shamanic realms, and communicate with the spirit world in doing so. However, what exactly constitutes a trance is hard to pin down and depends on how you define the term. As such, the dividing line between shamanism and animism is blurry and far from settled and agreed upon.

This does mean that at certain points in this book, some readers may think that I should be referring to animism and not shamanism (and at other times, the reverse). Interesting whilst it may be to try and pin down precise definitions, though, doing so is complex and not really relevant to what this book is about. Rather, the point here is that, in order to really understand shamanism, we need to try and experience the world as an animist does. This means not just *believing* that everything around us is alive and conscious but *experiencing* it in that way. It means not just *believing* that we are part of an interconnected, living whole, but *experiencing* this for ourselves.

Peeling Back the Layers

All of our human hunter-gatherer ancestors were animists. All of them. All over the world, and for hundreds of thousands of years. This is because being an animist, perceiving and experiencing the world in that way, is our true and natural state. It is at the heart (and Soul) of what we are meant to be.

For most of us, though, having been raised in the modern world and living the way we do, experiencing the world as an animist is only going to be possible to some degree. Maybe if you abandoned living a modern-day lifestyle and went to live in the wilds and managed to completely immerse yourself in an animist way of life then *maybe*, after several years, you might rewire your brain enough to perceive and experience the world as our ancestors did. I am not wholly convinced, though. But in any case, renouncing the modern world and living in the wilds as an animist is not something most people realistically can or want to do. Given human population levels being what they are now, it is not a realistic option for people to choose to do *en masse* in any case. Nor would doing so help us answer an important question about both animism and shamanism: how do we make them practical and useful *for the times we live in now?*

These days, the reality is that we probably cannot fully experience the world in the way that our animist ancestors did. For what we have done with domestication and the Fall has changed not only the world around us but us, too. It has changed the way in which our brains are wired. Nevertheless, we can train ourselves to perceive the world in a *more* animist way and retrain our brains to think *more* animistic thoughts.

It should be clear by now that the Taker society has a very different mindset and way of seeing the world to that of animism and shamanism, and that it has a profoundly different relationship with the other-than-human, too. In learning shamanism, this is something that needs to be fully grasped and addressed. For much of Taker thinking is not only different to shamanic thinking, it is *inimical* to it. The problem, though, is that we are *steeped* in Taker thinking. We are raised in it, and so immersed in it that we usually do not know anything else. It is habitual to us and is our default way of thinking. So much so that, most of the time, we do not even realise we are thinking this way, and just how profoundly messed-up its underlying premises are. That is, until we wake up to this and begin the conscious and deliberate process of freeing ourselves from it. It is only by doing this that we can begin to understand what shamanism truly is.

Wearing your Clothes Back-to-Front

In truth, it is not just us modern people trying to learn shamanism who need to free ourselves from the thinking of the culture that we live in. Deprogramming from the stories of the culture that you have been raised in is an essential part of training to be a shaman any-where, and this has been true throughout human history. Shamans were people who lived at the margins of the culture to which they belonged. They were both part of their tribe, and yet distanced from it. This distance was not because shamans live in some rarefied "spir-itual" state, and that the day-to-day concerns of everyday life were somehow "beneath" them. Not at all. In fact, to think in that way is a very Taker way of viewing "spiritual" people and their relationship to society. It is symptomatic of the way we have been programmed to see Spirit and matter as separate, and that in order to be "spiritual" we must transcend the physical realm.

Because they knew that Spirit and matter are not separate, and that everything is sacred, shamans did not withdraw from the physical world. Nor did they renounce human society. For the role of the shaman was, and still is, *to be of service.* The shaman was distant enough from the tribe to be able to see the tribe objectively and see the tribe's stories for what they are, and yet still close enough to it to be able to help when needed. In this way, part of the role of the shaman was to shape the stories that make a culture what it is, and in doing so, keep the tribe healthy and on the right path.

For this reason, in most cultures, part of shamanic training involved periods of time doing things in ways that they were not normally done, in order to shake the trainee out of social norms. For example, an apprentice shaman might have to wear their clothes back-to-front or inside-out. They might have to walk backwards. They might stand whilst everyone else sat, sit when everyone else was standing, shout when everyone else was being quiet, or be silent when everyone else was being noisy. In addition to these kinds of things, they would be given information no one other than the shamans knew, and which changed the way in which they saw the world. That included being told the stories that everyone else in the tribe believed to be true were not in fact "true", but there for social cohesion and to keep the tribe in right-relationship with the other-than-human.

This did (and still does) come with costs, which is why indigenous people sometimes say, "Who on earth would want to be a shaman?". And indeed, it is not a path that most people want to take. Most people choose to live in blissful ignorance. However, if you really want to understand what shamanism is, and if it is a path that you truly want to walk in this life, then that means waking up and facing the nature of the culture that we are living in now.

Seeing Taker Society for What it is

The Taker society that we are living in is, from a shamanic perspective, a deeply psychopathic one. As we grow up in it, through the process of socialisation and domestication, we adopt ways of thinking and seeing the world that are *profoundly* un-shamanic. Things like:

- Thinking that we are more intelligent or conscious than other species.

- Dividing the world into living and non-living things.

- Materialistic thinking.

- Excessive consumption.

- The idea that we can use and abuse other animals, plants, and the Earth as we wish.

- The idea of "ownership".

- Taking everything and leaving nothing.

- The way we think the world revolves around us, and that even the gods and the goddesses are obsessed with us (to the extent that they even are bothered about things like what we eat or what we get up to in our bedrooms).

- Our tendency to think in hierarchies.

- Thinking that inequality is normal and okay.

- Oppressing sections of society.

- Violence.

- Thinking that the spirits are "just" imaginary and not real.

And so many other things.

The institutions within society usually reflect these things. There are some honourable exceptions, but on the whole, things like political parties, banks, companies and corporations, organised religions, schools, hospitals, businesses, clubs, committees, the media and so on, are usually based on these unhealthy Taker society thoughts and values.

Generally, characteristic of the dominant Taker society is that:

1. It is a hierarchy run by charismatic leaders (often by narcissists, sociopaths and psychopaths).

2. These leaders often have little or no real accountability.

3. These leaders seek to manipulate, exploit and coerce those below them. They usually do this by keeping people divided against each other, or united in the persecution of a minority group or groups.

4. The leaders take more than is their fair share.

5. The leaders undermine or even persecute those who threaten their authority.

6. People who do not buy into the dominant culture are seen as weird or threatening.

7. The culture tells people that what it says is right, and that this is how things are and always have been. It writes history. It sets and controls the narrative and is resistant to change or challenge.

8. The culture is bad for the mental and spiritual health of its members (and sometimes, even their physical health).

These are all characteristics of a cult.

However, also characteristic of a cult is that it tends to be a minority thing, at odds with normal society and divergent from the consensus and the majority. Now, you may think this characteristic of cults cannot apply to the culture we live in, because this culture *is* the majority, not the minority. It is what is normal, and it is the consensus.

However, this is what Daniel Quinn calls "The Great Forgetting"— the myth that Taker society is normal and how things have always been. This is one of the destructive myths Taker society tells us, and one we need to free ourselves from. Instead of believing it, we need to step back and see the bigger picture.

We need to do what Quinn refers to as "The Great Remembering". We need to remember that Taker society is only a few thousand years old. It makes up only a small percentage of human history. Looked at in this bigger context, it is *Taker society* that is the minority. *It* is the thing that has diverged from the consensus; the thing that is completely at odds with the tens of thousands of years of Leaver culture that proceeded it.

It is also destructive and self-destructive. It is a way of thinking and acting that is out of touch with reality, preposterous and delusional. It persecutes those who dare challenge it, and those who do not fit in and adopt its beliefs, values and lifestyle. And it is bad for the spiritual, mental, emotional and physical health of its members. It is run by charismatic, narcissistic and psychopathic leaders, with little or no real and effective accountability. These leaders exploit the rest of the population, leading to massive inequality in the distribution of resources. According to a report by the Organisation for Economic Co-operation and Development, just 5% of the world's population own 71.6% of world wealth, and only 1,266 of the world's richest people own as much as the bottom 60% of the world's population (over four *billion* people). That report was done in 2012. Since then, the indications are that the inequality gap has grown worse.

The Taker Society is a Cult

Looked at in this way, and in the wider context of human history, the psychopathic Taker society we live in fits all the criteria that defines a cult. Nothing about it is "normal". And, in the relatively short period of time it has been around, the Taker society—the Taker *cult*—has brought us the Anthropocene extinction: the *human-created* mass extinction of our brothers and sisters (the other species we share this world with). It has brought us to a place where we are also facing the possibility, even probability, of our own extinction, by our own hands.

Remember, to practice shamanism is to try and wake up and see the truth, the things that most other people in a culture do not want to see. So, let's face the reality. The Taker society is not even *just* a cult.

It is a death cult.

Right now, it is killing species at around *1,000* times the normal rate of extinction. On top of that, the majority of wild species that have not gone extinct yet are facing catastrophic decline in their numbers. It is also destroying the environment on which our own lives depend, threatening our own survival. Looked at in this way, the Taker cult is not *just* a death cult.

It is a *suicidal* death cult.

And we are living in it. We have been raised in it and indoctrinated into it.

The survival of literally hundreds upon thousands of species of plants and animals, and our *own* survival as a species, depends upon our waking up and seeing the truth about the dominant culture. There is no rehearsal in dealing with this. This really is an emergency. We *have* to wake up.

It has always been the shaman's role to be awake, to be able to watch over society and how humans are living in relation to the more-than-human world. Their role is to unflinchingly face things as they are; to be prepared to look into the darkness and see the things most people choose not to see. Doing that is the definition of the word "shaman"—someone who can see in the dark and see the things that other people cannot, or will not, see. For when things go wrong, when humans stray off the path and turn away from what is in accordance with Great Spirit, it is, and always has been, the role of the shaman to wake people up, to heal their wounds, and to provide the healthy stories that help people come back to right-relationship.

Being able to See what Shamanism really is

Doing that these days involves waking up from the spell of Taker cult thinking. The problem, though, is that, for most people, Taker thinking is unconscious. It is a set of ideas, values, stories, beliefs, opinions and preconceptions that people bring to how they perceive the world. It shapes and colours what they see around them. This usually means that, when people are learning something new, they unconsciously bring Taker perception to the process. Learning shamanism is no exception to this.

You may be lucky enough to live in a place where shamanism survived to the present day, and so can learn directly from people practicing an unbroken lineage. However, for most people in the West, shamanism is a broken lineage, something that we are trying to piece back together. In the process of reinventing shamanism and making it relevant to our modern-day lives, the danger is that we unconsciously bring Taker thinking to that process. Indeed, my experience is that this is exactly what happens most of the time; a lot of present-day shamanism is, to varying degrees, infected with Taker society thinking.

Waking Up

Remember, Taker society started around 11,000 BC with our adoption of totalitarian agriculture. Then, starting around 4,000 BC, in a process the author and psychologist Steve Taylor calls "The Fall", we begin to move *en masse* into fortified settlements. This leads to the birth of the first city-state cultures, which gradually evolve into the dominant culture we now live.

Words are important, as they define and shape how we perceive things—something the dominant culture understands and knows only too well. For Taker society calls the period from 4,000 BC to the present day "civilisation". As I said in the last book, the word "civilisation" is from the Latin civilis ("civil") and related to civis ("citizen") and civitas ("city"). So, the literal meaning of the word is "city culture". In terms of the way in which we use the word, though, it has far more meaning than just that. If you look the word "civilisation" up in dictionaries, the definitions include things like: "an advanced stage of social development and organization"; "a human society that has highly developed material and spiritual resources and a complex cultural, political, and legal organization" and "the peoples or nations collectively who have achieved such a state"; "the comfort and convenience of modern life"; "excellence in thought and manners and taste" and "intellectual refinement"; and even in one dictionary "the people slowly progressed from barbarism to civilization".

Conversely, the adjective "uncivilised" means being not socially, culturally, or morally "advanced". It is a derogatory term, and synonymous with being rude, uncouth, crude, barbaric, savage and ignorant.

Do you see what is going on here? It is the dominant culture, through language, instilling in its members (in *us*) the idea that as a culture it is "better" than the hunter-gatherer cultures that preceded it. Most people these days grow up believing this. It is just a "fact" they do not even question and accept as being true.

It is, though, complete and utter crap.

The Myth of Taker Supremacy

As I write this, a few months ago a fundamentalist Christian missionary was killed by members of an Andamans Island hunter-gatherer tribe. In case you do not know, the Andamans Islands lie in the Bay of Bengal, between India and Mayanmar. They are home to the Andamanese, a group of indigenous people that include the Jarawa and Sentinelese tribes. The Sentinelese are generally isolationist and have had little contact with any other people. They tend to kill any outsiders on sight. They still live a hunter-gatherer lifestyle. The Indian government protects the Sentinelese's right to their privacy.

The reason the Sentinelese are so hostile to outsiders is that they have learnt to be. It is, a matter of survival for them. In the past, a succession of Malays, Burmese and Chinese slavers raided the Andaman Islands, capturing and selling the islanders as slaves, and so the islanders learnt to fear and hate outsiders. Then the British arrived, the master colonialists. The Sentinelese witnessed what then happened to the other tribes they shared the Islands with. In 1858, the number of indigenous people (excluding the Sentinelese) in the Andamans was conservatively estimated at 4,800. After the British arrived, due to a combination of disease epidemics, colonialists encroaching on their land, and periods of deliberate massacre, the population is now estimated to be below 700. They are on the verge of extinction.

The Indian government classes the Sentinelese as a Particularly Vulnerable Tribal Group (PVTG) and, to protect them from diseases to which they have no immunity, all contact with them is forbidden. Under Indian law, it is illegal for anyone to be within five nautical miles of the islands. This did not matter to John Allen Chau, though. Chau was a 26-year-old fundamentalist Christian missionary from the U.SA. In 2019, he paid some local fisherman to take him to the island where the Sentinelese live. Before arriving on the island, he wrote: "Lord, is this island Satan's last stronghold where none have heard or even had the chance to hear your name?". He wanted to bring the news of his Taker cult sky religion to these "uncivilised savages", even if that probably meant bringing fatal diseases to them in the process. "Saving" them was what mattered, even if it meant killing them all in the process.

On arriving at the island, the Sentinelese shot him dead in a hail of arrows before he even got off the beach.

Many people might think Chau's actions to be, at best, appallingly misguided. Some people might think his actions to be stupid, or even criminal. To some people, though, he is a martyr. Indeed, in earlier times he would probably have been made a saint. In the media, although the consensus seemed to be that the whole incident was unfortunate and regrettable, there were also those who called for the ban on contacting the Sentinelese to be lifted. It was high time, such people argued, that the Sentinelese be shown the benefits of joining the modern world. In short, it was time that "civilisation" be brought to these wild, primitive and ignorant savages; time that they became tamed and domesticated like us. This is Taker cult thinking. Like the Borg in Star Trek, the Taker cult thinks that all other peoples and cultures must be forcibly assimilated and turned into drones. For indigenous peoples, history shows this never goes well.

Taker Genocide

In the case of John Allen Chau and the Sentinelese, it was the missionary who died. Usually, though, in encounters between the Taker cult and indigenous people, it is the indigenous people who die. In 1491, it is estimated that the indigenous population of the Americas was around 145 million people. A mere 200 years later, the arrival of the Taker cult had reduced the number of indigenous Americans by an appalling 90-95 percent, or by around somewhere between 130 to 138 *million* people.

In Australia, the British colonists regarded the indigenous Aborigines as vermin and sometimes even hunted them for sport. The number of Aborigines declined by a staggering 84% after British colonization. Similarly, the Maori population of New Zealand declined by 57%. The first nations population of British Columbia in Canada decreased by 75%. And the Americas, Australia and New Zealand are just the genocides of indigenous people that most people are familiar with. The Russians slaughtered the indigenous peoples of Siberia, killing 90% of the indigenous Kamchadals and 50% of the Vogules people, for example, and exterminated some ethnic groups entirely. The Japanese did much the same to the indigenous Ainu, Oroqen and Hezhen people, amongst others. Similar Taker cult genocides have happened in Vietnam, the Congo, China … in truth, all over what we absurdly call the "civilised" world. For this is what "civilising" indigenous people usually means to the Taker cult—killing them and taking their land.

It happened here in Europe, too. People often assume that when the Taker agriculturalists arrived on their lands, the indigenous European hunter-gatherer people simply took up agriculture too. For remember, we are brought up being told that agriculture is a better and easier way of life than hunter-gathering. Given that, it would be natural to think that on seeing agriculture, hunter-gatherers would be delighted and only too happy to exchange their (supposedly) harsh life-style for the (supposed) benefits of agriculture. In fact, though, DNA testing of current Europeans shows that only a tiny percentage of indigenous European DNA remains. The truth is that what happened in places like the Americas and Australasia happened here. The indigenous hunter-gatherers of Europe were all but wiped out.

It is not as if this is all in the past, either; that it is all just "history". Taker cult genocide is still being waged *right now*. As you read this, it is happening in Bangladesh, Brazil, Colombia, Congo (DRC), East Timor, Guatemala, Irian Jaya/West Papua, Myanmar, Paraguay, Tibet and other places.

Genocide is what the Taker cult does. Let's not forget it is not just humans this death cult does this to, either. It does the same thing, but on an even bigger scale, to our other-than-human relatives.

Coming Back to Sanity

Remember, words have power. They shape and define how we perceive things. To call the Taker cult a "culture" normalises it. It lets it off the hook. For whilst the word "culture" can simply mean something like "the way of life, customs and beliefs of a particular group of people", in our minds we associate it with the word "cultured". The meanings of "cultured" include things like accomplished, civilised, genteel, polished, educated, and refined. The antonyms of the word "cultured" include barbaric, barbarous, uncivilised, ungenteel, unpolished, and unrefined. Surely though, compared to the Leaver cultures, it is the *Taker* cult that is all these things.

The Taker cult is insane. It is an illness. It seems to me that to call it a "culture" or "civilisation" is to normalise it and give it a legitimacy that it in no way deserves. It is to buy into its own propaganda, and it gets in the way of our waking up and seeing it for what it really is. For these reasons, I will be referring to Taker society as the Taker *cult* from now on.

The Normalisation of Violence and Abuse

I do understand that even entertaining the idea that we are living in a suicidal death cult is not exactly a comfortable thought. In teaching students, it is something that sometimes I see people resist even considering.

I think there are a number of reasons for this resistance. As a psychotherapist, I have many times heard clients who are new to therapy describe their childhood as "normal", even if it clearly was not normal at all. One reason for this is that, as children, we usually have nothing to compare our childhood with. We grow up thinking that what is happening around us, and *to* us, is "normal". It is what we are familiar with, and all that we know. This is less often the case when there has been sexual abuse in childhood, as even as children we can sense there is something deeply wrong with what is happening. It is also less often the case when there is extreme violence in childhood. But sexual abuse and extreme violence aside, we have a great capacity to normalise what happens in childhood and not fully appreciate its impact on us. Take physical punishment, for example. People often say that their parents regularly hit them, but it "obviously" did not do them any harm because they have "turned out alright". However, if someone has grown up to think that using physical violence on people who are defenceless and weaker than you is okay, then they have really not "turned out alright" at all. Their childhood has damaged them in terms of normalising and accepting violence.

Thinking that it is okay to hit children is indeed the norm in most parts of the world these days. The Taker cult tells us that without corporal punishment, children will grow up to be lawless and out of control, with no manners and no respect for their elders. Like most Taker cult thinking, though, it is simply not true and (as with many things) all that we have to do is look back to our animist ancestors to see it for the nonsense it is. In his book, *"The World Until Yesterday: What Can We Learn from Traditional Societies?"* the historian Jared Diamond points out that although corporal punishment existed in some hunter-gatherer cultures, it was rare. Most hunter-gatherer adults did not hit children. Yet, those cultures were the most emotionally and psychologically healthy human societies the world has ever known, and are characterised by children growing up to be well-adjusted adult members of their tribe.

Take a moment to let this sink in. Modern humans, Homo sapiens, are around 200,000 years old as a species. The Taker cult is a little over 11,000 years old. However, as I explored in the *"The Shamanic Journey"*, it was not until the emergence of the first city-states and empires, around 6,000 years ago (the Fall), that the violence inherent in Taker thinking really kicked in. Taking round figures then, this means that for around about 195,000 years or so, that is 95% of the history of our species, we mostly raised children without hitting them. Yet people grew up to be high-functioning members of the societies in which they lived, societies that were characterised by excellent physical, mental, emotional and spiritual health compared to ours.

The fact is there is nothing necessary or normal about using violence against children. Doing so is something that only comes in with the emergence of the Taker cult. It comes in with the Taker cult, because violence is what the Taker cult does: violence towards children, towards each other as adults, towards animals, plants, and towards the Earth herself.

The Taker cult tells us this violence is normal; that it is our natural state and an inevitable fact of life. That is a lie. We need to remember (the Great Remembering) that history shows us the opposite. There is nothing normal about the violence of the Taker cult. It is not our true nature, but a sickness.

Emotional Neglect

In terms of violence, there was no sexual abuse in my own childhood, and no physical abuse to speak of either. My father only ever hit me once and, afterwards, he felt so bad about it that he never did it again. What my childhood *was* characterised by was emotional neglect. Whilst the basics of my physical needs were met, the neglect of my emotional and psychological needs was extreme. My mother suffered with major anxiety issues and agoraphobia and spent virtually all her time shut in the kitchen, which was out of bounds to me. She had a borderline grip on reality, a very fragile personality, and periodically had "nervous break-downs". My father suffered from periods of severe depression and had PTSD from his time as a soldier in the Second World War. He spent all his time either at work, holed up in his study (another place that was strictly off-limits to everyone else), or else sitting, glowering at the television with nobody else being allowed to speak—the only time we ever spent "together" as a family. Pretty much the only time my parents spoke to me was to tell me off or to criticise me. Other than that, they had absolutely no interest in me. They never played with me. Not once. They never hugged me. I never had a single bed-time story read to me. They never asked me how my day had been. They went to their graves knowing almost nothing about me.

From both being a psychotherapist, and from being a client in psychotherapy myself, I understand the enormous impact and damage that such a childhood has. However, as a *child*, I did not know that, for to me it was just "normal". I did know that I was deeply lonely, but everyone else in the family seemed to be deeply lonely too, and I thought that is just how life is, and how things are.

Whilst such childhoods may not be the norm these days, as a psychotherapist I have worked with enough people over the years to know that, they are, to varying degrees, not that uncommon either. It is also true that, not so long ago, they would have been the norm, in the days when children were meant to be "seen but not heard". Plus, until relatively recently, of course, children as young as seven were sent to work in appalling conditions in factories and mines, with no thought whatsoever given to their emotional or psychological needs.

As with violence in childhood, though, if we look back to hunter-gatherer cultures, we see a very different picture. In these pre-Fallen cultures, childhood neglect was rare to the point of being virtually non-existent. As Jared Diamond explores in his book, hunter-gatherer child-rearing is characterised by keeping children close, and quickly responding to their emotional needs and well-being. As such, there are countless examples of anthropologists studying hunter-gatherer tribes from all over the world and describing the children as "unusually happy and well adjusted". "Unusual", that is, compared to our children.

Not everyone these days has had an abusive or neglectful childhood, of course. I do really know that! You may have had a genuinely happy and well-adjusted childhood. If you have children yourself, then you may be giving them a happy childhood too. In which case, that is marvellous. We need much more of that in the world. However, the childhoods of the hundreds of psychotherapy clients that I have worked with over the years were not happy. I have also taught hundreds of people shamanism over the years and not all of them, but certainly the *majority* of them, would not describe their childhoods as truly happy either.

Given how my parents treated me, my own childhood certainly was not a happy one. In saying that, I am not criticising or judging my parents. It is simply the truth of what happened. My parents behaved as they did, and were as they were, because of their own childhoods. Both had shockingly neglectful parents themselves who, in turn, came from parents who had neglected them in childhood too, and so on back through the generations. The point is that, things like abuse and neglect are endemic in the Taker cult. Most people are raised in this and, because they do not know any better, pass this on to their children. So, the cycle of violence, abuse and neglect that characterises the cult gets passed down the generations and rolls on and on.

The importance of the Great Remembering, of looking back to our animist ancestors and how they lived, is twofold here. By putting things in a larger context, it can help us realise that these things really are not normal at all. Plus, by showing us a different way of being, a way that was healthier, it can give us a template to work with and show us what we need to do to heal.

Denial as a Survival Mechanism

As well as simply not knowing any better, another reason people often describe their childhood as normal even if it was not, is to do with survival. This is because for a child in a dysfunctional family, it is often simply too psychologically and emotionally dangerous for them to face the truth of what is going on around them. Instead, a child may tell themselves that their parents must "love them really", or they may make excuses for their parents, or pretend to themselves that things are not really that bad. Or they may simply shut off and block things out. It is often only as adults, once people are out of their childhood situation and no longer dependent on their parents for survival, that they can really face the truth of how things were (but even then, even as adults, most people continue to deny, avoid, make excuses, pretend or forget).

Another reason people make excuses for their dysfunctional family and childhood is a version of Stockholm syndrome. Usually, people think of Stockholm Syndrome as to do with terrorism. It is, of course, a condition in which hostages develop a psychological alliance with their captors as a survival strategy during their captivity, even though the alliance is irrational in light of the danger the victims are in. The term "Stockholm syndrome" came from a case in 1973 where Jan-Erik Olsson, a convict on parole, took four employees of a bank hostage, in Stockholm, Sweden. He negotiated the release from prison of his friend Clark Olofsson to assist him. Together, the two of them held the hostages captive for six days. When the hostages were eventually released, none of them would testify against either captor in court. Instead, they began raising money for their captors' legal defence.

Stockholm syndrome is a survival mechanism. It happens because the victim's need to survive and keep on the captor's good side is stronger than their impulse to hate their captor. The term is now used to include not just what can happen in hostage situations, but also to victims of human trafficking, prisoners of war, and, yes, victims of domestic or child abuse. As a psychotherapist, some version of Stockholm syndrome is exactly what I see when I witness some client's defending the behaviour of their parents or their dysfunctional family.

A Big Thing to Face

All these mechanisms of denial can apply to our relationship with the Taker cult too. Like a child growing up in a dysfunctional family, we grow up in the Taker cult not really understanding just how dysfunctional it is. To us it seems "normal", and just "the way things are". Only a few percent of people from dysfunctional and abusive families find the courage to get into therapy and face the truth of what really happened to them. For it does take courage. Indeed, the author and psychiatrist Scott Peck in *"The Road Less Travelled"* says that such people are amongst the bravest people in the world (and having spent much of my adult life working with such people, I agree with him). Similarly, only a few percent of the people in the Taker cult wake up and face its true nature.

It is scary, and can feel overwhelming, to face up to the reality of what we are living in. Most people just do not want to do it. They prefer to keep taking the blue pill and living in denial. And not *just* in denial. Like people suffering from Stockholm syndrome, people defend the Taker cult. They say things like, "Look at all the good things it has given us. Look at things like modern medicine, safe housing, warm showers, and so on".

It is true that not everything that has come out of the Taker cult is bad. Halfway through writing this book, my partner was diagnosed with a serious illness. It was the kind of thing that, in days gone by, would have been a certain death sentence. Instead, she received treatment that, really, borders on the miraculous, and she can now go on to enjoy many more years of a hopefully long and happy life. I too am here because of modern medicine. It has saved my life on at least two occasions now. Without it, I would have been dead long before I got to write this book.

"And" Not "But"

In defending their abusive or neglectful parents, clients often use the word "but" to make excuses. For example, "Yes, those things they did were awful, *but* then they used to do these nice things too". Or, "Yes, they abused me, but deep down I know they loved me really". The problem is that using the word "but" like this usually gets in the way of fully taking on board what really happened, and the effects and impact of it. As long as a client is in denial like this, then any recovery will only be partial. In this case, as a therapist, one of my aims is to help the client reframe their thinking, in terms of their using "and" instead of "but". For example, "Yes, my parents may have done nice things at times, *and* the other things they did were still abusive". It is a seemingly small change, but one that makes a massive difference.

People who defend Taker cult sometimes do so by saying that anyone who attacks it should be doing something like living in the woods, wearing bearskins and foraging for their own food. They say that if you criticise capitalism and consumerism, then you are a hypocrite if you live in a house with central heating and own a mobile phone. I am a hypocrite, apparently, for criticising the Taker cult whilst typing this book on a laptop (seemingly, I should be writing the book on parchment, using a quill pen made from a bird that I hunted myself using a stone and sling, and using homemade ink). The thing is, not everything in the modern world is bad. I enjoy having a safe home with clean, running water on tap. I enjoy being able to have a warm shower in the morning. I love how my laptop means I can access an incredible amount of information at the touch of a button, and means that I can get the message of Therapeutic Shamanism out to people literally all over the globe. *And* though (*"and"*, not "but"), there are clearly things about the way we are living now that are deeply wrong.

It is important, too, to not romanticise hunter-gatherer life. There are lots of things about it that would have been really tough. It would have been physically dangerous. There would have been parasites to deal with, and no antibiotics, fungicides or vermifuges. There were dangerous wild animals around. Food would have been scarce at times. Lots of children would have not made it to adulthood, and lots of women would have died in childbirth. And whilst we do know that most hunter-gatherer tribes had good mental and emotional health, people are people, and there are bound to have been tensions and conflicts both within and between tribes. And though (another "and", not "but"), it is simply true that in hunter-gatherer, animist thinking we can find the answers to many of the problems we now face. Animist thinking can heal the broken relationship that we have not only with our each other, but with the more-than-human world, too.

In any case, as long as human population levels remain as they are, then our future does not lie in all of us abandoning technology and going to live in the woods by foraging. For one thing, if billions of us left cities and tried to do that, it would be a disaster for the countryside and completely unsustainable. Rather, it is about waking up to the reality of the situation we are in, having the courage to unflinchingly face the things that are wrong and which need changing, and coming up with radical and new solutions. And whilst the solutions need to be new, the healthiest template on which we can base them on will usually be found in the wisdom of our animist, Leaver-culture ancestors.

Different Kinds of Shamanism

Animist thinking is the cure for the sickness that is the Taker cult. To really find that cure, though—an animist way of perceiving and being in the world that works in our modern-day lives—we need first to look to *pre-Fallen* animism. For not all present-day animism or shamanism is free of Taker cult thinking.

For most Westerners, shamanism is usually something that they "bolt on" to Taker cult thinking. People can learn to do shamanic journeys, find their Power Animal, have great experiences with their Guides, and do shamanic healings for others, all without questioning their (unconsciously held) Taker thinking. People variously add shamanism on to things like New Age beliefs, theistic thinking, Celtic or Norse Mythology, Druidry, Yoga and so on. Now, these are all things that undoubtedly have their own good points and values. *However,* they are all nevertheless still products of totalitarian agricultural, domesticated and Fallen societies, and so, whatever their good points are, they also show the hallmarks of that unhealthy way of seeing the world.

It is crucial to realise that, these days, this is true to some extent even of much indigenous shamanism, for virtually all existing shamanic societies are *agricultural*. Genuine hunter-gatherer shamanic cultures have all but gone. Even the few animist nomadic societies that are left are usually herders, practicing animal husbandry and not hunter-gathering. This means that, animist or not, they are to some degree still Fallen societies, affected (and infected) by domestication and

Taker thinking. As such, they inevitably practice a different kind of shamanism to that practiced by their hunter-gatherer ancestors.

Before going further, I want to make clear that this is in no way to single out present-day animist societies for criticism. Far from it. Whilst still showing signs of Taker cult thinking, such societies still have a much healthier relationship with the Earth and with the more-than-human than the societies that abandoned animism and shamanism altogether. As such, we owe a truly incalculable debt to them for keeping shamanic and animist knowledge and practices alive. They really have been the wisdom-keepers through the dark times of domestication and the Fall.

My criticism is not of existing shamanic societies. It is of Taker cult thinking, in *all* its various forms and guises, and *wherever* it is found.

Taker thinking can Infect Shamanism

The extent to which modern-day indigenous shamanic societies have been influenced by Taker thinking will vary, depending on how recently they have adopted an agricultural lifestyle. In places like North America and Australia, colonisation by the Taker cult is a comparatively recent thing, and so it is not that long ago that people were still living as hunter-gatherers. This means the indigenous, pre-agricultural knowledge, practices and ways of thinking can still be relatively intact. In other shamanic societies that exist now, though, the indigenous people adopted agriculture a long time ago. This is true of pastoral (herder) animist and shamanic societies, such as in parts of Africa, Mongolia and Siberia, Scandinavia and so on. In Mongolia, for example, herding was adopted by the indigenous people several thousand years ago. Herding, although still nomadic, is based on a *very* different relationship with animals and the earth to that of hunter-gathering.

Likewise, many people consider empires such as the Inca, Aztec and Toltec to be shamanic. Arguably that may be true, depending on how one defines shamanism. They were, though, undeniably Fallen societies, and show all the characteristics of the Taker cult, including being largely city-based, based on massive inequality, extremely hierarchical, run by psychopathic leaders, patriarchal, violent, militaristic, and so on.

The point I am trying to make here is that, just because a society is practicing a form of shamanism or animism, these days that does *not* necessarily mean that it is free of Taker thinking. There are many societies that we consider shamanic that are heavily Taker-based, and their shamanic practices reflect this.

To give an example, Taker-based shamanic societies usually practice animal sacrifice. In shamanic societies in large parts of Mongolia, Siberia and Africa, for example, sacrificing animals to the spirits is common-place, and indeed in some places regarded as essential in shamanic work. I have had several conversations with a Mongolian shaman, who claims to be able to trace his shamanic lineage back 27 generations. He is utterly scathing of Westerners practicing shamanism without performing animal sacrifice as, in his opinion and shamanic tradition, working with the spirits must involve blood sacrifices. If you do the maths, though, the reality is that his "lineage" only stretches back a few hundred years, whereas agriculture has been practiced in Mongolia for thousands of years. This makes his version of shamanism one that is heavily influenced by Taker cult thinking, to the extent that he thinks that owning and farming animals, and then sacrificing them to the spirits is intrinsic to shamanism; that it is the *only* way to practice shamanism.

This is simply not true. Whilst there *may* have been some hunter-gatherer cultures that practiced animal sacrifice, I do not know of any. Certainly, *if* the practice did exist then it was extremely rare. For one thing, hunter-gatherers did not have "spare" animals lying around. It is agriculture that produces such surplus. Much more importantly, though, hunter-gather people would simply not dream of "using" animals in this way, because their relationship with animals was not hierarchical. Animals were not property or commodities to be used as humans saw fit.

Another example of the difference between the way our hunter-gatherer ancestors practiced shamanism, and how it is practiced in modern-day Taker-influenced shamanic societies, is the issue of possession (as in, "being possessed"). Most people think the notion of possession is central to shamanism, and that performing de-possessions (removing unhelpful spirits from people, objects or places) is a major aspect of shamanic work. In many forms of shamanism that exist these days, that is indeed the case. However, as I discussed in the previous book in this series, the anthropologist Michael Winkelmann, in *"Shamans, Priest and Witches: A Cross Cultural Study of Magico-Religious Practitioners"*, points out that hunter-gatherer societies generally do not experience possession. Similarly, in *"Altered States of Consciousness within a General Evolutionary Perspective: A Holocultural Analysis"*, the anthropologists Erika Bourguignon and Thomas L. Evascau point out that possession experiences are generally only found in *agricultural* societies, and in societies that are characterised by social stratification and hierarchy (so, not in hunter-gatherer cultures).

Possession is a symptom of the Taker cult. It describes a relationship between things that is based on inequality, power-over and ownership. Hunter-gatherers did not own anything much at all. It is only with the adoption of agriculture that we see the idea of ownership emerge (indeed, ownership is at the heart of Taker thinking). With agriculture we began to acquire possessions—things that we "own" and have power over. In turn (due to the massive soul-loss and power-loss that ensued with our separating ourselves from the natural world), we became susceptible to being possessed ourselves—other things having power over us and owning us. Dealing with this then became central to shamanic work, and so the practice of de-possession emerged, and has become synonymous with shamanism in modern times.

This development had other effects, too, in terms of the way shamanism was practiced. In hunter-gatherer times, shamans worked with their guides but were rarely, if ever, possessed by them. This is in marked contrast to the kind of shamanism practiced in agricultural times, where being voluntarily possessed by one's guides became a normal way of working. The result of this was the emergence of very different practices to those used by our hunter-gatherer ancestors, and a very different relationship with the more-than-human world.

Pre-Fallen, Fallen and Post-Fallen Shamanism

Essentially then, there are three different kinds of shamanism, belonging to three different eras, with three different ways of thinking and relating to the world around us. The first of these is pre-Fallen shamanism. This is the kind of shamanism that we practiced for tens of thousands, probably even hundreds of thousands, of years. It is shamanism that is entirely free of Taker cult thinking. It is Leaver culture shamanism.

When Taker thinking enters a society, the result is often that shamanism dies out altogether (to be replaced by the sky religions). If, however, shamanism survives, it is then changed by the contact with Taker thinking. This is Fallen shamanism—the shamanism practiced in agricultural, hierarchical societies, and characterised by the myth of human supremacy. The extent of this change varies from place to place. Whatever the degree of Taker influence, though, the point is that the shamanism practiced in such societies is different from the shamanism practiced before the arrival of agriculture, and has a different relationship to the other-than-human (as we have seen, this includes things like an emphasis on depossession work, working by inviting in spirit possession, animal sacrifices, hierarchical thinking, and so on).

The third type of shamanism is only just emerging. It is very much part of what Steve Taylor describes as the post-Fallen recovery—the regaining of our sanity and compassion for each other as humans and for the more-than-human world. Because of this, it is *ethical* shamanism. It is also shamanism that is not solely based on traditional practices, but adaptable, flexible, and relevant practices. In developing it, we are doing what our pragmatic and highly-adaptable hunter-gatherer ancestors always did, which is to take shamanism and make it relevant to the times in which we live. What makes an approach to shamanism a post-Fallen one, though, is not just whether we can use it in our modern-day lives, but whether it *specifically* helps with our post-Fallen recovery. For, as we have seen, not all contemporary approaches to shamanism do this, in that they have accepted and adopted Taker-cult thinking, to varying degrees. By contrast, post-Fallen shamanism has practices and knowledge that help us identify Taker thinking, and which show us how to heal from its damage.

What Stories shall we Choose?

Shamans say that things are as they are because of the stories they tell themselves. Societies are the same. What a society is like is determined by its stories. Hunter-gatherer societies were ecologically sustainable, well-adjusted and healthy societies, because hunter-gatherer shamanism, free of the taint of Taker cult thinking, told good stories, stories based on kinship, non-hierarchical thinking, empathy and right-relationship. Everything that has gone wrong with society can be traced back to abandoning those stories and values. Clearly, if we are to stop slaughtering the other species we share this amazing world with, and if we are to survive as a species ourselves, we need much better stories than the ones the suicidal Taker death-cult is telling us.

Where can we find these healthy stories we so desperately need? The answer is, *from our ancestors*. Not from our recent ancestors, though. Not from the Victorians, or even the "ancient" Greeks, Romans or Egyptians. Not from the Celts, the Vikings or the Druids. Not from The Inca, the Mayans or the Aztecs. Not even from Fallen shamanic societies, either. Sure, there are bits and pieces we can usefully learn from them—there is usually *something* of value in most things if we look hard enough. In the end, though, the healthy stories, the truly healthy stories and values we need, are not going to be found in Taker thinking. We need to reach further back than that. That is why, although I have studied many different kinds of shamanic societies, my interest has always been primarily in the shamanism practiced by pre-agricultural hunter-gatherer cultures.

All hunter-gatherer tribes looked to the Ancestors for guidance. The Ancestors were the wisdom keepers, the standard to measure the current tribe against, and the basis upon which decisions were made. That is how we lived, successfully and healthily, for thousands upon thousands of years. We need to do the same. To do this, we need to look not to our recent ancestors, but to the heathy shamanism of our Ancestors. We need to recover that knowledge and wisdom, and make it relevant to the times in which we now live.

Healthy Templates

Ancient shamanic knowledge contains a set of archetypal templates. As we shall see in the subsequent chapters of this book, these templates provide the outlines for the healthy stories we need. It took me a while to fully realise this personally. But these days, when I look at what is wrong in society and wonder what would make things right, I find the answer almost always lies with our hunter-gatherer ancestors. If I think, "What would the ancestors do?" or "How would this have worked in a hunter-gatherer tribe?", then things usually fall into place. For the answer is almost always there in the form of a healthy template. It is then just a question of working out how to apply whatever it is to modern day life.

This works in personal life too. If I am faced with decisions in my life, I ask, "What would my hunter-gatherer Self do here?", and then think about how to translate that and implement it in a way that works in modern-day life. Doing this does not work for all the small stuff, of course. It does not help with choosing which brand of fridge or car to buy (although it can help you make ethical choices as to which brand you choose, and even about whether you really need whatever it is in the first place). It does work for most of the big stuff, though, and for a surprising number of things throughout each day. The key to being able to do this, of course, is knowing your hunter-gatherer Self. This is about finding your true, deep Soul. That is something we will come to in the next chapter. Indeed, it is at the heart (and soul) of what this book is about.

Wild Boars and Acorns

A while ago, I did a shamanic journey where I became a human. Not a modern domesticated human (that is all too familiar) but the kind of wild human we are meant to be, and that we once were. As usual, I started the journey at my Axis Mundi, carefully hollowing-out and leaving behind as much of my middle-world identity and stories as possible. I was then taken by my guides to the lower-world. We emerged into an ancient oak forest. The first thing that struck me was just how vivid everything was. My journeys can vary from being insubstantial and dream-like, more about impressions than defined and concrete things, through to being very detailed and precise. I never know what to expect. This journey was surprisingly detailed and multi-sensory from the second I stepped into the lower-world. I felt the moss and twigs under my feet. I felt the temperature of the air. The forest was full of sounds. The smells of the forest filled my nostrils. The movement of the leaves in the wind was making ever-shifting dappled patterns of light on the forest floor.

In the lower-world, I am used to being burnt, buried, dismembered or dissolved. I am used to having organs removed, the organs being healed with plants or stones, and then replaced. I am used to intrusions being removed by biting, sucking, singing, swarming or smoking. And all sorts of other things. If you are familiar with journeying, then you will know the kinds of things I am talking about. In this journey, though, almost none of those things happened. I did have a very vivid encounter with Wild Boar, though. We stared into each other's eyes for a long time, and she took me to meet her piglets. She then placed an Acorn in my heart which was (of course) perfect healing for what I was going through at the time, exactly what I needed. But other than that, none of the usual kind of things happened. At no point in the journey did I shapeshift into another Animal, or become a Tree, a Mountain, the Wind or anything else.

Instead, I stayed human. Not a dulled, domesticated modern-day human, though. Instead, I felt *intensely* alive and present. All my senses were clear and heightened. I felt intimately and deeply connected to the world around me, and everything around me itself felt vibrantly alive. I was free of the stupor of domestication.

I could identify dozens of different smells. Plus, I understood what the smells meant, and what each sound meant. I could read the weather. I knew what the patterns of the clouds and the wind direction meant. I knew about every plant and animal that lived in the forest. I felt no sense of separation. I belonged there. The forest was not something I was visiting, or observing from a place of separation, disassociation or superiority. I was *part of* the forest. Like the trees, the mosses and lichens, the birds and the insects, the rocks and the sunlight, and all the other myriad of things, I was a part of what the forest itself was made of.

I had woken up. I was experiencing the world as an animist. I was experiencing the world as we used to experience it, as we are *meant* to experience it.

Shamanism can Wake you Up

Shamanism is not a magic cure. It will not always work to heal your bad back or your anxiety, your diabetes or your depression. With those sorts of conditions and diseases, like any other healing modality, sometimes shamanism works and sometimes it does not. No healing modality works all the time or can cure everything.

There is something, though, that shamanism does do reliably. If you do the practices, they *do* change you. Bit by bit, surely and steadily, they wake you up and bring you back to life, back to who you were meant to be. That is what this book is about.

Exercise 11: Becoming Human

Take some time to really use your imagination to think about what it would be like to experience the world as a hunter-gatherer in pre-Fallen times.

Imagine yourself back in a pristine landscape, one from before agricultural times, the kind of landscape that your hunter-gatherer ancestors would have known.

As you do so, allow yourself to become aware that this landscape is much more alive than the ones you are used to in your modern-day life. It is much, much richer in species. It is *full* of different species, of plants, insects, birds, and other animals. And it is not just abundant in terms of the number of *different* species. Each individual species is more plentiful, too. There are ten times more mammals around you, hundreds of times more birds and amphibians, thousands of times more insects and flowers. It is rich with life.

The air is completely unpolluted. The water and soil, too.

You are alive to the world around you. Absolutely present (not distracted with thoughts about work, or remembering the shopping, or listening to something through your headphones as you walk along, or staring at a television or your phone). You are in the present moment, not apart from the world around you, but a living part of it.

You notice things. You notice plants. You really notice them. Because they are important to you. They are your food and your medicines, and your teachers. You never just walk past a plant without noticing it. You notice broken twigs, and when the wind changes direction. You notice different smells. You are alert to sounds.

You are a hunter-gatherer.

All your senses are heightened and more finely attuned. And you know what all the things that you are perceiving mean. You can read the world around you. It is full of food, medicines, opportunities, meanings and stories.

You are an animal. A rare one, though, for human animals are few and far between. You are dressed in animal skins. You skilfully hunted, killed and skinned those animals yourself. Your relationship with animals is a deeply intimate one. They are your food, your clothing, your shelter, and your teachers. You know their scents and how they taste. You know their droppings and the tracks they make, and how to track them or avoid them. You know how they live, and how they die. You live among them, are one of them.

You prepared the hide of the clothing you are wearing. You cut it into shape using a stone knife you had made. You made a needle from an animal bone and thread from animal sinews to make the prepared hide into clothing. You know how to do all these things. Everything you need is in the world around you. You know how to find and knap flints, how to make stone tools, where to find medicines, and how to make fires and build shelters.

You are evolved for running long distances. You are an endurance runner, who can run after prey for hour after hour, wearing them down. You also know how to move silently when needed, and how to imitate the calls of birds and other animals.

You are, literally, made for all this. This is what your body is evolved to do. Your body is at home here. This is your world. You are a part of it. A part of a bigger whole.

You belong here.

This is home.

Now, prepare yourself for doing a shamanic journey, in whatever way works for you.

Start the drumming.

Go to your Axis Mundi and hollow-out as usual.

Then, go to the lower-world and experience the joy of being this wild, fully-alive human being.

Repeat this exercise as often as you wish!

CHAPTER FOUR

Finding Your Deep Soul

Each Person is a Multitude

Most people see themselves as being a single "self", a single "I" they think of as being who they are. The reality is much more complex. Each of us is made of several different parts of self, each part having their own needs, drives, agendas and stories. As we go about our daily life, we are constantly moving our sense of self from one part to another, usually without being consciously aware we are doing so. For example, people often come to therapy because they have an internal conflict, with different parts of them feeling, thinking and wanting different things. As a therapist, when listening to a client it is often clear they are unconsciously moving backwards and forwards between these different parts. Helping a client become aware of this allows them to separate their internal parts out and negotiate a healthy resolution to the conflict between them.

Like psychotherapy, shamanism also understands that we are made of different parts-of-self. Far from having the single "soul" that most people in the West think they have, shamanic cultures understood that we have several different types of "souls" within us. The number of these varied, depending on how each culture divided things up. Some cultures recognised us as having as few as three parts, whereas others recognised as many as fifteen or more. Whatever the number, it was understood that each has a different function. Some must stay in the body as they give the body life, and the body dies when they leave. Others can leave the body without causing death, such as the part that can travel the shamanic realms, or the parts that get lost when we suffer from soul loss.

The Main Parts of Self

Although we can divide the parts-of-self into any number of sub-divisions, in this book I am going to concentrate on the four primary ones. From a shamanic perspective, each of these four corresponds to (and is an aspect of) one of the main shamanic realms. This means, as we shall see, that each part has different needs. Shamanically, to live a healthy and balanced life, each part must be honoured and accepted, allowed to express itself, and its needs addressed and met.

In going through the different parts, it is important to understand that, whilst at one level everything is part of a greater whole, at another level, some parts have more sense of individuality than others do. Because of this, I am going to differentiate between "Soul" and "Spirit". Although the two words are often used loosely and interchangeably by people, I am going to use the word "Soul" to refer to parts-of-self that have more of an identity as individual beings, and "Spirit" to refer to the part that has the least individuality. In addition, I am also going to differentiate between "Soul"—lower-world, and "soul"—middle-world. This should become clearer as you read on.

The four main parts are:

Our upper-world Spirit. This part of us is pure consciousness. It is a fragment of Father Sky (or God, if you like), in the same way that a water drop is part of the ocean, or that a spark is part of a fire. This part of us likes to soar and transcend; to rise above things and see the bigger picture. It likes to be free of the concerns of the middle-world and of everyday life. One of the reasons people often experience positive benefits from having a regular meditation practice is that, in meditation, we are connecting to this part and allowing it to do what it needs to do. This part also needs us to live in a way that is ethical and moral, kind and compassionate. If we do not live in this way then this eats away at us, and this part of us becomes ill.

Our middle-world self (or soul). This part of us corresponds to the shamanic middle-world. It is both a *personal* and a *collective* construct. It is made of the stories we tell *ourselves* about who we are, and of the stories *society* tells us. It is the domesticated, socialised part of us. It is also the part that most people identify with as being who they are. It includes our ego (our inner self-identity), and our persona (the face or mask we present to the outside world). It is also made up of two other sub-parts. These are "head" and "heart", and each of these needs two things. Head needs to understand, and it needs to feel understood. Heart needs to love, and it needs to feel loved. In order to try and meet these needs, the head and heart make up stories. They make up stories about things like love and loyalty, duties and deceptions, motivations and meanings, rights and wrongs, all of which we weave into our middle-world story of who we are.

Our physical body. This corresponds to the *physical* middle-world. This part of us needs to have its physical needs met. It needs clean water, warmth, healthy food, fresh air and shelter. It needs to know that it is safe from harm, and to have somewhere it can rest and sleep. It also needs to be allowed to do what it was designed to do, which is to move around (instead of sitting at a desk, or in a car or on a sofa for most of the day). In our culture we tend to think of the body as not us, but something that we inhabit; a "vehicle" for the soul, a kind of biological car that we drive around in. In fact, many people these days are barely in their bodies at all, but ungrounded and living in their heads. The body is *far* more than just a vehicle though. Remember, in shamanism, everything has a soul, is alive and conscious and can be communicated with. Everything has its own unique qualities and gifts, and that goes for the body, too. Our bodies are a conscious part of us; a part of us that has its own wisdom and intelligence.

Our lower-world Soul. Unlike our upper-world Spirit, which is not so much an individual as a part of a whole, a spark of Father Sun within us, our lower-world soul is our true Self-identity. It is part of Mother Earth, but it is also the unique *individual* that Mother Earth intended (and still intends) us to be. The Jungian psychologist James Hillman said that, whilst our Spirit loves the peaks and dazzling heights, our Soul wants to lead us to the valleys and the depths. When we follow our Soul, we experience a sense of "deepening". Unlike our middle-world self, our Soul is not a collection of human-made stories. It is the untamed and undiminished part of us, free of Taker cult domestication. This part of us needs to live a life that is authentic, a life that is true to our Soul. It needs to express itself in the world and be allowed to blossom and thrive. It *must* be connected to nature. Without connection to nature, it withers and weakens. Sadly, though, since we domesticated ourselves and turned our back on the lower-world and nature, it is a part of themselves that most people do not even know exists. It is finding this part of us that this chapter is about.

Our (Healthy) Inner Tribe

Understanding these parts shows us that, contrary to what most people think, there is in fact no one single "self", no single "I". Rather, we are ourselves a community, an inner tribe. Any healthy tribe is one where all tribal members feel welcome, respected, and have a voice. It is also one where there is a balance between meeting the needs of the individuals within the tribe on the one hand, and meeting the needs of the tribe as a whole on the other.

Understanding the needs of the different parts of our inner tribe, and keeping a balance between them, is essential for health. We need to get to know each of our inner parts, listen to them, and honour their needs. In doing this, we need to be mindful that we do not bring Taker cult thinking to the process. For hierarchical Taker cult "spirituality", of course, tells us the "highest" and most "noble" part of us is our upper-world part. It tells us that the lower-world and middle-world parts are "corrupt" and not to be listened to or trusted. It tells us the story that we must deny them and "transcend them" and focus on the "light" and "enlightenment".

I have already discussed what is wrong with this story, so I will not labour the point here. I would just add this: there is a saying in shamanism, "Does it grow corn". It means, "Never mind the dogma, does it *work?*", for generally shamanism is a dogma-free and pragmatic path. A more useful version I find, though, is to ask not just "Does it grow corn?", but "What *kind* of corn does it grow?".

The hierarchical value judgements of Taker cult "spirituality" can be hard to break free of. If you do not buy into them then you are often looked down on by those who do, pitied even, as someone who is less "evolved" and who has yet to "raise their vibrational level". This is because hierarchical "spirituality" is exactly that—it is *hierarchical.* Looking "down" on people and judging how "evolved" people are comes with the territory.

If you ever find yourself getting caught up in the spell of hierarchical "spirituality", then remember this spell-busting question. Ask yourself, "What kind of corn does this grow?". Compared to the tens of thousands of years of non-hierarchical animist spirituality that preceded it, in the brief few thousand years of its history, the answer is that Taker "spirituality" clearly grows *terrible* corn. Corn that makes us ill.

Any thorough exploration of what shamanism tells us about our upper-world Spirit, and about the nature of the upper-world itself, needs a book of its own, and will be the subject of the next book in this series. The focus of this current book is to explore what shamanism tells us about our lower-world Soul, and how to find it, connect with it, and cultivate it in our lives. To explore that, we need first to understand more about the difference between our middle-world *soul*, and our authentic lower-world *Soul*.

The Ego (Middle-World Soul)

As I said, the middle-world part-of-self is what most people think of if asked to describe themselves, for it is the part that tells us (and other people) stories about who we are. For example:

> *"I am Paul Francis. I am British. I am a white Caucasian. I am male. I am a psychotherapist, shamanic practitioner, teacher and author. I am good at cooking. I am not good at drawing. I live in Wales and I do like laver bread, but I am not that keen on rugby. I am a father and a partner. I have never driven a car (and have no wish to ever learn). I am an introvert. I am a cat person, not a dog person. I love the country Iceland. I do not like grapefruit."*

These things are all factually true on one level. On another level, though, they are also just stories. They are the kind of stories that, for the purposes of going about our everyday life, we tend to take at face-value. However, if you begin to look at them more closely, they are much less substantial than they first appear. For example, what does it mean to be male? Ideas about it vary a lot from society to society, and from individual to individual. "British" is a human construct, too, and one that people find hard to define and agree on. "Wales" and "rugby" are human constructs. I tell myself that I am not a dog person, but there are bound to be dogs out there somewhere that I could grow to love (I guess). Cars and driving are human-made constructs. Partner, parent, teacher, psychotherapist … all human-constructed roles. What does it mean to be a white Caucasian? It is a story that comes with all sorts of history and baggage (and privilege). The introvert-extrovert scale is a human construct. Lots of people do agree that I am a good cook, but somebody (with poor taste, obviously!) may hate my cooking—it is all subjective after all. I really do not like grapefruit, but there is lots of interesting research that suggest that food likes and dislikes often have their origin in psychological associations (so again, human constructs), and I can certainly trace my dislike of grapefruit back to my childhood and my mother (it is a long story!).

Now, it is very important not to think that, because these things are constructs, that means they are not real. Doing so is a common mistake that comes from sky-focused spirituality and its denial and dismissal of the middle-world. In "spiritual" social media groups, I regularly see people being very insistent that the "self" is just an illusion and that it does not really exist (ironically, though, often doing this in an ego-driven and opinionated way). They argue there is no "self", as "self" implies duality and separation (in the sense that it means "*this* thing, separate from *that* thing"). They argue that duality is an illusion, because, as any truly "enlightened" person would know, everything is in fact one.

On one level, this is indeed true. In shamanic terms, everything is indeed part of Great Spirit. *And* (not but), on another level, separation is real, too. Just because at a quantum level everything is energy, this does not mean that at another level things are not physical and solid. They are two different levels of reality; one does not cancel the other out. You can believe all you like that separation is an illusion and that everything is just energy, but if you step in front of a moving bus then you will still get run over and experience the reality of physical matter.

In regaining our animist worldview, it is important to see this dismissal of the middle-world by sky-orientated spiritualities for what it is. It is a symptom of spiritual bypassing which, as we looked at earlier, is itself a symptom of distress, a neurotic response to unresolved psychological wounds. At the same time, it is also a story the Taker cult wants us to believe for, if as it says, the middle-world is not alive and does not matter, then we are free to plunder it as we please.

The Middle-World is Real!

At one level, everything is indeed one. *And,* at another level, things are separate. Both things are true. Physical things in the middle-world are real, and pretending otherwise does not make this any less true. This is not just true of physical things, either. Although not physical, ideas can be real and have a life of their own, with all too real consequences and effects. Look at things like religions and political ideologies. Look at the ancient stories behind the conflicts in the Middle East, or the five-hundred-year-old stories behind the troubles in Northern Ireland, or the fourteen-hundred-year-old stories behind the conflict between Sunni and Shia Muslims. Totalitarian agriculture is a human story, a thought-form that has lasted for over *twelve-thousand years* and one that has had very real and profound effects on nearly all life on this planet.

Our non-physical middle-world part-of-self is a story, too (or more accurately, a collection of stories, beliefs, opinions, concepts and other human-made thought-forms). However, because it is composed of stories, you will often hear sky-based spiritualities (and not just the organised religions but some New Age "spirituality", too) saying that the ego is not real; that it is just an illusion. Again, though, looked at from the perspective of Great Spirit, "self" and separation disappears, and all is indeed one. *And* though, back in the everyday middleworld, the ego is very much a real thing. It *really does not* go away by trying to ignore it or by denying its reality. Quite the opposite, in fact. For, as the saying goes, "What we resist, persists". Even worse, when we try to deny parts of our self, we create what Jung called "The Shadow". Rather than go away, the denied part becomes stronger and out of our conscious control, a "monster" we see as "other" to us, and which stalks us (which is why people who deny the reality of the ego, far from having no ego, often end up having an ego that seeks to dominate and control—a "guru-complex").

The other thing that sky-orientated spirituality often tells us is that the ego needs to be "transcended". Again, this is true up to a point. The ego does need to be reined in, as an ego out of control is indeed a monster. The sky-spiritualities tell us that the way to do this is to focus on our upper-world Spirit. The problem is, though, that this can result in a top-heavy, disembodied and ungrounded spirituality with all the negative consequences that I have already discussed. Instead, shamanism shows us that we need to rise, but rise *rooted*. If we are to *healthily* rein in our middle-world self, then as well as needing to ascend, we need to descend and cultivate our connection with our lower-world Soul.

Trying to transcend both our middle-world self and lower-world Soul by focusing primarily on our upper-world Spirit, unsurprisingly often results in becoming overly-detached, other-worldly, and ungrounded. This may work fine if we can live in a monastery or as a hermit in a cave, or in some other way "renounce" the world. It usually does not work, however, if we choose to live in the middle-world in an active and engaged way. Indeed, this is why, with the Fall and the rise of the sky-orientated religions, for the first time in human history we see the emergence of things like monasteries and hermitages. These had never been needed before, because focusing on the upper-world part-of-self in this unbalanced way, and becoming disembodied and dissociated as a result, is something that pre-Fallen people had never done.

The truth is that, unless we wish to withdraw from the world, then our middle-world self is necessary and has its rightful place. The ego is not "bad", it just needs to be of service and not in charge. From a shamanic perspective, it is the tool through which both our Soul and Spirit can express themselves and be of service to the world.

Nature and Nurture – Soul and Environment

As I said earlier, shamans say things are as they are because of their stories. Something is a stone because of "stone story", something else is being a tree because of "tree story", and as humans, we are as we are because of our stories, and so on. The question is, what is the "something" that is being these different things?

The "something" is Mother Earth. Everything in the lower-world is a part of her. Mother Earth, the Feminine Principle or Yin, contains within her *all* the Stories; the Stories of everything that ever was, is, and could be. She is the *potential* for everything and yet, on her own, nothing can manifest. For these potentials to manifest, Yin and Yang must come together. When Father Sky (the restless, energising masculine Principle, or Yang) seeks out and finds Mother Earth then, from the body of Mother Earth, a Soul is born.

In the lower-world, the Soul is what something was born to be. It is its truest nature; the *essence* of it. It is also both the blueprint for how it could manifest in the middle-world (its seed-potential), and it is the drive to try and become that thing (its actualising tendency). Looked at in this way, things are as they are because of the Stories that *Mother Earth* tells them to be, for those Stories are from Mother Earth (and everything is a part of her body being told a Story).

The Stories we Make Up

Remember, when it comes to the physical middle-world, things are as they are because of the interaction between two factors: their Soul on the one hand, and the physical environment around them (and how they respond to it) on the other. So, rocks are sculpted by water, trees are shaped by the wind and the direction of sunlight, animals by the availability of food and the presence of predators, and so on.

As is usually the case when it comes to humans, things become more complicated. Remember, humans are shapeshifters. Other than us humans, most things are happy to be what they are and have no curiosity or desire to be anything else. Stones are happy being stones, trees are happy being trees, eagles being eagles, and so on. We, though, are a restless, curious and inquisitive species, who wonders what it is to be something other than what we are. We wonder about how things work, about what causes things, and about what things mean. In doing so, we make up our own stories. We become shaped not just by the story of our Soul, and how that is shaped by the physical environment, but also by the stories we invent for ourselves; human *middle-world* stories.

When it comes to making up stories, we are *exceptionally* good at doing this. The stories we spin can be captivating and seductive. We can tell stories that are so entrancing and beguiling that, no matter how preposterous they are, no matter all the facts and evidence to the contrary, we still believe them. We can tell stories that enchant both ourselves and each other; spells that we become seduced and bewitched by.

Think about some of the stories that different religions spin, stories that can often be "unbelievable", and yet stories which millions of people take as being literally true. Think, too, about the stories of charismatic politicians, the stories of narcissists, sociopaths and psychopaths—often lies and empty promises, but ones that people still fall for. Then there are the fictitious stories spun by the media. The fictions that we tell ourselves; fictions like how someone in our family must love us "really" because (so the story says) "we are family" and "blood is thicker than water", despite all the evidence to the contrary. The story we may tell ourselves about how our partner does not mean to behave as they do (until they do, and we double down on our story, again and again). The stories we tell ourselves about how we are not good enough or lovable enough, or how we must achieve more to prove ourselves, or how we will never amount to much and so there is no point in even trying. The story that we are ugly. The body-shaming stories. The unconscious stories—that alcohol, binge eating or buying new things will make us feel better; the story that we must keep busy and never relax; the story that it is not safe to open up or be vulnerable.

Not all the stories we make up are dysfunctional, of course, for we can make up good ones, too. We can make up ones that uplift us and inspire our lives. Stories that can make us laugh and cry; that can motivate us to be better people and do good things. Stories that are good for our Souls. Stories of love, redemption, courage, bravery, compassion and kindness.

Our stories are what bond us and bind us. Societies are formed from them and defined by them. They make up the norms, mores, folkways and taboos that create social cohesion and allow societies to operate successfully; they are the glue that holds societies together. They are also what defines how we try to fit into human society, and find a role and purpose within it. Stories like teacher, plumber, engineer, musician, husband, wife, parent, friend, gay, straight, goth, punk, democrat, conservative, Christian, Muslim, Hindu, football-fan, golfer, law-abiding, rebel, joker, and so on.

Not all Stories are Equal

Our ability to make up stories is not in itself good or bad. It is, in any case, in our nature. It is part of the gift of being human, part of what we are and what we do. What is important is how we use it. To use it well, it is crucial to understand the difference between *our* stories, and the Stories that come from Mother Earth.

Earlier in the book, I suggested an exercise to help you think more like an animist. It involved looking around you and allowing the possibility that everything around you is alive and conscious. I suggested you try doing the exercise outside in nature, and doing in human-made environments, too, and that you notice the difference between the two. If you did this, you might have found that it is easier to experience aliveness in natural things than it is to experience it in human-made things. If so, this is a common. In teaching, I have found that *generally* people find it easier to experience aliveness in things like mountains, boulders, waterfalls and the wind than they do in things like chairs, shoes, cookers and so on. We generally experience nature as being alive (which, in turn, helps us to feel more alive), and human-made environments as being much less so. There is plenty of research these days that backs this up, research which shows that spending even short periods of time in nature has significantly positive benefits for our mental health and well-being.

Generally, we find being in nature to be good for the Soul. The reason for this goes back to the stories that make things what they are, *and where those stories come from.* To understand this, we need to pull together three threads that we have discussed at different points in the book so far.

First, remember the analogy that all the Peoples (Human, Animal, Standing, Plant and Stone) are part of a great "tree" and that individuals in the middle-world are like the tips of twigs, protruding into physical reality from the lower-world. Remember how something manifests in the middle-world is a result of the interaction between its lower-world Soul and the middle-world environment into which its Soul is protruding.

For example, an individual horse is formed from its Soul projecting from the lower-world into the physical middleworld. How the physical horse takes form depends not just on the Soul's blueprint, but on how the blueprint is influenced by environmental factors. Then, if we follow the horse's Soul back into the lower-world, we find that it converges with other individual horse's Souls, to form the Horse Oversoul branch. This branch is part of the larger Mammal branch, which itself stems from the trunk that is Animal. Together with the other two great trunks of Plant and Stone, Animal makes up the great "tree" that is the Peoples in the lower-world, and which grows out of Mother Earth.

Second, remember that everything in nature is made from the body of Mother Earth; that everything is literally a part of her. Remember that the reason something is *this* thing rather than *that* thing is because of the Story that Mother Earth is telling that part of her body to be. In this sense, the Souls and Oversouls are Stories told by Mother Earth.

Third, remember that everything physical in the world, whatever *else* it may be, is made of the Stone People, too, in terms of the chemical elements it is built from (a horse is both a horse and a physical body made from the Stone People). Remember, though, that the Stone People are not *just* the chemical elements—that is just their simplest form. They are also things like Quartz Crystals and Mountains, Stars and the Sea.

Drawing these threads together, we can see that an individual horse in the physical world is the product of two sets of Stories. One set of Stories is the horse's individual Soul, and the Oversouls that it is a part of: Horse, Mammal, and Animal. The other set of Stories are those that make the Stone People that its body is made from: Carbon, Nitrogen, Oxygen, and so on. Both sets come from the lower-world. They are Mother Earth's Stories. They are her bringing the world into being.

Like a horse, a mobile phone is also made up of two such sets. One set is the Stories of the Stone People, the chemical elements that it is made from. The other set are the stories that make it a mobile phone (including the phone's brand, the model, and so on). However, only one of these sets is from the lower-world and from Mother Earth—the Stone People Stories. The other set (the phone's make and model etc.) are stories that are human-made and of the middle-world. In the lower-world, there is no "Mobile Phone" Story. There is no "Samsung" Oversoul, no "Galaxy 10+" sub-branch. This is because, good though we are at telling *stories*, we have no power to create *Stories*. In other words, we cannot create Souls. Only Mother Earth can do that.

What this means is that the things we create, aside from the chemical elements they are made from, have no connection with the lower-world. It is important to remember that this does not make them any less alive. As we discussed earlier, to shamans *everything* is alive, and so anthropologists reported indigenous people talking about the soul of the machete or of the outboard motor. What they did not talk about, though, is the *Soul* of the machete.

In other words, the things we create have middle-world souls, stories that define them and make them what they are. They do not have lower-world Souls, though, and as such (aside from the elements that they are made from), they are disconnected from Mother Earth. They are not *soul*-less, but they *are Soul*-less. Natural things, however, the things created by Mother Earth, are full of Soul.

To understand how this connects to the different parts-of-self and the quest to find our true Soul, it is necessary to realise that, whilst human-created things do not have a lower-world Soul, they can still be *modelled* on Soul. They can be an expression or representation of something more natural. For example, a mobile phone represents nothing natural. It has no connection with nature or the lower-world. A beautiful painting or sculpture of a horse, though, may convey something of its Soul.

Generally, the closer something human-made is to the Stories in the lower-world, the more we are moved by them. Because the closer something is to Soul, the more it calls to our Soul, too. This is why mobile phones do not move our Souls, but great art can. It is why some paintings can move us more than others (because the great ones convey something of Soul), and the same is true of stories, poems music or films. It is why informal gardens often feel more Soulful than formal ones do. It can be why some buildings feel better to us than others, why natural materials may feel better than synthetic ones, and why heavily processed food feels less nourishing than food made from fresh ingredients. Things that are closer to Mother Earth's Stories are "food for the Soul", whereas things that are far from her Stories feel "Soul-less" and dead.

This is true when it comes to the stories that make up our middle-world self, too. Our middle-world self is meant to be modelled on our true nature, on our lower-world Soul. To lead a Soulful life, our middle-world self needs to be an expression and representation of our Soul in our earthly life. The more this is the case, the better we feel. The further away our middle-world self is from our Soul, the worse we feel.

The problem is, of course, that most of us are raised these days with no notion of what their Soul is (or, even, that it exists at all). However, our Soul can be found. Once we find it, we can begin shaping our middle-world self around it. We just need to know where to look, and what it is that we are looking for.

Initiation

To take part in the human middle-world, we need a middle-world part-of-self. This was true for our hunter-gatherer ancestors, too, for them to be able to live and function as a member of a tribe. But, in this, there is a huge difference between our ancestors and us. In a hunter-gatherer tribe, the available roles that people could adopt would have been far fewer in number. Crucially, too, the roles would have been ones that were much closer to Soul. Like a great work of art representing Soul, their middle-world lives could be an expression of Soul, of what it is to be truly Human, as Mother Earth intended. By contrast, in the modern world, many of the roles we adopt are *at best* pale reflections of Soul, and most of the time, nothing to do with Soul at all. In domesticating ourselves, we abandoned Mother Earth's Story of what it is to be Human and remade ourselves according to our own made-up stories. In doing this, we suffered massive Soul-loss, and (until we heal ourselves of this), whilst we have a soul, we have no more Soul than the other Soul-less things we create.

Whilst hunter-gatherers had middle-world selves that were more in line with their lower-world Souls, they nevertheless recognised that, in growing up, we are still constructing a middle-world self. They understood that we can become lost in the stories this part of us tells. Because of this, as I said earlier, around the time of adolescence they had initiation ceremonies. These were designed to dismantle the middle-world identity that someone had constructed in their childhood, and replace it instead with a new identity. An identity rooted in their Soul and which grew from it, in the same way that Soul itself is rooted in Mother Earth and grows from her.

I also mentioned that, because we no longer have such initiations, my Guides told me it was essential for my shamanic development that I did one. However, although this was many years ago now, it still did not happen until I was in my late 30s. Up until this point, for all the years I had spent in therapy, meditating, doing sweat lodges, encounter groups, shamanic journeys, and countless other things, I still had not met my true and authentic, lower-world Soul. In fact, I had no idea it was missing in the first place, or even that such a part of me existed at all. Of course, this also meant my middle-world self was not deeply rooted in my Soul. For all that I had worked hard on my personal and spiritual development, up until this point, I was a tree with shallow roots.

As I was soon to discover.

The House I Built on Sand

I grew up in a nuclear family of six people. My designated role in the family was to be the scapegoat and the outsider. Mostly, whenever I spoke, I was either ignored or attacked. It was made clear to me that I was not welcome in the family. Any efforts I made to join in were always rebuffed. It was a deeply lonely childhood in terms of human contact. My solace, and my sanctuary, was nature. For a few years in my childhood we lived in an isolated, ramshackle vicarage with several acres of neglected gardens. I spent as much time as I could outside, climbing trees and hiding in dens. I studied the names of flowering plants, mushrooms and lichens. I examined the contents of owl pellets and made plaster casts of animal footprints. I watched shrews, ant colonies, newts and staghorn beetles. In those days, I did not yet have the conscious awareness I do now, the awareness that everything is alive. I was yet to fully wake up to that. At some level, though, I did know that in nature I was safe. I had a sense I was being looked after. I often had a sense of the presence of a fox at my side, looking after me. The feeling of being looked after was particularly strong around one particular old pear tree, in whose branches I used to feel protected and held.

When I was fourteen, we moved into a city and I managed to get a job that kept me busy after school and on Saturdays. This allowed me to spend as little time at home as possible, and I developed a good set of friends both at school and through work. The next twenty or so years of my life had their ups and downs, as life does. Mostly, though, they were great, both in terms of my social life and in my personal and spiritual development and learning.

During that time, I had an experience that stayed with me, although I would not understand its significance until many years later. One day, when I was in my early thirties, I went for a walk on my own. Nothing too unusual in that, except that this day I went walking in a remote and less visited part of the Welsh mountains. A couple of hours into the walk, I began to realise that I had not seen a single other human being, nor passed a house, nor heard any sign of human habitation. The further I walked, the more the lack of human sights and sounds began to feel oppressive. I began to feel uneasy. Some of this unease manifested as thoughts, like "What if I get lost?", or "What if I twist my ankle and there is no one around to help me?" (to put this into context, this was long before the time of mobile phones and google maps!). Some of my unease was more visceral, though, and much deeper than just anxious thoughts. As I tuned into what I was feeling, I realised that I no longer felt safe in nature. I had spent most of the last eighteen years or so around people, working, socialising and partying. I had become, without realising it, disconnected from nature. Whereas in childhood, nature had been my safety and my refuge, now the wild was an alien and unsettling place to me. I had become urbanised, humanised and domesticated.

Looking back on that experience, it is *so* far away from who I am now. These days, spending a day in nature, away from humanity, is my idea of absolute bliss. At the time, though, shortly after having that experience, I soon got sucked back into the human world; back into work, parenting and socialising. Nevertheless, the experience stayed in the back of my mind and niggled at me. A year or so later, I was in a new relationship. My new partner had been born and raised in London and knew pretty much *nothing* about the countryside. One day, I took her walking in the fells in the Lake District. She was genuinely terrified. The cronking of ravens made her jump out of her skin as she had no idea what the noise was. The open spaces and the sheer size of the mountains freaked her out. If we crested a ridge on the hills and startled some sheep, she was ten times more spooked than the sheep were. She was terrified by the open expanses and the ever-changing weather. She did gradually get over her fears and started to fall in love with the place. Watching her reminded me of my own experience a year or so earlier and got me thinking again about how disconnected I was from nature (and how disconnected from nature humans generally had become).

A few years later, my life fell apart. I went through a series of events that left me with severe post-traumatic stress disorder. As well as the shock from the events themselves, I was also deeply shocked by how bad a state I was in. Given all the work I had already done on myself, I thought I would have been more robust, and yet I had gone from being happy and confident to being so suicidal that just staying alive was an hourly struggle. I talked to my therapist about this, and her reply turned out to be pivotal in my recovery. She likened the work I had done previously to my having built a house. She said that, given my lack of a healthy childhood, once I had left home I had sensibly built a new and safe house to live in. Good though this house had been, it had a hidden problem. It was built on a fault line. I could have got through my whole life without realising this, she said. However, the events that happened had triggered the fault, causing the house to come crashing down. The first job in therapy was to clear the rubble, in terms of dealing with the immediate issues facing me. Once that was done, then we could begin to dig into the foundations. In doing so, we could discover what the underlying fault had been, and so what needed to be done in order to rebuild more securely.

She turned out to be right, but not quite in the way that she intended.

Digging Down to the Soul

She was right about the house. From a shamanic perspective, the house was, of course, my middle-world self. Through the therapy I had done in my 20s, I had dismantled the rickety and leaky shack that my childhood had provided me with, and built a much better home in its place. This is what therapy is good at. It helps us deconstruct any dysfunctional parts of our middle-world self, and replace them with healthier ones. She was right too that, although I had built a good house, I had unwittingly built it on a fault-line. And in rebuilding, she was also right that I needed to dig deeper this time than I had before, to find out what had happened and how to rebuild in a better way. For her, this meant exploring my childhood in more depth because, as a psychodynamic therapist, she believed it was in that layer the roots of the problem were going to be found. In this, though, she was only partially right. What I was about to discover was that, to get the *full* answer, I had to dig much deeper still. Much, *much* deeper.

Think of therapy as being like an archaeological dig. It starts with a building (or the remnants of one). This is someone's constructed, middle-world self. The ground this has been built on consists of layers of history. The uppermost layers are the person's recent history. It is these layers that people usually start with exploring in therapy, as it is usually a current issue that prompts people to begin therapy in the first place. If people stay with the process of scraping these layers back, then what is usually revealed is the issue that brought them to therapy has deeper roots, roots that go back to the layers of childhood. It is in sifting through these earlier childhood layers things can be discovered that, when pieced together, show the deeper and truer story, and the work that needs to be done.

Although psychotherapy can go deeper than these childhood layers, usually it does not, and this was certainly the case with the psychodynamic therapist I was seeing, who referred *everything* back to my childhood. Whilst I gained a lot from the work we did together, I had already done a lot of work on my childhood earlier on in my life, so my hunch was that I needed to explore deeper still. Underneath the childhood layers, the next layers down are those of earlier generations. Since my therapist did not have the knowledge or skills necessary to go there (and no interest in doing so, either), I began to look for other ways to explore these layers. Doing so led me to epigenetics, the work of Bert Hellinger and Family Constellations (which we will explore in a later chapter when we look at family and tribal structures), and other avenues. It included shamanic work, too, for shamans have always known that we are affected by many generations of ancestors before us, and so I set about learning how to journey down timelines and do family and ancestral healing.

In doing this, I realised that below the layers of my more recent ancestors, there were even deeper layers. Historical and collective layers. My family carried wounds that went back hundreds of years. On my father's side, for example, we were descended from Border reivers—raiders from the English-Scottish border country, whose history goes back as far as the late 13th century. It is not a happy inheritance. The reivers constant raiding and fighting gave us the word "bereaved", so much misery did they cause. Their behaviour affected many generations of people who came after them, hundreds of thousands of people.

I began to see that, collectively, we are carrying wounds that go back even further still. In terms of the land in which I live, this meant back to the layers of the Dark Ages, and further back still, to the Romans and the Celts. Even back as far as the Beaker People. These were the first agriculturalist to arrive in Britain and, as is the way with the Taker cult, the people who slaughtered the hunter-gatherers that they found here, and who began to clear the land for farming. These layers carry wounds which still affect us to this day, the wounds of domestication and the Fall.

From the Beaker People, right up to the present day, the layers are full of the noise of humanity. They are full of human-made stories, stories than can largely drown out the Stories of nature. Below these Taker cult layers, though, are quieter layers; layers that are more about nature and almost free of human middle-world noise. It is these layers that Daniel Quinn refers to when he talks about the "Great Forgetting", for the Taker cult buried them so deeply that, for a long time, we forgot they even existed. Luckily now, though, we are seeing the beginning of the "Great Remembering", as more and more people realise these layers put things into a larger context. They show us the deeper and truer picture of what happened, and they hold the answers to what needs to be done.

In exploring these deepest layers, we can find something else, too. Underneath all our personal history, deeper than the layers of our childhood and those of our family and ancestral stories, underneath all the layers of the Fall, underneath *all* this domestication, our Soul is waiting for us.

It is in these quieter and simpler layers that we can find something our animist ancestors knew through-and-through, with their heads and their hearts, with their bodies and their Souls. We can find what it is to be Human. Not our middle-world stories about being *human*, but the Story from Mother Earth. Out truest and deepest Story.

To do this is to finally come home. For as Bill Plotkin says, our Souls really are not separate from nature, but *part of it*. Our Souls really are both of us *and of the world*. They really are both *in* and *of* the world, "a distinctive place in nature". As our wise animist ancestors also knew, our Souls are a potential. They wait for us to discover them and claim them. And, *because* we are part of a whole, part of Mother Earth herself, it is true, the world cannot be full until we become fully ourselves.

A House Built on Soul

In saying all this, I want to be crystal-clear about something. I am *in no way* saying that shamanism is better than psychotherapy. In the way that it is usually practiced, psychotherapy has its limitations and blind-spots, *and that is true of shamanism, too*. Although there is some overlap between them, each can also do things the other cannot do well. In this way, both have their place. Psychotherapy is good at replacing the unhealthy stories of our middle-world self and replacing them with healthier ones. It is good at creating healthy souls, but rarely will it help us find our Soul. Without shamanism, but with the help of therapy, I know I would have been able to build a new and improved house to live in; a sturdier one with better foundations. It would not have been the same kind of house that I did go on to build, for I still would have not met my Soul. But it is perfectly possible to live a life without Soul. It is after all what most people these days are doing. It is even possible to live a good life in that way, but it is nonetheless a life missing something.

I want to be clear about this because the idea that shamanism is better than psychotherapy is a common one in the shamanic community. It is a wonky thought, and one that leads to people not getting the kind of help they really need (I come across *a lot* of people in the shamanic community who could really do with psychotherapy). This is why these books are about *therapeutic* shamanism. Because these days, in our complicated human-made middle-world, both psychotherapy and shamanism have things to contribute. Neither is a good substitute for the other. Rather, they complement and enhance each other, and each has much that it can learn from the other.

Another thing I want to be clear about is that the process of finding your Soul does not have to be a dramatic one. You will often here it said in the shamanic community that people come to shamanism, or to finding their Soul, through near-death experiences or similar traumatic events. This is sometimes true, as such experiences can sometimes involve the death of an old way of being, allowing a new way of being to emerge. However, there are other paths, too, gentler and steadier ones, but ones that are equally effective. My own path was a traumatic one, but having experienced it, there is absolutely nothing that I can recommend about doing it that way and knowing what I know now, it is not a path I would choose again. That is why, as both a shamanic practitioner and a psychotherapist, I am keen to teach shamanism in a way that is effective and yet manageable; in ways that are grounded and trauma-free and which avoid unnecessary drama.

Those things being said, we can turn now to the practice of journeying to find our Soul. As we explored earlier in the book, having accurate prior knowledge can really help in journeying, as without it we can bring wonky middle-world stories with us, that colour and distort what we experience. That is very much true here, too, and so in seeking our Soul we need to have some idea about what it is we are looking for. One essential thing to know is that Soul is an Adult. The problem is that most people these days do not know what a real Adult looks like, so we need to address this next.

Real Adults are Rare

There is a reason why, in all hunter-gatherer tribes, people waited until adolescence before beginning the process of finding their Soul. This is because finding your Soul is an initiation into *Adulthood*. It is about stepping into being your authentic, *Adult* self. For our animist ancestors, doing this was not a problem, for children were raised by people who were real Adults and who modelled and embodied Adulthood. When the time came, adolescents knew exactly what they needed to step into to make the transition.

When it comes to us doing this, however, we have a problem. The problem being that most people these days do not know what an Adult is. What we think of as being adult are "grown-up" things such as getting a job, "settling down", having a mortgage, and so on. These things may (or may not!) be what being a modern middle-world *adult* is about, but they have nothing to do with what being an *Adult* is about, for our Adult Soul is of the *lower-world*. And these days, of course, most people are cut off from the lower-world and have little or no knowledge of its existence—the place, the *only* place, where their Soul is to be found, for our Soul *really is* of the lower-world. It *cannot* be found in the upper-world or in exploring Spirit. Nor can it be found in the human-made stories of the middle-world.

In addition, as I said earlier, because of our lack of initiation ceremonies, most people are stuck in the middle-world identities they settled on when they were little, unconsciously playing out childhood patterns in their "adult" lives; effectively children in adult bodies. The consequence of all this, and the truth, is that in this day and age, real Adults are rare. I have met only a handful in my life and, in teaching, I have found that most people really do have no idea what the qualities of a real Adult are.

What an Adult Really is

To begin addressing this, what follows is a list of the qualities I see as being characteristic of an Adult. In compiling the list, I have drawn on the qualities I have observed in my Human lower-world Guides, and from what they have taught me about Adulthood initiations. I have also drawn on what I know from anthropology, and from psychotherapy (particularly from Rogers, Maslow, Reich and Jung). The list has also been road-tested in several training groups over the years and has been modified and refined by them. It continues to be work in progress, however, and I am not claiming it to be a definitive list. Like everything in this book, I am simply offering it as suggestions, so feel free to add things or remove things as you see fit.

In reading through the qualities, some may seem obvious, though some may seem less so. For instance, one characteristic listed is "Does not take more than their fair share of resources", and another is "Seeks to distribute resources fairly". Given that we live in a culture that sees the acquisition of wealth as one of the hallmarks of being a successful grown-up, these two qualities of Adult may not seem obvious. What is important to remember is that we are looking here at what an Adult would have been in a hunter-gatherer culture. We are looking for the healthy template in the layers below those of the Taker cult. Most people these days tend to think of adulthood as being about things like "standing on your own two feet" and being "independent" and able to "support yourself". This is because the Taker cult is all about separation and isolation. In an animist tribe, being Adult was about *inter*dependence, not independence. This is because the experience that we are all interconnected is at the heart of animism. It is also because the survival of the tribe depended on the Adults operating from a place of interdependence.

Remember, viable hunter-gatherer tribes were small units, consisting of as few as 20 people, and not more than around 200. They lived in a literally hand-to-mouth way, and alongside dangerous wild animals, and with little or no personal space or privacy. Hunter-gathering could be precarious. It is worth remembering that not so long ago there were other hominid species besides us, including the Neanderthals and the Denisovans, all of whom went extinct. We ourselves came close to extinction at times. Genetic analysis suggests that around 70,000 years ago, for example, there were as few as 2,000 of us Homo sapiens in the entire world. We survived because we cooperated with each other.

In order to survive, a hunter-gatherer tribe had to be a high-functioning team, where people got on with each other, trusted each other, and had each other's backs. Any tribe where there was interpersonal strife, factions and resentments would not have survived. Because of this, things like sharing resources fairly, so that there was no resentment and so that everyone got what they needed, were not just *desirable* traits, but *essential* traits of being an Adult. This is why, from all over the world, there are accounts in anthropology of indigenous people saying that if they had any surplus then they *had* to share it. The world over, this was an essential trait of being an Adult; keeping surplus for oneself was to behave like a child. So, too, traits seeking to "enhance social cohesion" and being "inclusive rather than divisive" are not just desirable, either, but intrinsic to being an Adult. Looked at in this way, the essential qualities of an Adult describe not an individual, but a *role* within a community; an *essential* role if that community is to be a healthy and high-functioning one.

Here is the list.

A True Adult:

1. Is grounded, present, and embodied.

2. Has a good degree of self-awareness.

3. Is reality-orientated.

4. Is willing to face the truth and see the world as it is (rather than how they would like it to be, or how they think it "should" be).

5. Is willing to accept responsibility for their own choices, actions and behaviour.

6. Is open to learning from their mistakes.

7. Is open to feedback.

8. Sets and maintains appropriate and healthy personal boundaries.

9. Is willing to step into and own their personal power and authority. Does not unhealthily hand their power over to others.

10. Knows the limits of their power.

11. Uses their power wisely and constructively.

12. Seeks to empower others where possible and appropriate.

13. Is reliable and dependable.

14. Is congruent.

15. Is in touch with their feelings and emotions. Can show vulnerability when appropriate.

16. Can ask for help and support when needed.

17. Is empathic and compassionate.

18. Can engage in healthy parenting when appropriate (including nurturing, setting healthy boundaries, teaching and protecting).

19. Is a good role-model.

20. Has healthy self-control and self-discipline (mental, emotional and physical).

21. Contributes constructively to their community.

22. Supports others.

23. Treats others with respect and dignity, including the other-than-human members of the community, too.

24. Seeks to enhance social cohesion.

25. Is inclusive rather than divisive, and accepting of difference (whenever possible and appropriate).

26. Is willing to act for the greater good when necessary, rather than purely for personal gain.

27. Does not take more than their fair share of resources.

28. Seeks to distribute resources fairly.

29. Is competent in their chosen roles and tasks.

30. Lives ethically, honourably, and with integrity.

As I said, I am not claiming this is a definitive list. There may be things you disagree with, and other things you think should be included. The point here is not whether the list is "right" or not. Rather, it is to think about the issues, and in doing so, strip away wonky Taker cult ideas about adulthood, ideas that would otherwise get in the way when it comes to journeying to find your Soul. To help with that, here are a couple of exercises.

Exercise 12: How Adult Are You?

Take some time to go through the qualities of an Adult and reflect on how they apply to you.

Be honest with yourself in doing this. It is not an exercise in beating yourself up, though. It is an exercise in being Adult. That means facing the truth and being open to feedback (from yourself). It also means being compassionate and empathic with yourself, too. For, given the lack of healthy modelling in this culture, if you are even halfway towards being an Adult already, then you are doing well.

When going through the list, take your time. Really reflect on each of the qualities.

In doing so, if you find ones that need developing in you, make a note of them. Then, take each of these one at a time. With each one, take as much time as you need—a day, a week, a month, a year—however long it takes, to reflect on it as you go through your daily life. Practice it and notice how it feels to be coming more from that place.

Exercise 13: How Many Adults Do You Know?

Looking at the list of Adult qualities, think about how well they apply to people in your family, or in your work environment, or in other groups you belong to.

Then, try to think of as many people as you can who you feel embody the qualities of Adult. These can be people you have met in your life, famous people, or even fictitious people.

Notice how rare true Adults are (compared to hunter-gatherer tribes, where every adult was an Adult).

Reflect on how much we need Adults back in the world.

Reflect on how that means it is *your* responsibility to choose to be an Adult in *your* life.

Meeting your Soul

In a moment, I am going to go through how to journey to meet your lower-world Soul. In order to do the exercise successfully, though, there are just a few other things that need clarifying first. One is that there really is no point doing this exercise unless you feel ready. Becoming an Adult is a process, not an event, and will take time. *However,* you really do need to be ready to begin that process for it to work. If you embark upon it when you are not, then you are setting yourself up to fail. So be honest with yourself and take your time to do any needed preparation first.

It is also important to understand more about what it is you are looking for, so that your intent in the journey is as clear as possible. It is important to be clear what you are looking for is an Adult *Human*. Because your true lower-world Soul is not some abstract thing.

It is not going to look like a glowing ball of energy, or a fairy, or some kind of winged beast. Your lower-world soul is *You*. The specific, individual healthy Human Being that you were, and are, meant to be.

Probably the easiest way to understand this is to think about what you would be like as an Adult had you been raised in a healthy hunter-gatherer tribe. Brought up by parents who knew how to be good parents. Raised in a high-functioning, well-bonded, emotionally-intelligent and supportive group, and by people who wanted to help your Soul blossom. An Adult who spent their childhood playing outside and in nature. Who lives a life where their body can do what it is designed to do, and what is healthy for it. An Adult who is free of possessions (objects), and of possessions (things they are possessed by). Someone who is free of soul-loss and of power-loss. Who experiences the world as an animist, as an inter-connected being, alive to the aliveness of the world around them.

If you had been raised in this way, what would you be like? What would be your role and place be in the tribe?

This is the person you are going to meet. They need to look something like you, as they are, after all, the lower-world blueprint for your body too. They will almost certainly be healthier and fitter, as hunter-gatherer lifestyles were physically active, and, contrary to what most people think, the diet was often healthier than most modern-day ones. Sometimes, they may not be the same sex as you are in this physical world, though, but only if this feels right to you and makes sense.

On that last point, things feeling right to you is crucially important with every aspect of meeting your lower-world Soul. Maybe in your life you have met someone you click with. You feel at ease with them and feel they "get" you, and that is almost as if you have known each other for years. Or maybe you have known someone for years, someone who you feel does grok you, and who you feel at ease with. The thing is, though, that no matter how much a "soul mate" they may feel to you, no matter how much of a kindred spirit, they are still someone else. Your Soul, on the other hand, is you yourself, the person who you should feel, at some level, the most kinship with. Depending on how far your middle-world self is from what they are like, they may feel strange to you at first, like someone who has lived another life altogether (they have!). *And* though, at another level, if they are your Soul, then there will be a deep familiarity about them too. That is why it is important that your Soul, in the form of the lower-world hunter-gatherer you are going to meet, feels right to you. If not, then move on and try again, either in the same journey or in another journey later on.

In doing the journey, it is of course crucial you are definitely in the lower-world since, because your Soul is *of* the lower-world, that is where they are to be found. Remember then that the lower-world is the realm of wild nature. It is entirely free of any signs of human domestication, including agriculture. There is no farming. No fields or hedgerows. The people there do not own herds. Remember that the humans in the lower-world are Stone Age People. So, your Soul will not be wearing any metal jewellery or carrying metal knives. Any clothing they are wearing will be made from animal skins or natural fibres.

Exercise 14: Meeting Your Lower-World Soul

The intent of this journey is to go to the lower-world to meet your own Adult Soul.

Prepare yourself for doing a shamanic journey, doing whatever works for you.

Start the drumming.

Go to your Axis Mundi and deliberately and consciously hollow-out. Take your time doing this.

Then tell your Guides you wish to be taken to the lower-world to meet your Human lower-world Adult Soul. When ready, set off to the lower-world with your Guides.

As always, follow your Guide's lead and directions. Remember, you are looking to meet Yourself as the Adult you would have ideally grown up to be in a healthy hunter-gatherer Tribe. Once you do meet them, do take time to check out if things feel right, and check with your Guides too. If things do not feel right, then set off with your Guides again and keep looking.

When you do find your Soul, greet them. Then notice details about their appearance—their hair, the colour of their eyes, the shape of their nose, what they are wearing, if they have any jewellery or tattoos etc. Make them as solid and detailed to you as you can.

Ask them their name (your lower-world name).

Then, ask them if there is anything they wish to show you, or anywhere they want to take you (staying in the lower-world). Generally, spend time with them and get to know them.

If it feels right and appropriate, you could also try becoming them—shapeshifting into them and noticing how it feels to be them.

On the call-back, bring them back with you, either alongside you, or by bringing them back with you into your physical body.

Afterwards, as always, write down what happened in as much detail as you can remember before your left-brain starts to erase bits from your memory.

Growing into what you were Meant to Be

"To think about the Soul, to think about it at least once in the confusion of every crowded day, is indeed the beginning of salvation."
– Georges Duhamel

Meeting your Soul is the beginning of a process. Having met your Soul, the process then involves allowing your Soul to start shaping your middle-world life. To do this, you need to begin to cultivate the habit of checking in with it. Ask it what it would do, and for its advice. Your true Soul is, of course, a wild and free animist hunter-gatherer, because that is *literally* what we are designed to be. Because of that, though, you may think your Soul has little to offer that will be of practical use in your daily life, given how far our lifestyles are from those of hunter-gatherers. If so, then I can only say that from my own experience and from watching students, I have found the opposite to be the case. The Soul provides an anchor that stops you drifting and getting lost in the stories of the human-made middle-world. The human middle-world is cluttered and "sticky", and this can be true of our middle-world self, too. If we let it, our middle-world self can draw us in and entangle us with its stories and dramas. By contrast, our Soul is a calm, clear and wise voice. When we listen to it and centre ourselves in it, much of the noise and clutter of the middle-world just drops away. We gain perspective.

We can gain this perspective and healthy degree of detachment from the middle-world by being centred in our upper-world Spirit, too, of course. This is because both Soul and Spirit transcend the middle-world. As well as healthy detachment, though, Soul brings something else. It brings answers. Answers about how to live in the world and about who to be in the world. Soul provides the healthy Templates on which to base an authentically-lived life. Your middle-world self will then need to translate and adapt these Templates, to make them relevant and useful in your everyday life and the environment in which you live, but doing that is the correct and healthy role of the middle-world self. By being the channel through which the Soul can flow into the world, rather than being lost and adrift in human-made, middle-world stories, the middle-world self becomes anchored in Mother Earth and part of her again.

As well as referring to your Soul for guidance, another important practice is to regularly shapeshift into *being* your Soul. This does not work if it is only done in your head. It must involve your *physical* body. You need to *feel* what it is like to be that wild and free hunter-gatherer; shapeshift into them in a *somatic* way. By doing this, gradually your Soul becomes more embodied and present in your daily life. If you do this, then, little-by-little, you will find your default notion of who you are gradually shifts from being your middle-world self, to being your Soul instead.

These practices actually work. Along with the other animist and shamanic practices, they really do start to change how you experience the world and wake you up to its aliveness and interconnection. It is simply a matter of doing them. That is all it takes (and, as a bonus, they are mostly fun and enjoyable to do).

And, in doing them, not only do you gradually become whole yourself, but by taking your rightful place in the world, you are helping the Earth herself to become whole too.

CHAPTER FIVE

Finding Your Tribe

You Belong to a Lower-World Tribe

As well as individual lower-world Guides, at some point in your sha-manic journeying you will meet your lower-world Tribe. In shaman-ism, these people are sometimes referred to as your "Ancestral Kin". You may unexpectedly meet them one day whilst doing a shamanic journey, or you may deliberately ask your Power Animal to take you to meet them.

Like your lower-world Human Guides, your Ancestral Kin are not your individual biological ancestors. They are not ancestors, but An-cestors. Working with individual biological ancestors is middle-world work, and as such it is outside the scope of this particular book (I will explore it in later books). Ancestral Kin are not individuals from the middle-world, though, but of the lower-world, representatives of Human. As with your main Human lower-world Guide, your Tribe may be of an entirely different race and culture to you (alt-hough they do not have to be, of course). They may be of the same tribal culture as your main Human lower-world Guide, but not nec-essarily. It does not matter either way.

Your Tribe shows you how you are part of Human, and what it is to be loved and part of a healthy human tribe. The Tribe, and the place where they live, is somewhere safe you can go for healing. It is a place you can go to learn from Guides who specialise in particular areas of shamanism. You can also go there just to enjoy hanging out, as a respite from the human middle-world and the Fall; a place where you do not have to worry about paying bills, problems at work, emails, or ethical dilemmas about what food or products to buy. You can go there to experience and remember how we used to live, in right-relationship with the Earth and the other Peoples, living a sustainable and simple life.

Importantly, this Tribe is also a place you can go to experience what it is like to be part of a happy, well-adjusted and supportive community. It is a place you can go to heal wounds created by difficult or dysfunctional human relationships. Maybe you have never felt really welcome in the human middle-world, or that you have a place here. By going to your Ancestral Kin, you can experience what it is like to be part of a tribe where you really belong, and are loved, valued, accepted, and truly treasured. Maybe you never felt safe in childhood. Again, you can journey to your lower-world tribe and experience what it would be like to be part of a human family who absolutely have your back covered and keep you safe. Maybe in childhood you felt like you had no voice or power, or that nobody was interested in you or wanted to spend time with you, or that you always felt you had to fight and be on-guard. Maybe as an adult, you have never quite found your place in human society, the place you fit in and truly belong and are loved and valued. Maybe you find the office politics at work in your wider family exhausting. Whatever the wound is in terms of relationships with people and human society, you can travel to your lower-world tribe and experience what it is like to not have that wound. Doing this can be profoundly healing. Plus, you can do this as often as you need and as many times as you want, until the wound is healed or no longer troubles you. For your lower-world Tribe will *always* be there for you, whenever you want them or need them.

Our Lack of Healthy Tribe

Whilst spending time with a lower-world Tribe can be immensely healing, to be able to do this you need to know what hunter-gatherer tribes were actually like. Otherwise, as we have explored earlier on, you will inevitably tend to use imagery and concepts you are familiar with. I find that people often think tribes were some version of a modern-day extended family, or like a small present-day community. In fact, they were very different to either of these things. In order to visualise and experience being part of a Tribe, then, it will help to have some understanding of hunter-gatherer tribal structures to draw upon. So, we are going to explore this first.

In terms of families, it is important to understand the modern nuclear family is actually a recent invention. It is not how we have lived for the vast majority of human history, and in that sense, it cannot be said to be natural to us, as some people would have us believe. Exactly how recently we started living in nuclear families is a matter of scholarly debate, but at the most it is only within the last few hundred years. This is only a tiny percentage of the tens of thousands of years of human history—about one four-hundredth of it! It is also a way of living that is already looking to have been a failed experiment, as nuclear families increasingly are becoming no longer a norm. Prior to nuclear families, people tended to live in extended families or larger communities (villages and so forth), and prior to the adoption of agriculture, for the majority of human history, people of course lived in tribes.

In a tribal culture, you would have been living with people you knew well. It is only after the Fall that, as we move into towns and cities, we began living side-by-side with people who we were not related to and who were effectively "strangers". Living in close proximity to strangers brought new stresses and anxieties. This is because the maximum size for a high-functioning, cohesive and psychologically healthy human group is around 150 members. This is known as "Dunbar's Number", and is biologically hard-wired into us. When the group becomes bigger than that, stresses and tensions begin to emerge and so, in hunter-gatherer times, when this happened the group would split into smaller, less stressful ones.

Most animals are territorial to some extent. Some animals are solitary and keep away from all other animals of the same species. If such animals are forced to live in close proximity, they will experience anxiety, and conflict will usually result. But even animals that are sociable and live in groups usually are territorial and avoid other groups. In animals like wolves, lions, chimpanzees, hyenas, and us humans, the pride, pack, troupe or tribe usually has its own territorial space. This is true even of things like ant colonies and hives of wasps and bees. If another group encroaches on a group's space, the result is usually tension and conflict.

As humans, we are both social animals and territorial by nature. Most human conflicts and war arise as a result of the proximity of strangers and competition for resources. This is, of course, another reason why in hunter-gatherer cultures conflict was much rarer than in modern times, as in those times the population density was dramatically less than it is now, and so encountering strangers would have been a rare event, and there would have been much less competition. Compare this with how many strangers you see in a day spent in a town or city, or when using public transport. Hundreds of strangers, possibly even thousands. This is radically different to the life of our tribal ancestors, who might go for months or years without seeing the face of someone they did not know.

Take a moment to imagine what it would have been like to go hunting and gathering as part of a healthy human tribe you had grown up in. It would have been physically tough for sure, and at times even dangerous. In terms of the *human* side of it, though, you would have been doing it with people you knew and trusted, and you knew had your back, and with people who enjoyed working together—a high-functioning, co-operative team. Now, compare this with the modern version of hunting and gathering for many people. It consists of navigating a commute with thousands of strangers, working in a competitive environment with people you would maybe not choose to spend time with otherwise, and then navigating a crowded shopping centre or supermarket to get your food and other goods. Biologically, we are simply not evolved to comfortably cope with living in such close proximity to so many strangers. Living as we do now goes against hundreds of thousands of years of human evolution, against millions of years of being an animal. It is not natural to us, and results in stresses, often leading to conflicts and violence. In order to try and manage these stresses, we have had to evolve things like laws, police forces and prisons, diplomacy and treaties. But if you look back at the astonishing levels of violence and warfare in the last 6,000 years of city-state societies, it is debatable whether our attempts to manage conflict have been all that successful.

Plus, to manage the anxiety of being surrounded by strangers, we have had to do all sorts of things like medicating our anxiety with alcohol or prescription drugs, putting locks on our doors, having passwords and other security features to protect what is ours, having hedges and fences to mark our territory and for privacy, avoiding making eye contact with strangers, being wary about going out alone at night, keeping our wits about us in crowds and public places, and so many other things. To cope with it we also try to seek out and join an interlocking network of "tribes", such as: our colleagues at work, church, the golf club, our Facebook "friends", the group of friends we socialise with, and so on.

The thing is that usually these modern-day "tribes" are transitory. Friends, work colleagues and neighbours all come and go. You may be somebody who has a group of lifelong friends who stick by you. If so, then you are lucky because that is less and less common these days. Indeed, one of the ironies about "social" media is that it was meant to help us feel more connected, but it is having the opposite effect. A recent YouGov poll, for example, found that 27% of millennials (people born between 1981 and 1996) have no close friends,

25% them have no "acquaintances" and 22% (or 1 in 5) have no friends at all. This compares with ("only") 15% of Generation Xers (people born between 1965 and 1980) who reported having no friends, and 9% of Baby Boomers (born between 1946 and 1964) who said the same (still a staggering 1 in 10 people, though). We know from anthropology that in hunter-gatherer times, 0% of people would have reported having no friends, and that most of their friends would have been close ones. Another study done for The Economist magazine and the Kaiser Family Foundation found that more than 22% of adults say they often or always feel lonely, lack companionship, or feel left out or isolated. And in another study, done in 2010 for the American Association of Retired Persons, the number of adults who reported they regularly or frequently felt lonely was a staggering 40 to 45% (this compares to between 11% and 20% who said the same thing in the 1980s). Again, in hunter-gatherer times this figure would have been zero.

The Loneliness Epidemic

A common misconception about loneliness is that it is about being alone. In fact, loneliness and being alone are not the same thing at all, for loneliness is something that can affect people when they are surrounded by others, and even when they have a good social network. Loneliness (as opposed to solitude) is about the quality rather than the quantity of relationships we have. It is perfectly possible to have lots of friends and family and yet find that your need for meaningful human contact is still not being met.

As well as confusing it with being alone, another misconception about loneliness can be that it is the result of poor personal skills. In reality, studies show that teaching social skills has only a modest effect on levels of loneliness. The reason we are seeing a rise in loneliness is not due to a lack of social skills. Nor is it due to being alone.

With nearly eight billion people on the planet, we have never been more surrounded by people. We can move from "tribe" to "tribe"— from work colleagues, family, friends, the gym, and so on—at will and in a way that no hunter-gatherers could. Social media gives us the ability to "connect" with hundreds of people. Yet several studies show that social media use, far from increasing a sense of connectedness, can actually increase the sense of loneliness in people. All the evidence is that we have never been lonelier and are becoming more so. Loneliness is a modern-day epidemic. Clearly, something has gone very wrong with our inter-human relationships.

This is a major issue, for loneliness triggers in us the same primal alarm bells as things like hunger, thirst, physical pain and danger. This is because we evolved to be social animals; animals who form strong bonds and cooperate to provide mutual aid. In hunter-gatherer times, although you would have known how to survive for a while on your own, being alone long-term would not have been viable. You *needed* a tribe if you were to survive for any length of time. As such, we are hard-wired to perceive loneliness as a physical threat; a threat to our very existence.

There are many studies that show how loneliness has a negative impact on our health. It raises levels of stress hormones, disturbs sleep patterns, increases inflammation and allergic responses throughout the body, decreases the ability of the immune system to fight off infections, and is associated with greater levels of heart disease, strokes and diabetes. Some studies suggest that it increases your risk of dying early by around as much as thirty percent, and that it can be as damaging to your health as smoking cigarettes. As such, alongside soaring rates of obesity, loneliness is the major physical health problem of our time. It is another sign of just how much we have lost our way. This is, though, another thing that shamanism can help us with, by providing healthy templates on which to model things, as we shall see.

Leaving your Middle-World History Behind

As part of growing up and constructing our middle-world identity, we adopt a relationship style. It may be to be the strong one, or the needy one, the listener, the sensible one, the joker, and so on. Likewise, in relationships our pattern may variously to be guarded or trusting, independent or co-dependent, volatile, aggressive, passive, self-centred, distant, clingy, critical, tolerant, sensitive, insensitive, stubborn, flighty, and so on.

When it comes to journeying to the lower-world to meet our Tribe, whilst such patterns are not *necessarily* problematic, they can be. For example, I see students who, because of their middle-world history, have learnt to be overly independent and in control. When they come to me and ask why something went wrong in a journey, I ask them if they were paying attention to their Guides. Invariably, they were not. Other people's relationship style is to hand their power away too much, and they do this with their Guides. They never really step up and take their full part in journeys, and so they never learn to feel confident about what they are doing. Other students, because of their pasts, have problems letting love in because they are scared of getting hurt, or because they do not feel worthy. Even though the reality is that their Guides would never hurt them or let them down, they still bring this middle-world pattern with them. They keep their Guides at arm's length and do not really commit to them and so do not get the depth of healing and teaching they could. Other people are suspicious, and so have trouble trusting their Guides.

The more we can be aware of our middle-world relationship styles and scripts, the more we can stop them getting in the way of our relationship with our Guides. Not only that, but by not being caught up in our scripts, we can then also ask our Guides for help with healing them. We can ask them to help heal wounds that led to us feeling that we must be in control, or afraid to step into our power, or afraid to be vulnerable, and so on.

It is not just our relationship stories we need to be aware of and try to leave behind in seeking out our lower-world Tribe, though. There are a couple of other things that, if they are not aware of them, people tend to take with them, and which then distort their experience of Tribe. One is the story of nuclear family that I mentioned earlier. People tend to think of hunter-gatherer tribes as having been made up of a collection of nuclear family units. This was very rarely the case. Rather, children were usually raised by *all* of the adults in a tribe, and not just by their biological parents. As a child in a tribe, you would have been free to hang out with whatever adult or adults you felt closest to. When it came to sleeping arrangements, in *some* tribes people slept in groups based loosely on direct "family" (children sleeping with their biological parents). More common, however, was that the whole tribe slept in the same area. In other tribes, all the men would have slept in one area, and all the women in another area. This did not mean that biological link between parents and their children did not matter (as we shall see later, it still needed to be acknowledged and honoured), but that it had a different context and emphasis. To see your lower-world Tribe clearly, then, it is important not to think of nuclear family units.

Another story that people often take with them is around the almost total lack of privacy in tribal cultures. In the modern era, most of us value our privacy. We lock our doors, have fences between us and our neighbours, enjoy the privacy of our cars, and heave a sigh of relief when we get home and can shut the door on the world. In the film *"Tawai: A Voice from the Forest"*, the explorer and filmmaker Bruce Parry says that, before he was about to spend a long period of time with a hunter-gatherer tribe, he was worried about how he would cope with the lack of privacy and space. After being with the tribe, though, in the film he reports that he had not felt the need for privacy, because he found it so easy to be around such peaceful people and in a group with no interpersonal tensions and dynamics going on. People who have spent time around hunter-gatherers often report similar experiences to Parry's. This is important to understand, if you are to truly grok what being in a healthy Tribe is like. Our modern need for privacy is a product of the Taker cult. It is a result of things like the stresses of modern population density, and the state of most peoples' mental and emotional health.

Hunter-gatherer people often say that we modern people are crazy. When they say "crazy", they do not mean this as a figure-of-speech. They mean it literally, because in comparison to hunter-gatherers, our mental health is terrible. Of course, there are individual exceptions, but *collectively* this makes modern-day people much harder to be around than hunter gatherers were. It means, again with exceptions, that our groups (workplaces, committees, families, and so on) tend to be much harder work to be in. I am aware in saying this that I am an introvert, and so I am well aware of how stressful I find being around people. However, there is a base-line level of stress these days that is there in even the most sociable of people. We *all* do things like lock our doors and windows, have passwords for our phones and bank accounts, are careful if we are out alone at night in a city, and so on. We all have to manage difficult people in our workplace, family, or other groups that we are in.

People sometimes say that if you put a frog in a saucepan of cold water and bring it slowly to the boil, then the frog will sit there till it dies. It is, of course, an analogy for how we can become so used to things that we do not notice them even if they are bad for us. When it comes to being around other people, there is a basic level of stress and unease these days that we think of as being normal. Like many things in the Taker cult that we think of as normal, though, when we look at hunter-gatherer cultures, we can see it is not normal at all. It is not how we used to be.

The Drama Triangle

When it comes to going to the lower-world to experience healthy Human relationships and Tribe, another middle-world thing we can take with us and which can get in the way is what is known as the "drama triangle". The term originates from the psychotherapy known as Transactional Analysis, developed by Dr. Eric Berne. It works like this. Somebody feels like they are the victim, and that somebody else is persecuting them. A third person then steps in to "rescue" the victim. Often this is done by the "rescuer" turning on the "persecutor". Now the "persecutor" feels like they are a "victim", and that the "rescuer" is being a "persecutor" themselves. More people now get sucked in, and the whole situation begins to escalate out of control. The drama triangle destroys communities. It rips families apart. It can be passed on for generations, centuries even. It can even operate on a mass scale—the conflicts in the Middle East, Northern Ireland, the Balkans, the Cold War, religious conflicts—conflicts all over the world.

The thing is that, in the drama triangle, *everyone* ends up feeling aggrieved and that they are the victim. Everyone in it thinks it is the "other side" who should apologise, and that them doing that will resolve the situation. Believing this, though, is *precisely* what keeps a drama triangle going. Instead, the truth is that a drama triangle *only* stops when people within it have the courage to put their grievances down and stop looking for things like apologies, justice or retribution. This is the immense thing that Nelson Mandela did on his release from prison, and what people did in the Truth and Reconciliation process that followed. It was people doing that which led to the end of the Troubles in Northern Ireland.

If one person within a drama triangle stops playing the blame-game, and then the other people involved follow suit, the cycle can come to an end. Of course, though, sometimes not everyone is able or willing to do this. However, whenever we find ourselves in a drama triangle, we always have the option of walking away from it. Other people can continue to play if they wish. That is up to them, and their responsibility and choice. Irrespective of what the other people decide to do, we can still choose not to play the blame-game anymore ourselves.

If you think back to the qualities of a true Adult, it becomes clear that the drama triangle is a game played by children, not by Adults. Remember, and Adult is willing to see things as they *are,* rather than how they would like them to be, or how they think they "should" be. They are willing to accept responsibility for their *own* choices, actions, feelings and behaviour. They are willing to step into and own their personal power and authority, and do not hand their power over to others (this includes not expecting other people to make them feel better, or to make things right for them). They set and maintain appropriate and healthy personal boundaries. They are willing to own their mistakes and learn from them. They use their power wisely and contribute *constructively* to their community and seek to enhance social cohesion. They are willing to act for the greater good when necessary and are a good role-model. None of these qualities of Adult are compatible with playing the drama triangle.

This is why you will not find the drama triangle being played in your lower-world Tribe (or anywhere else in the lower-world, or upper-world, for that matter). It is a middle-world game. It is, though, one that we are surrounded by in this world and so, like our other wounded experiences of human relationships, it has the potential to discolour and distort what we experience in the lower-world. As such, it is important to be aware of it and, as much as possible, not take it with us when we go to meet our Tribe.

The drama triangle is not, of course, something any true lower-world (or upper-world) Guides will help you play. What they can and will do, if asked, is help you to walk away from any drama triangle you find yourself in. They can help you with any healing necessary for you to be able to do this, and can model healthier ways of being too.

How to Live with Other People

We know that tribes were not like nuclear families. We know, too, that tribal people felt little or no need for privacy, because they were free of the tensions, anxieties and conflicts we are used to these days. We know they were mostly free of mental health issues, and of loneliness. These things tell us what tribes were *not* like (essentially, they were not much like anything that we are used to). What *were* they like, then? How were they organised? What healthy templates can they provide, in helping us come back to a saner way of living with each other?

What we know from anthropology can go some way in helping us to answer these questions. However, there is much we can learn from psychotherapy, too. In studying tribes, anthropologists look at how tribes are organised, but they are not necessarily focused on what makes them *psychologically* healthy. Because of that, in looking at models of healthy human groups, I am going to start off by looking at the work of Bert Hellinger, a German psychotherapist, and explore what this tells us about healthy tribes. Although Hellinger was studying modern-day families rather than hunter-gatherer tribes, his work uncovered archetypal templates that underlie *all* healthy human living arrangements. In this, his work can help us pick out what it was about the way that tribes were organised that tended to make them so psychologically healthy.

Hellinger's original work involved looking at the different roles that people have in families, and the dynamics between them. He developed a unique way of working called "family constellations". The work has evolved into many different forms these days, but the original form looks something like this:

The work is done in a group of people. One person is the "client". The client starts by setting up a representation of their own family, the "constellation". To do this, the client asks people in the group to represent the various members of their (the client's) family. So, the client will ask one group member to represent their father (the client's father), another person to represent their mother, and then other people to represent each of the significant members of their family. This includes asking a group member to represent the client themselves. As the representatives are chosen, the client arranges them in the room in relationship to each other. Some may be standing, others sitting. Some may be facing each other, or some may have their backs turned. Some may be spatially close, and others may be further away from each other. Some may be making eye contact, while others may be looking away. In the purest form of constellation work, the representatives are told nothing about the person who they are representing, nothing about that person's personality or any other information whatsoever. All they know is that they are representing either the father, the mother, the sister, and so on. Having set the constellation up, the client then withdraws and is allowed no further input other than to just observe. The chosen representatives then take some time to tune into what they are feeling and experiencing and then slowly begin to give voice to that. For example, the person representing the father might say, "The father is feeling sad that the mother is so far away from him". The person representing the grandmother might say, "The grandmother is feeling that she would like to be closer to her grandchild but is worried that her son-in-law would object". And so on. As well as speaking, the representatives also move at times, changing the spatial relationships between them, moving closer or further apart, changing who they are stood next to, turning to face someone or turning away, and so on. What happens then is sometimes extraordinary. What started off as (usually) a tableau of despair, misery, tension, hostility, isolation, fear, loneliness, and all sorts of other things, then sometimes changes into something that palpably feels and looks much healthier and resolved.

When a constellation does resolve in a healthy way, this can be healing not just for the client, but sometimes for other family members, too, and even for the family as a whole. In this, the work demonstrates that we really are all part of larger wholes, and that what affects one part affects the whole. Of course, constellations do not always come to a happy resolution, but even when they do not, they can still be of great help in terms of the client's healing, as they often turn up surprising information and insights. This is because, in becoming the representatives, people report that they enter a trance-like state. Along with the stripped-back language that is used when doing constellation work, and the emphasis on feelings, intuitions, and spatial relationships, this gets underneath the content and stories about what is going on and reveals deeper patterns and truths.

When constellations *do* resolve, though, they reveal patterns that go beyond what is relevant to a specific family. Hellinger noticed that healthily-resolved family constellations had characteristics in common; that when families are healthy, they are following certain universal patterns. He said that: "There is an ancient order that works inside us, that controls much more than we are aware. Good order comes about when peace has been made for the whole system.". He called this good order the "Orders of Love" (he is using the word "orders" here in the sense of a sequence, and not in the sense of rules or commands). He noticed that, when families follow these ancient patterns, love flows. When they do not follow them, families are unhealthy and full of pain.

There are a number of these patterns. They describe the healthy roles within a family, and what constitute healthy relationships between family members. When I first came across these patterns in the form of the "Orders of Love", I could see that Hellinger was on to something. However, as he described them, the patterns never felt *quite* right to me. In part, this was because, at the heart of

Hellinger's Orders is essentially a nuclear family. A mother and father standing together, grandparents behind them in supportive roles, and the children arranged in front of the parents in order of age, and so on. I spent a number of years trying to resolve this. When it came, the solution was, as it often is, to think about how things would have worked in hunter-gatherer times. It involved my reaching back past the Taker cult and thinking how the patterns would have worked not in modern-day families, but in hunter-gatherer tribes. In doing that, the healthy Patterns became clear.

Discovering the healthy Patterns would not have been possible only by looking at the anthropological data, for as I said, how tribal structures contributed to psychological health was not something anthropologists would specifically have been looking out for (especially not in the days when there were still true hunter-gatherer tribes to study). The Patterns only emerged when I brought Hellinger's insights together with what we know about pre-agricultural shamanism—an example of the many ways in which psychotherapy and shamanism can complement each other and have a lot they can learn from each other.

Not all tribes would have conformed to *all* the Patterns. From anthropology, I am well aware of that. On a psychological level, though, just as with families, the more a tribe followed these Patterns, the healthier the tribe (and the individuals within it) would have been.

The Psychological Patterns of Healthy Groups

Most of what follows applies to healthy tribes and to modern-day family units. However, much of it can be applied to other human groups, too, such as workplaces and larger communities. Also, when it comes to the sections on parents, remember that in a hunter-gatherer tribe, the "parents" would generally have been all the adults in the tribe.

In a healthy group:

1. **The costs of belonging do not outweigh the benefits (except for parents – see 2 below).** Obviously, belonging to almost any group involves a series of costs and benefits. This is true whether it is about belonging to a family, a workplace, a religion, the gym, or to society as a whole. Ideally, the equation between costs and benefits should always add up. Any group in which the costs of belonging outweigh the benefits is a dysfunctional group and unhealthy for the people in it.

2. **Parents give more to children than they get back.** Parents owe children because it was the parent's choice to take on that role. Children, however, do not intrinsically owe parents anything, because if someone enters into a relationship without freewill and informed consent, then ethically nothing can be required of them. Because of this, the parent-child relationship is not meant to be an equal one. Giving more than you get back goes with the job of being a parent.

3. **Children have the right to expect love from their parents. All other love from someone within a group (including from one's own children) is earnt by one's behaviour and is not demanded, expected or assumed.** Children need love in order to grow and thrive. Because of that, in choosing to be a parent, part of the responsibility that goes with the role is to try and do one's best to show your child love. Parents cannot *demand* love from their children, however. The love from a child towards their parent is not a given, but something that the parent needs to earn. It is not something that can be commanded or expected.

4. **When people take the benefits of being in the group, then they are willing to meet the costs (responsibilities).** This

gets broken many times in modern families. Some family members may pay more in costs than they get back in benefits, in which case they have the right to leave if they wish. Other family members may take without being prepared to meet the costs, making the whole family dysfunctional, because inequality is toxic to communities.

5. **Responsibilities and rewards both increase with growing up. Older children have more responsibility, and so are given more, younger children have less responsibility, and so are given fewer benefits.** In a tribe, as you grew up you would be given more responsibilities, but in turn you would be given more benefits (more authority and voice in the tribe, more respect, more autonomy, etc.). This Pattern is often broken in modern families, with the youngest child being spoilt and given the most whilst having the least responsibilities.

6. **All adults are equally Adult.** Once children are adults, age no longer matters. The youngest does not remain in a permanent state of childhood in relation to their siblings, nor does the eldest remain in a permanent state of having extra responsibilities and rewards.

7. **Everybody takes responsibility for their own actions and their consequences.** In a healthy group, everyone needs to grow up and take responsibility for their own actions, thoughts, feelings and behaviour.

8. **The Drama Triangle is not a game that people play.** Drama Triangles poison groups and simply have to be stopped (or, ideally, never allowed to develop in the first place). Stopping them is often the role of "elders"—people old and wise enough to put aside their own grievances and see what is good for the group as a whole, and able to rein in younger, hotter heads (in this and in other ways, elders are vital to groups, and so we will look at eldership in detail in the next chapter).

9. **Parents are Adults.** As we saw in the last chapter, though, our lack of initiation ceremonies and model of healthy Adult means that many children these days are raised by people who are themselves still children (albeit, in adult-sized bodies).

10. **What is between parents is kept between the parents (and never put onto the children).** Children are not used as weapons in disputes between the parents/adults or asked to take sides. Nor are children parent's emotional support or best friend (that is an adult role). To put a child in those positions robs them of their childhood, and their need for (and right to) a grown-up parent figure.

11. **Children are allowed to be children.** They are only given responsibilities, knowledge and information that are appropriate to their age.

12. **The Adults are the people in charge.** Although the children's opinions, ideas and concerns need to be respected and listened to, the Adults are the people in charge and able to step up and make Adult decisions when needed.

13. **In relation to children, elders (grandparents) step back and are behind the adults (parents), supporting them.** Adults decide, elders advise. Child, adult and elder are three different roles and stages in life. Tribal cultures understood this well. In such cultures, children were very much allowed to *be* children and enjoy their childhood. Decisions were made by the Adults. The role of the Elders was to support the Adults. In a family, when a grandparent does not step back, and instead interferes with the parenting, this undermines the parents, with negative consequences for the family as a whole.

14. **The masculine and the feminine are both honoured and treated with equal respect.** Generally, tribal cultures practiced a fair degree of gender division, with men and women having

different roles in the tribe (although the extent of this would vary tribe to tribe). In the majority of tribes, though, although there were different roles between the sexes, no one gender had dominance over the other. Each gender (and the associated roles in the tribe) was respected equally. It is also the case that in most of these cultures, the gender roles were not rigid. People were free to choose what gender they wanted to live as (including being gender-neutral). In a healthy tribe, what was important was not biology, but to respect and honour the masculine and the feminine equally, because inequality leads to dysfunctional groups.

15. **Adults take responsibility for teaching and modelling healthy masculinity and femininity.** Children learn about healthy masculinity and femininity from adults.

16. **Couples relate equally, and do not try and change each other.** People can only thrive in relationships when they feel their partner respects, loves and values them for who they are. Nobody thrives on a diet of criticism, or by being made to feel they are a disappointment or failure. This is important not just for the individuals involved, but because the health of a couple's relationship affects any groups to which they belong.

17. **All sides in a group are given equal respect.** Obviously, getting on with everyone in a group is not always easy, and it may be necessary to draw boundaries on things like behaviour, length of contact, and so on, but actively disrespecting people in groups damages the group a whole.

18. **Previous partners are honoured and respected.** This is similar to the last point. Previous partners are a fact, and actively disrespecting them creates fractures and damages the group as a whole. It also is disrespectful of your partner's history and their choice of previous partners. Again, though, healthy and appropriate boundaries may be necessary.

19. **In adoption, the biological parents are honoured and acknowledged.** There is a mass of evidence that denying, disowning or disrespecting the biological parents can have negative effects on an adopted child. If you tell a child that their biological parents were bad people, then deep down, what is that going to make the child feel about themselves and the genes they carry? And if you do not tell them anything about where they came from, how can they make sense of who they are, and of what may be "theirs" and what may be "not theirs" (i.e. inherited)?

20. **Parents respect their offspring's choice of partner.** Disrespecting your son or daughter's choice of partner, or meddling in the relationship between them, can only ever lead to fractures and disharmony. You may not like or approve of their partner, but actively disrespecting them damages the group as a whole.

21. **Sexual activity is treated with respect and its power understood.** Sex is rarely cost-free and often has consequences in groups (which is why all societies have rules around sexual behaviour). To varying degrees, sex creates energetic entanglements. These rarely just go away of their own accord, and if they do not then they need to be acknowledged and resolved (the process of doing shamanic disentanglements is covered in detail in the previous book in this series). Addressing this issue is particularly important when we enter a relationship with a new partner (or, ideally, *before* we enter into a relationship with a new partner!).

22. **In a new sexual relationship, the new partner comes first.** Obviously, if someone allows a previous partner to come between them and their new partner, this will damage the new relationship. Ideally, in order to enter a new relationship, we need to be as clearly disentangled from the old one as possible. Any children with the previous partner still need to be fully honoured

and respected, though, so that may mean that a total disentanglement is not always possible, in which case there needs to be healthy and appropriate boundaries to protect the new relationship.

23. **Every member of a group is acknowledged (even the dead).** In a family, this does not mean that we need to include or even be in contact with every family member. Rather, it means the existence of a family member, their place in the family and their effect on it, needs to be fully acknowledged and faced. When people are not acknowledged, it casts an unconscious shadow over the family. In constellation work, Hellinger discovered that this even means abortions and miscarriages. The dead child, and the associated and unresolved grief or shame around them, can cast a deep shadow over families until they are acknowledged, and any feelings are faced and resolved. *However*, this does not mean that all family secrets must be told and be out in the open, as there are situations where total honesty may do more harm than good. Decisions need to be based on honestly weighing up the costs and benefits.

24. **People's histories are acknowledged and respected.** This is similar to the last point. What has happened to people, why they are the way they are, needs to be acknowledged, so that it can be understood and respected. That includes people facing up to and acknowledging their own histories, too. For example, as a very young man, my father fought in the Second World War. For a considerable period of that time he was in special forces, fighting behind enemy lines in what was then called Burma. This involved witnessing, and doing, some *truly horrific* things. Like many men of his generation, he never spoke about it when he came back (although, in shamanic terms, a large part of him never really did come back from the war, as part of him was stuck there still, in those terrible events). As well as him never speaking

about it, no one else in the family was allowed to mention it. My parents were great believers in never talking about anything much, but especially not about feelings or about the past. They firmly believed that skeletons should be kept in closets. In being unacknowledged in this way, my father's unresolved history—his PTSD, for that is what it was—had a devastating effect on the family as a whole, and on the mental health of all of us in it. It was not until he was in his 80s, when he was still waking up screaming at night, and long after all his children had grown up and left home, that he finally sought out some specialist counselling. He began to open up about what had happened to him and, in doing so, he began to get better. A weight began to lift off not just him, but off the rest of the family, because repressing histories damages groups, and acknowledging histories opens up the possibility of healing.

25. **Endings are resolved and honoured.** When endings are not fully acknowledged and resolved, they leave unfinished business and lingering entanglements. Things become stuck and stagnant, and there can be no healthy new life. Endings need to be fully faced, acknowledged, processed and resolved. This is not just true of deaths of family members. It includes *all* endings—the ending of relationships, the endings of the various stages of life, the ending of old roles and ways of being. For our own health, but also for the health of the groups we belong to, we need to know when, and how, to let go.

Reflecting on the Patterns

I know from teaching the Patterns that sometimes people can have strong reactions to them. Sometimes people react to them as if they are some kind of a judgemental list of commands. They are not. They are simply descriptions of how healthy groups operate. They are not rules, but a set of guidelines or principles for consideration. There is no judgement about whether you follow them.

People also sometimes complain that they seem too idealistic, or just not possible. To which my reply is that they *are* ideals. That is the point of them. They are things to aim for. This does not make them black-or-white choices, though. Rather it is a matter of degrees— the closer a group is to the Patterns, the healthier the group will be. In terms of *how* achievable they are, that depends on circumstances. Clearly, they are not impossible to live by, because, to a large degree, they *are* how we used to live. The degree to which they are achievable in a specific modern-day group is another matter, given things like mental health issues, domestic violence and abuse, family histories, and other factors. They do, however, give us something healthy to aim for.

Most of the time in teaching them, I find people usually sit there nodding in agreement as we go through them, because they are mostly common-sense and hard to disagree with. However, people often sit there gasping, too, as they realise just how far away from these healthy Patterns their own experiences of family and groups have been, because the Patterns do highlight how far we have strayed from what is healthy.

The Patterns are an example of the kind of wisdom the elders and shamans in a tribe held, wisdom that kept the tribe healthy, for as I have said, there is far more to shamanism than just doing shamanic journeys. Shamanism is also a role in society, and part of that role is to hold and share the knowledge of how to live in right-relationship with each other. By knowing the Patterns, we might be able to nudge our family, workplace, or other groups that we belong to, towards healthier ways of being. Or, we may not be able to, for sometimes people in groups do not want to change. In that case, though, if we just try to model our own lives and behaviour on the healthy Patterns, then we will have done enough. We will have done the only good thing that, in the end, anyone can do. We will have tried to live an honourable Human life. And when death comes, we will be an honourable ancestor.

Getting Ready to Meet your Tribe

As well as their relevance to our daily lives, and potentially to the groups we belong, the Patterns can be of great help when it comes to meeting our lower-world Tribe. They can help us hollow-out from our own history of family and groups, and from the Taker cult's dysfunctional stories of how groups should be, so that we do not take those things with us into the lower-world and allow them to distort what we find there. The Patterns also help us to know what a healthy Tribe is like, so that we know what we are looking for when we journey. To help with this, then, there are four exercises below, in preparation for the journey to meet your Tribe.

Exercise 15: Reflecting on your Childhood Experience of Family and School

The intent of this exercise is to honestly face the pattern of relationships we experienced in childhood. You will probably get the most out of this exercise if you write it down as you do it, rather than just doing it in your head.

Think back to your childhood. Go through each of the Patterns in turn. With each one, as honestly as you can, reflect on whether that healthy Pattern was present or not in your family as you grew up. Remember, it is not being disloyal or judgemental to write that a Pattern was missing or broken. It is just facing things as they were.

After doing this with your family, do the same thing with your experience of school, reflecting on each of the Patterns in turn (some may not be applicable to school, of course).

Exercise 16: Reflecting on how you Coped with Family and School

Having honestly faced and reflected on your childhood experience of group, this next exercise is to raise awareness of how you *responded* to those experiences and how they shaped and moulded your middle-world self. Again, you will probably get more out of this by writing it down as you do it.

Reflect again on your childhood history of family and school, as uncovered in the last exercise. This time, ask yourself how you responded to those experiences? What role or roles did you adopt, or what mask did you put on?

What messages did you take from them about yourself?

Whatever it was that you shaped into, reflect on how you might let this get in the way of meeting your Human Tribe, and what it is that you need to do in that case.

Exercise 17: Reflecting on your Current Family and Other Groups

Having honestly faced and reflected on your childhood experiences of groups, and the ways of being that you adopted in response to them, this exercise is to bring that awareness into your *present-day* life. Again, this will probably be most effective if written down.

Go through the Patterns one-by-one and reflect on how they apply to your <u>*current*</u> *family situation.*

Reflect on the Patterns and how you behave in the situation. Is there anything you wish to begin to change?

You can repeat this process with any other group you belong to in your current life.

Exercise 18: Healing your Wounds around Groups

If there is anything that has come out of the last exercises you want to change in yourself, you can journey and ask for healing. In doing this, remember that <u>ethically you cannot do anything to anyone in a journey without their explicit permission and prior consent.</u>

Think about the healing you want to ask for. Try to frame it as clearly as you can. As well as healing a wound, it may involve an extraction, a disentanglement, or so on. It may also involve getting help with cultivating healthy qualities (i.e. becoming more able to be vulnerable, more assertive, less self-critical, less of a perfectionist, more kind-hearted, or so on).

Prepare for journeying as usual.

Start the drumming.

Go to your axis mundi and hollow-out. Tell your Guides what you want help with.

With your Guides, go to the lower-world to receive the healing.

As usual, write the journey down on your return, and research it as needed.

Meeting your Lower-World Tribe

The rest of this chapter is focused on a set of journeys to guide you through the process of meeting your Tribe. The first journey is the one to initially meet them, and the journeys that follow build on this, deepening your connection to them. After reading through what is involved, if you do not feel ready to meet your Tribe, that is fine. It is important that you meet them when the time feels right.

When doing the journeys, try to be mindful of the last exercises and what you could inadvertently bring with you in terms of your history with human groups. Try to leave your middle-world history at your axis mundi when you hollow-out.

Exercise 19: Meeting your Lower-World Tribe

The intent of this journey is to go to the lower-world to meet your Human Tribe, and to get some healing.

Remember they are a Tribe of Humans living as they would have before agriculture and domestication. As such, as always with lower-world journeys, there is no metal-work, no domesticated animals, and so on. Be alert for middle-world signs bleeding into the journey.

Remember that your Tribe are Humans living according to the Patterns of Healthy Tribe.

Prepare yourself for doing a shamanic journey as usual.

Start the drumming.

Go to your Axis Mundi and deliberately and consciously hollow-out.

Tell your Guides that you wish to be taken to meet your lower-world Human Tribe. Set off with them to the lower-world.

As always, follow your Guides' lead and direction.

Once you meet your Tribe, introduce yourself to them. Usually, one or two of them will be more in the "foreground" in the journey, and others more in the background.

Ask the names of anyone who seems prominent in the journey.

Pay attention to the details of their appearance—their hair, the colour of their eyes, what they are wearing, if they have any jewellery or tattoos, and so on. Make them as solid and detailed to you as you can.

Notice, too, the details of where they live, the details of their dwellings, the tools they use, and so on (as always, watching for any middle-world things bleeding in, and filtering it out if it does).

Ask them for some healing, or if there is anything they wish to show you or anywhere they wish to take you (staying in the lower-world).

On the call-back, thank them and tell them you will be back. Then return back to your physical body.

As always, write down what happened in as much detail as you can remember.

You may want to repeat this journey a few times, as often as you like, really, spending time to get to know your Tribe.

Healthy Connection with Children, and with Being a Child

If you are someone who in any way had a difficult childhood, then spending time with your lower-world Tribe can be very healing. And even if your childhood was a happy one, there is still much to be gained from experiencing what it would have been like to have had a childhood free of conventional schooling and the trappings of modern-day life; to experience what it would have been like to have been raised by animists.

Exercise 20: Meeting the Wild Children

The intent of this journey is to go to the lower-world to spend time with the Children in the Tribe. There are two ways of doing this. You can spend time with them as an adult, playing with them. Or you can journey and experience what it is like to be a child and part of a happy group of Children. Children who are allowed to run free and who spend their lives immersed in nature. Children who are being raised in a healthy Tribe, by healthy Adults and Elders. Whichever way you choose to journey, the intent of the journey is to play!

Prepare yourself for doing a shamanic journey as usual.

Start the drumming.

At your Axis Mundi, deliberately and consciously hollow-out.

Tell your Guides that you wish to go to your lower-world Tribe and spend time with the Children.

Go to meet them in the lower-world.

Play!

On the call-back, thank them and return back to your physical body.

Write down what happened.

Exercise 21: Showing Gratitude to your Tribe

Think about a gift you could offer your Tribe to express your gratitude towards them. It could be a crystal, a carving, a flint knife, or some other object. It could be something you make yourself—a toy for the Children, a pipe for the Elders, a necklace, a poem you write, or a letter of thanks. Whatever you decide upon, it needs to be an actual physical thing, something that exists in this physical reality.

Prepare for doing a shamanic journey as usual. This time, though, hold the gift, or have it beside you when journeying.

In the journey, go to your Tribe and picture yourself offering the gift to the person or people in the Tribe for who it is intended, with love and deep gratitude.

After the journey, place the physical object somewhere visible and where it will remind you of your connection to your Tribe.

CHAPTER SIX

Wise Elders and Healthy Power

In understanding Tribe, and how different it is from what we are used to in today's middle world, there are a few remaining jigsaw pieces we need to put into place to complete the picture. We are going to look at these in this chapter. They are the issues of leadership, power and equality, and the essential role of the Elders in a healthy community. Doing this will help in two ways. It will again help with the inner-work of shamanism, by scraping away further layers of Taker cult stories and uncovering the deeper layers underneath. This helps us gain an even clearer, more hollowed-out experience of our lower-world Tribe and Human, and so of our own true Soul, too. Second, it helps with the outer-work of shamanism—the role of bringing healthier stories into the world around us.

No Need for Leaders

Most people think of tribes as being ruled over by a chief. Often this is because they are thinking of *agricultural* tribal societies, rather than hunter-gatherer ones. Although these two kinds of societies are in reality very different, it is a common mistake to lump them together. Sometimes it is not even a mistake but done deliberately because it suits people's agendas. For instance, the anthropologist Napoleon Chagnon, in his book *"Yanomamö: The Fierce People"*, paints a picture of the Amazonian Yanomami tribe as living violent lives. Chagnon argues that, in this, they are typical of hunter-gatherers. However, Chagnon knew that, whilst the Yanomami did *some* hunting and gathering, the majority of their food came from agriculture and had done for the last few hundred years. In this time, they had also been re-peatedly attacked by Spanish, Dutch, and Portuguese colonists, who killed them or took them as slaves, so they had learnt to become violent in order to protect themselves. Far from being representative of hunter-gatherers, the Yanomami's story is the usual story of the Taker cult and its effect on indigenous people. Nevertheless (and despite being widely criticised by other anthropologists for his re-search methods, his theoretical approach, and the interpretations and conclusions he draws from his data), Chagnon's book became influential. It is often cited by people because it fits the Taker cult narrative that hunter-gatherer people were "primitive" and savage (all part of "The Great Forgetting").

As we saw earlier, agricultural tribes, even ones that are still animist, show the characteristic problems of the Taker cult, whereas hunter-gatherer tribes show the characteristic positive qualities of the Leaver culture. There is, though, one exception to this I should men-tion. Anthropologists sometimes distinguish between "simple hunter-gatherers" (also known as "band hunter-gatherers"), and "complex hunter-gatherers" (also known as "collector societies"). In some regions of the world, the natural food resources were so plen-tiful that the land could support large human populations without the need for agriculture. This meant that in these areas, there was no need for people to be mobile to find food, and so they became set-tled and no longer nomadic. The result was that complex social structures evolved (hence the term "complex hunter-gatherers"), to manage disputes over access to food sources. Consequently, these societies, although they did not practice any form of agriculture, ex-hibited all of the same problems that agricultural Taker cult societies do, including hierarchies, inequality, slavery, mass warfare, and ... chiefs.

The truth is though that complex hunter-gatherer cultures were ex-tremely rare. So rare that usually only one example is ever given—

the communities of the Pacific North-West coast of America. Occasionally, the indigenous Aynu people of Japan are cited, too. In this, hierarchical hunter-gatherer cultures are very much the exception that proves the rule. Which is why, when anthropologists use the term "hunter-gatherers" unmodified, they are referring to the egalitarian, band varieties.

Another reason people usually think that hunter-gatherer tribes must have been led by a chief is because we are brought up to see the world through the Taker cult's eyes. Until we take steps to free ourselves from them, the stories of the Taker cult are the way in which we both perceive and make sense of the world around us. Most people are so used to society being arranged in a hierarchical way that they just assume that is the way it has to be, and they find it hard to conceive of any other way it could be done. Indeed, most people believe that, without top-down hierarchical government, societies would collapse, and the result would be anarchy.

Despite the Taker cult wishing us to believe otherwise, there is a difference between anarchy and anarchism. Anarchy is chaos, whereas anarchism is order without top-down government. It *is* government, but government through the cooperation of people who are truly equal, without the need for hierarchy. The fact is that hunter-gatherer tribes governed themselves successfully in this way. There was no leader who imposed their decisions on the rest of the group. The result, however, was not anarchy. Remember, no hunter-gatherer tribe would have survived if it were chaotic, as the lifestyle depended on there being a high degree of cooperation and order within a tribe. Rather than being imposed from above, in hunter-gatherer tribes, the necessary cooperation and order was achieved by respectful discussion, and then by reaching consensus. This was possible because the people involved were Adults (and, as we shall see, Adults who were also guided by Elders). There were no permanent leaders or followers in hunter-gatherer communities. Instead, people *temporarily* took the initiative, or were *temporarily* assigned authority, by consensus and according to the task at hand.

The assumption that tribes must have had chiefs comes from Taker cult thinking. It is the wonky thought that hierarchy is the only way of organising societies. It is a thought that is deeply ingrained in most people. So much so that, even if they can see how tribes and other small-scale groups can work in a non-hierarchical way, when it comes to larger organisations, such as large businesses, hospitals, schools, local and national governments and so on, most people assume that hierarchy is necessary. However, even at this level of organisation, there are better ways of doing things than traditional hierarchies, and ways that are much better for us.

As Frederic Laloux in his book *"Reinventing Organizations"* says, survey after survey shows that the majority of employees feel disengaged from the organisations they work for. Obviously, whilst some people do love their work, it is also a common experience for people to love their job but to feel ground-down by the organisation they work for; to feel disheartened by managerial decisions they have no say in, by power-struggles and office politics, by a lack of autonomy and so on.

Hierarchical institutions disempower the majority of the people in them, and there is a wealth of evidence that feeling disempowered leads to things like low self-esteem, anger, frustration, hopelessness, anxiety, and depression. It is not good for the Soul. Given this, hierarchy seems a ridiculous way to organise societies. Especially when hunter-gatherer cultures show us there is another way that works, and one that is better for people's mental, emotional and spiritual well-being, because the truth is that scaling-up from small-scale non-hierarchical models to large-scale ones is possible. In his book, Laloux looks at various pioneering organisations that have already done this. He describes how a non-hierarchical paradigm is emerging in businesses and organisations (in truth, of course, it is *re*-emerging, for it is a rediscovery of the ancient Patterns of healthy Tribe). He calls it a "soulful revolution" in the workplace.

The organisations that Laloux looks at, though, are just the tip of an iceberg. People all over the place are experimenting with organisational structures that are non-hierarchical, or at least *less* hierarchical. These include things like cooperatives, what Jacob Morgan in his book *"The Future of Work"* calls "flatarchies", flat-organisations, holacracies, and more. In these experiments, people are finding that all of these models have their pros and cons, and no one size fits all. Sometimes, in large organisations, there may need to be a balance struck between hierarchy and non-hierarchy. What we are seeing, though, is the beginning of a paradigm-shift, the realisation that hierarchy is not the only way of doing things, and never has been.

The inconvenient fact for the Taker cult is that, for the vast majority of human history, we got on fine without having leaders and were better for it. Given the Anthropocene extinction and the various other crises we find ourselves in, surely it is clear that Taker models of leadership have failed us. There are, and always have been, saner and better ways to organise ourselves.

Power-From-Within

Part of the reason hunter-gatherer cultures were able to function so well without leaders was because their relationship to power was different to ours. The author, feminist and neo-pagan, Starhawk, in her book *"Dreaming the Dark"*, describes our modern-day relationship with power as being one of "power-over" and "powerlessness". Power is not distributed fairly and evenly, but instead, some people have power over others (the powerless). She compares this to what she calls "power-from-within". Characteristic of power-from-within is that, when someone has it, they have no wish to have power *over* others, nor are they willing to hand their power *to* others.

Although she does not directly discuss them in her book, power-from-within is what hunter-gatherer cultures were based on. In those cultures, people were raised from childhood to have power-from-within. Think back to earlier on in the book, about the non-violent child-rearing practices of hunter-gatherers. Not only were children raised without physical punishment, they were shown trust and respect, and raised with kindness.

In her book, *"The Old Way: A Story of the First People"*, the anthropologist Elizabeth Marshall Thomas describes the child-rearing practices of the !Kung, or Ju/wasi, people of Africa's Kalahari Desert. She observed that children rarely cried because they had very little to cry about, and that if they ever were reprimanded, it was done in a soft voice. She described the children she saw in this way, far from being spoilt, as being sunny, cooperative, likeable, and "every parent's dream".

Hunter-gatherer parents did not hit their children or shout at them, because they had no desire to exert power over them. Rather, as the educational psychologist Peter Grey, in his excellent article *"How Hunter-Gatherers Maintained Their Egalitarian Ways"* observes, hunter-gatherer parents trusted their children's instincts. In other words, children were not powerless and dominated, but were raised with an experience of power-from-within, and so they grew up to be adults who felt little or no need to dominate others and were unwilling to hand their own power over, either.

Another interesting observation that Grey makes is that hunter-gatherers had an extraordinary degree of respect for the autonomy of others. They did not tell other people what to do, and rarely would offer unsolicited advice. This is utterly different from the way most people are today. On hearing that someone has a problem, the first response most people have is to offer their advice and opinion. As a teacher, I find that one of the hardest things with new students is not teaching them how to do shamanic journeys, but helping them get the power-dynamics right when they are working with people. By this, I mean getting them to stop problem-solving and offering advice, and getting them to properly *listen* to the person they are working with, instead.

This is why *Therapeutic* Shamanism draws so heavily from the practices of Person-Centred counselling, because the Person-Centred approach is rooted in the principle of respecting other people's autonomy. Rather than offering advice and opinions, it involves helping people explore their thoughts, feelings and intuitions, and in doing so, helping and allowing them to make their own decisions. In not coming from a position of power over clients, but a position of respecting and trusting clients' autonomy, clients begin to discover and trust their own power-from-within. In this, it is rooted in what turns out to be an ancient hunter-gatherer way of being. However good the intentions may be, practicing shamanism (or most things, for that matter) from a position of power-over is a Taker cult way of being.

Before moving on, as an aside, I want to address the issue of any parents who might be feeling bad about their own parenting skills, having just read that last section. To any parents reading this (and I speak as a parent myself), please be kind and compassionate towards yourself. I often think that by the time we truly get the hang of parenting in this culture, our kids are already grown up. As parents, most of us learn parenting on the job. This is because, with our lack of initiation ceremonies and model of healthy Adult, most of the time we were ourselves raised by parents who had little idea what they were doing. By contrast, when a hunter-gatherer became a parent, they knew exactly what to do, as they had healthy Parent modelled to them for all their lives. They also had a whole tribe around them for support, literally an entire tribe's worth of people. Not only that, people who embodied equanimity and the Patterns of Healthy Tribe.

People who did not engage in the drama triangle. People who willingly shared, supported and cooperated without strings attached. People with excellent mental health. They were also living a much simpler life, and one in which it was much easier to live in right-relationship and an expression of Soul. As parents, they did not have to deal with issues of bullying, social media, school discipline, homework, body shaming, pornography, homophobia, gender inequality, exam pressures, and so on. Nor did they have to cope with any of these kinds of issues as a parent, whilst at the same time juggling work issues, mortgages and bills, and the thousand-and-one other insane pressures of being a modern-day adult. Given all this, if you have done an even half-decent job of raising your kids, then what you have done is heroic. I praise and respect you for it and invite you to take some time and praise yourself for it, too.

Fiercely Equal

Hunter-gatherers did not just practice and embody genuine equality, they *fiercely* protected it, too. Maybe, even, it turns out, with weapons. Christopher Boehm is a cultural anthropologist who has spent his career studying human and primate communities. In his book, *"Hierarchy in the Forest"*, he compares human hunter-gatherer societies with those of our closest biological relatives—bonobos, chimpanzees, and gorillas. Boehm observes that our relatives' societies are far more hierarchical than human hunter-gatherer societies were. This may be because humans are just more egalitarian than other apes. However, Boehm finds little evidence for this and points out that many humans want power, and most dislike being dominated.

Boehm points out that all ape societies, including human ones, have similar underlying power dynamics. Some individuals want power over others. If they try and achieve this, a power struggle ensues. There are two possible outcomes. One is what Boehm calls "stable dominance", where the norm is social hierarchy with periodic changes in who is at the top of the pecking order. This is how all chimpanzee, bonobo and gorilla societies are organised, and our present-day Taker cult society, too, of course. The other possible outcome, the one that was practiced by our human hunter-gatherer ancestors, is "reverse dominance hierarchy". This is where, in a power struggle, the members of a group come together to oppose any attempt by an individual to impose their dominance on others.

Reverse dominance hierarchies use various levelling mechanisms. Usually, these include the group teasing any individual who tries to dominate or who becomes too egotistical. If that does not work, then ridicule and shaming will be used, and then disobedience (people will simply refuse to cooperate with the person who is attempting to dominate), and ultimately, if needed, the person will be ostracised or cast out of the tribe altogether. Coming from a place of equality and equanimity is one of the costs, and one of the benefits, too, of belonging to a healthy Tribe.

In addition to these social levelling mechanisms, Boehm proposes another interesting one—the development of projectile weapons. As far as animals go, humans are physically pretty puny compared to the majority of animals we used to hunt. Physically, we are much weaker than our existing cousins—chimpanzees, bonobos and gorillas—and much weaker than the Neanderthals were. Yet, out of all of them, we have become the dominant species. One of the various reasons this came about is that we developed weapons that we could use from a distance. This allowed us to safely take down animals were much stronger than us, giving us an enormous advantage over other ape species (including other hominids like Neanderthals). Boehm points out that it also meant we could take down other humans who were stronger than us, too. We could take out the bullies, if necessary, and the knowledge of that possibility alone might have been enough to keep in check people who might otherwise have sought to use their physical strength to dominate others in their tribe.

How true Boehm's theory about projectile weapons is, I do not know. I wanted to include it though, as, aside from it being an interesting idea, it does remind us not to sanitise hunter-gatherer lifestyles. Although they were not warlike, hunter-gatherers were not pacifists, either. They were, after all, *hunters*. Although they never hunted for "sport", they had no qualms about killing when needed. Obviously, they killed other animals for food and, if necessary, to defend themselves if attacked. Any attempts by someone to dominate in the tribe was *also* an attack, because it threatened the harmony and cooperation on which people's lives literally depended. Because of this, the egalitarian nature of the tribe was fiercely defended and so, if all other options had been exhausted, then any tribal member who persisted in trying to dominate would have been killed to protect the tribe.

Of course, these days, I am not advocating killing people who seek to dominate. We now have a range of sanctions available to us that were not viable options in hunter-gatherer times, such as prison, fines, restraining orders, and so on. The point is not the choice of sanctions, though, but just *how* seriously our ancestors considered the issue of dominance to be. They understood that tolerating it would be a disaster, and history shows how right they were. For the Taker cult is, of course, based on dominance, dominance that has given us endless wars, the subjugation of women, slavery, gross inequality, the exploitation of animals and of the land, and led us to the Anthropocene extinction itself.

Tribes need Elders

One of the ways wisdom like not tolerating dominance was held and maintained in a tribe was through the role of tribal Elders. Alongside the shaman, it was the role of the Elders to be the wisdom-keepers and guide the tribe. Understanding the nature of Elders is the remaining jigsaw piece we need to complete our picture of healthy tribe, so that is what we are going to turn to next.

You may be lucky enough to have had true elders in your life. Powerful and strong grandparents, or great uncles or aunts, or maybe someone outside of the family—a good parish priest, youth-club leader, boss at work, or so on. By "elders" here, though, I am not talking about powerful matriarchs or patriarchs who hold sway over their community, whether as family members, religious leaders or teachers, or other "pillars of society". Such people often demand and command respect, and often it is given to them. In this, they are coming from a Taker cult power-over perspective, and so they are not what hunter-gatherer Elders would have been like.

In our culture, it is often said that we should respect our "elders and betters". However, true Eldership is not something that comes automatically with age (and nor does being "better", either). Physical age no more makes on an Elder than it makes an adult an Adult. In the absence of ever having been an Adult, most elders in our culture are *still* children in adult bodies.

What is an Elder, then? Remember, in hunter-gatherer communities, it is the Adults' role to make the important decisions for the tribe, which they do through discussion and consensus. An Elder is someone who once held that Adult role, but who has come to the point in their life where they have stepped back into an advisory and supportive role, instead. As I said when we looked at the healthy Patterns, Adults decide and Elders advise.

The role of the Elders in a healthy tribe was a crucial one. The Elders were the older and *truly* wiser voices that kept the tribe steady and on track. They were truly wiser as a result of the years they had spent letting their authentic Soul, and the healthy Story of what it is to be Human, shape their middle-world selves. More than anyone else in the tribe, the Elders embodied Soul, and not just their personal Soul, but the larger Human Oversoul, too. They were the people least caught up in the middle-world; the "wisdom-keepers" who most understood what it is to be truly Human, as Mother Earth intended us to be.

The Qualities of a True Elder

What follows is a list of qualities of a true Elder. As with the qualities of Adult, and with the Patterns of Healthy Tribe, in compiling the list I have drawn from what I have observed from my own observation of Elders in both my middle-world life and from what I have observed and been taught in my lower-world Tribe, and from anthropology and psychotherapy, too. As with the other lists, this one has also been road tested over the years in various training groups, and has been modified and refined as a result. Like the other lists, it too continues to be work in progress, and again I am only offering it as suggestions.

A true Elder is someone who ...

1. Seeks to empower other people.

2. Supports the Adults in a Tribe.

3. Is concerned about the Children and about the future generations.

4. Is of service to their Tribe, and still active in their community.

5. Is still learning and fascinated with life.

6. Does not get drawn into the drama-triangle.

7. Knows how to listen.

8. Knows when to speak out, and when to hold their tongue.

9. Has useful skills, knowledge and wisdom to share. Is a knowledge and wisdom-keeper.

10. Understands the Patterns of Healthy Tribe and helps their tribe to not stray too far away from them (and can guide the tribe back to them if need be).

11. Can see the bigger picture and show healthy detachment and objectivity, especially when younger people are getting caught up in egos and emotions.

12. Is respected by others, and respects others.

13. Is largely at peace with themselves and with their history and has come to a place of self-acceptance.

14. Is willing to admit to mistakes made in their earlier years (and takes steps to put things right if appropriate, possible, relevent or necessary).

15. Has healthy self-esteem. Their opinion of themselves is not dependent on others. They do not need to seek validation.

16. Is no longer seeking to rise in authority or status.

17. Has modesty and can be healthily self-deprecating.

18. Is not attached to too much.

19. Is willing to face their own mortality.

20. Has a sense of what is important and what is not.

21. Is grounded and steady.

22. Is trustworthy and has integrity and morals.

23. Is willing to see and face the truth.

24. Is calm, patient and unflappable.

25. Is congruent and authentic.

26. Is compassionate and has a generosity of spirit.

27. Is empathic and emotionally intelligent.

28. Has a sense of humour.

29. Has a sense of hope (is not overly pessimistic or negative).

30. Has developed self-awareness.

31. Can have a positive, healing and transformative effect on situations, individuals and tribe.

32. Has presence, dignity and grace.

Meeting the Grandfathers and Grandmothers

There is something about just being in the company of Elders that is in itself comforting and healing. People often report that being around Elders makes them feel calmer and more grounded, less anxious, more at ease, more optimistic and hopeful. In hunter-gatherer times, of course, being in the presence of safe and wise Elders would have been part of your daily life. These days, though, in most people's day-to-day lives, true Elders are scarce or even absent altogether. In knowing your lower-world Tribe, you can have access to Elders whenever you want.

As well as providing a welcome respite from the modern-day human middle-world, and a safe sanctuary and place to convalesce and heal, spending time with the Elders has other benefits. The more time you spend with them, the more likely you are to become an Elder yourself as you grow older. In terms of the inner-work of shamanism, this means that in the last third of your life, you can embody and experience what it is like to feel free of the pull of the drama-triangle, to not feel attached to the opinion of others, to no longer be seeking to rise in authority or status, to feel not attached to too much at all, to have come to a place of self-acceptance, to feel at peace with yourself and your history. Plus, in terms of the outer-work of shamanism, as with the qualities of Adult, having a template gives us something to aim for. It means that, if we try to allow these qualities to shape and mould us as we grow old, we can begin to embody Eldership in the world, because the truth is that real Elders are vanishingly rare these days, and our communities desperately need them back.

Exercise 22: Meeting the Elders

The intent of this journey is to go to the lower-world to respectfully introduce yourself to your Tribal Elders and spend time with them.

In Tribes that practice differentiation of gender roles, the Elders may be split into the Grandfathers and the Grandmothers. Each group will have their own practices, ceremonies and body of knowledge. In other cultures, the Grandmothers and Grandfathers may spend a lot more time together as one group, perhaps only separating into gender-based groups for certain ceremonial practices.

In terms of who to visit in this journey, though, the Grandmothers or the Grandfathers (or both), it does not matter how you identify yourself in terms of gender when in the middle-world. In the lower-world, you are free to work with whoever you wish and be whatever gender you wish, too. After all, in journeying, you can shapeshift into being a bird, a tree or a waterfall, so shapeshifting into another gender is really not a problem! Plus, as I have said, in many tribal cultures, gender-roles and identities were fluid. In the journey, do whatever works for you, or whatever your Guides advise.

When you do meet the Elders, you can ask them for some healing, of course. Or you can simply be with them. One of the big qualities of the Elders is "being" rather than "doing". Rather than a busy journey getting healing, sometimes just sitting quietly with the Elders and being in their presence can be immensely healing in its own right. This can be especially true if you are someone who has trouble relaxing, or someone who feels they should always be doing something, or who leads a hectic middle-world life.

Prepare yourself for doing a shamanic journey as usual.

Start the drumming.

Go to your Axis Mundi and deliberately and consciously hollow-out.

Tell your Guides you wish to go to your lower-world Tribe and meet and spend time with the Elders (Grandfathers, Grandmothers, or both).

When with the Elders, either ask them for healing and teaching, and/or simply spend time in their presence.

On the call-back, thank them and then return back to your physical body.

As always, write down what happened in as much detail as you can remember.

CHAPTER SEVEN

Healing Our Mother-Wound

"We have forgotten the earth, forgotten it in the sense that we fail to regard it as a source of our life." – Fairfield Osborn

Our Forgotten Mother

In 2007, the Oxford University Press removed dozens of words from the Oxford Junior English dictionary in order to make room for more modern ones. The words removed were nearly all to do with nature. They included: acorn, adder, ash, beech, bluebell, buttercup, catkin, conker, cowslip, cygnet, dandelion, fern, hazel, heather, heron, herring, ivy, kingfisher, lark, leopard, lobster, magpie, minnow, mistletoe, mussel, nectar, newt, otter, ox, panther, pasture and willow. The words that took their place included: attachment, block-graph, blog, broadband, bullet-point, celebrity, chatroom, committee, cut-and-paste, MP3 player, analogue, and voice-mail.

This does not make Oxford University Press baddies. In making this decision they were merely reflecting the changes in the vocabulary of young people. What it illustrates, though, is how young people are becoming increasingly disconnected from nature.

When I was a child, my days were filled with catkins and conkers, hazels and herons, magpies and mice. I knew the difference between a cowslip and an oxlip, and between a crow and a raven. I knew that in spring, if the oaks came into leaf before the ash trees, then it was probably going to be a dry summer. "If the oak is out before the ash, then you can expect a splash. If the ash is out before the oak, then you can expect a soak". I knew the difference between a minnow and a stickleback. I was bitten by voles and shrews. I watched frogspawn transform into tadpoles and then into frogs, and caterpillars turn into butterflies and moths. I studied newts and great diving beetles, and knew what owls were eating by examining their regurgitated pellets.

This was because, as a child, I spent a lot of my time playing outside. In those days, this was the norm. In the 1960s and 70s, figures show that the majority of children played outside, and that 40% of them regularly played in nature. Since my childhood, though, this has changed. These days, only *10%* of children regularly play in nature and, horrifyingly, 40% of children never play outdoors at all. This is in spite of there being a proven connection between the decline in natural play and the decline in children's wellbeing. Antisocial behaviour, friendlessness, anxiety and depression are all known consequences. In addition to the negative consequences for mental and emotional health, a lack of outdoor play is one of the major factors associated with the rising obesity levels in children. According to Public Health England, the physical fitness of children is declining by a truly staggering and catastrophic 9% *per decade*.

We are raising generations of children who have less and less connection with nature. This is not just disastrous for us as humans. It is also terrible for the natural world, for if our children grow up to be adults who are not connected to nature, not even aware of it, then why should they care about it?

When I was young, the countryside was full of the noise of birds and insects. If you slept with your windows open, in the morning the bedroom would be full of moths and craneflies. Since then, though, bird and insect populations have plummeted. Why would children and young adults these days notice their absence, when they have never known anything different? Why would they know that these days the countryside is strangely silent (a silence that to me, is unmissable and terrifying)?

The Mother Wound (Personal and Collective)

In earlier chapters, we looked at how, in cutting ourselves off from the lower-world, we lost our right-relationship with the more-than-human world and turned our backs on the bountiful healing, teaching, and wisdom that is freely offered to us by the other Peoples. We looked at how uprooting ourselves from the lower-world meant that we lost connection with our own Souls, and lost the healthy Stories of Human, Adult, Tribe and Elder. There is another thing we lost, too, something we need to look at in this chapter. In abandoning the lower-world, we lost the healthy Stories of Mother. This created what is known as "the Mother-Wound", and it lies at the heart of the Taker cult.

Archetypes and Stories

To understand the Mother-Wound, we need to look at the concept of archetypes, what they are, and how they operate. The word "archetype" comes from the ancient Greek "archein", meaning "ancient", and "typos", meaning "pattern" or "type". So, the word means "ancient pattern". The great psychoanalyst, Carl Gustav Jung, used the term to describe universal, original and fundamental patterns residing deep within the Human psyche (or, as Jung described it, within our collective unconscious).

Originally, Jung described only four archetypes. These were all parts-of-self and, from a shamanic perspective, all aspects of the middle-world self. They are:

1. persona – the face we show to the world.

2. ego – our sense of self-identity.

3. shadow – repressed parts of us we deny, and which need to be brought into conscious awareness and integrated.

4. self – the adult self that comes about when persona, ego and shadow become integrated.

As his work developed, Jung talked about other archetypal motifs, such as the hero, wise-person, great mother, and so on, and this was then expanded on by other people.

Archetypes appear as themes that are common to all human cultures. As such, they seem to be hardwired into us as humans. In myths, for example, all cultures have stories that cover archetypal themes, such as overcoming a monster, going on a quest, coming of age, a journey and a return, love and betrayal, death and rebirth, and so on. Similarly, such stories contain archetypal characters such as hero, villain, champion, protector, care-giver, trickster, mentor, and so on. There are also archetypal events including things like birth, death, marriage, initiation, dreams, visions, battles, plagues, floods and storms. There are archetypal stages of life, too, and roles we play at different times, including Child, Lover, Adult, Mother, Father, and Elder.

In the later stages of his work, Jung began to see these archetypes as being human interpretations of something deeper and more ancient. He saw that archetypes have a dual nature. They exist not only in the human collective unconscious, but as patterns in something beyond human. There are *Archetypes*, Stories that exist beyond the human, and there are *archetypes*—human-made stories that are interpretations of the greater Archetypal patterns. Jung referred to these greater-than-human Archetypes as "psychoid Archetypes". He said that they are beyond human consciousness (we can only ever tell stories about them) and belong to a transcendent realm. He called the "psychoid unconscious". It is the layers where the self begins to become part of the whole, and where human becomes part of something greater.

Although we have no record of Jung doing what we would recognise as shamanic journeying, Jung's work was influenced by shamanism. Along with psychotherapy, this shamanic influence allowed Jung to explore the places where the human-made middle-world begins to give way to the lower-world. These are the layers that lie below the human unconscious; that below both the noise of our personal stories of self, and below our collective stories of separation. The places where we begin to remember we are both *in* the world, *and of* the world.

It was in exploring these layers that Jung realised that archetypes have their two aspects: their deeper and more-than-human pattern, and the human expression and interpretation of that. In this, Jung had discovered the two kinds of stories that we discussed earlier: the original, lower-world Stories from Mother Earth, and the human stories we use to express them. And so, too, he realised what shamans have always known, that the more aligned our human stories are with these ancient trans-human Patterns, the healthier our psyche will be.

The Mother Archetype

It is these ancient Patterns we have spent most of this book exploring, of course. We have looked at the archetypes of Stone, Plant, Tree, Animal and Human, and of Soul, Adult, Elder and Tribe. Jung lived before the development of things like eco-psychology and eco-therapy, when psychotherapists began to realise the importance of our connection with nature. Nor did he live in the days of group therapy, but instead worked with individuals. As such, he stayed with the layers where the individual human psyche begins to encounter the more-than-human. In doing this, though, he found something interesting. He discovered that we are programmed to seek out the Archetypal patterns in these layers. In order for our psyche to heal and be whole, we must find these Archetypes, encounter them, allow ourselves to be changed by them, and then healthily integrate them. This insight is of great help when it comes to understanding the Mother Archetype.

Earlier in the book, we looked briefly at how Mother Earth and Father Sky (or Yin and Yang, Goddess and God, Shiva and Shakti—whatever terminology works for you), are the two great creator energies that bring the universe into existence. They are the sacred Feminine and Masculine, and the sacred Mother and Father.

Mother and Father exist both outside of us and within us. They exist independent of us, as energies that are far beyond what is human. They are also parts of our unconscious we are programmed to seek out, yearnings we need to fulfil. The one we need to seek out first is Mother.

Before going further, it is important to clarify that in talking about Mother here I am referring to the Mother *Archetype*, and not necessarily to *biological* mothers. The Archetypal role of Mother, the ancient Pattern, is to be someone's first relationship in the world, the first thing they attach to. It is also their primary caregiver; their first experience of nurture, love, support, comfort, safety and protection. In this, they are also their first experience of the Feminine—qualities such as being receptive, nurturing, supportive, gentle, soft, loving, compassionate, heart-centred, egalitarian, cooperative, and so on (in comparison to more Masculine qualities, such as healthy detachment, assertiveness, self-reliance, protectiveness, objectivity, and so on). In this, a child's first experience of "other" in the world is of Mother and of the Feminine.

This is the idealised Pattern. How well an individual mother matches that Archetypal template is another matter. It is also important to say that the person who plays the role of mother for a child may or may not be that child's biological mother, of course. Nor does that person necessarily even have to be female, as "Masculine and Feminine" and "male and female" are not the same thing.

Our Yearning for Mother

All of your human ancestors had mothers. As humans, given how vulnerable we are when born, and for many years afterwards, our survival depends upon us seeking out and finding someone to act as a "mother" to us. Because of this, the need to find mother is hardwired into us.

If we survived into adulthood, it means we found someone who at least met our basic survival needs. To thrive rather than just survive, though, we need more than this. As children, we need to feel loved, welcomed, and wanted. We need support, encouragement, good advice, comfort and safe boundaries. As we saw when we looked at hunter-gatherer childrearing practices, this is largely the experience of mothering that children in those tribes would have had. These days, though, obviously whilst it is the experience that *some* children have, it is not always the case.

When Mothering is Good Enough

Healthy parenting is best done by people who are Adults, and by people who follow the healthy Patterns of Tribe. Given our disconnection from both Adult and the healthy Patterns, compared to hunter-gatherer societies, it is no wonder there is so much dysfunctional parenting in society these days.

In studying modern-day parenting, the English paediatrician and psychoanalyst Donald Winnicott recognised the existence of what he called "the good enough mother". People often assume he coined the phrase because perfection is impossible and all a mother can ever be is "good enough". What Winnicott meant was something subtler.

A "good enough mother" is one who gets the balance right between emotionally holding a child too tightly, and holding them too loosely.

Mothers who hold their children too tightly are *overly* attentive. This usually stems from the mother's own unfulfilled emotional needs. In keeping their child too close, they do not allow the child to grow and reach proper emotional maturity and independence. As a result, the child may react passively, remaining overly-bonded to their mother even as an adult, and in a permanently infantilised state. Or the child may react by rebelling against being mothered and grow up to become an adult who finds it hard to be vulnerable or form secure attachments with other people. They may even come to loathe and feel aggression to their mother, and even women as a whole.

In contrast, Winnicott said that some mothers hold the child too loosely. This may result in the child not feeling safe and welcome. They never really arrive and take their place in the world or their body. Instead, they feel anxious and ungrounded, with little sense of belonging. In growing up, this can variously lead to them becoming clingy, needy, demanding, and in constant need of reassurance, or dutiful and subservient in order to buy love. Their boundaries are often poor, and they may hand power away, or try to exert excessive control over their friends and partners in order to try and keep them close. In other cases, children who have been held too loosely may react by avoiding feeling vulnerable. Their boundaries become rigid and they avoid commitment and intimacy. Having not felt loved enough as a child for just being who they are, they may try to find self-esteem through what they "achieve", instead. They push themselves and the people around them, and fight causes and battles.

Within Winnicott's two main types of dysfunctional mother, there can be many subdivisions and patterns of behaviour. These include things like being narcissistic and self-obsessed, psychopathic, angry and aggressive, bullying, belittling and overly critical, timid and fearful, hypervigilant and anxious, dismissive and unsupportive, overly pushy, envious and jealous of their child, and even hateful towards them.

When Children are Hostages

Obviously, these examples of dysfunctional parenting can apply to fathers, too. This book, however, is about the lower-world and our relationship with Mother Earth, which is why I am primarily focusing on the Mother-Wound here. The nature of the Father-Wound is a big topic in its own right, and one that belongs in the next book, which explores the upper-world and our relationship with Father Sky.

I also want to be clear that looking at dysfunctional mothering is not an attack on mothers or motherhood. I say this because, from teaching, I know that sometimes people can *perceive* it as an attack. Sometimes this is because people wish they could make a better job of being a parent. They find being a mother hard work, and feel they are failing the standards they have set themselves. With respect to this, I would remind you of what I said earlier in the book. Given the state of the society we live in, the pressures we are under, and the relative lack of healthy role models and support, if you have done an even *half*-decent job of raising your kids, then as far as I am concerned, what you have done is heroic.

Sometimes, too, people get defensive about mothers and mothering because they think that criticising mothers is something that is *just not allowed*. The reason for this is that, if the parent-child relationship goes wrong, then it has the potential to effectively become a hostage situation and then the child can develop Stockholm Syndrome.

Remember, Stockholm Syndrome is where a hostage is held captive by someone who has power over them. The person in power is mentally and emotionally unbalanced and a threat to the hostage. In order to survive, the hostage has to make up stories to excuse the behaviour of the person in power, stories that the hostage then comes to believe as being true. If you think about it, this exactly describes what can happen in a dysfunctional childhood.

This can be why, even when there is evidence to the contrary, people buy into sweeping generalisations like "there is no love deeper than a mother's love for her child". Or the notion that all mothers must love their children (the truth is that sometimes they do not even like their kids, let alone love them). Or the belief that mothers love all of their children equally (again, this is by no means always the case). Or that once someone has a child, motherhood is something that comes naturally to them (whereas, in fact, some mothers never get the hang of it, and some mothers hate it). Or the story that people tell themselves that their mother was trying her best (again, this is not always the truth). Or the notion that, because of the sacrifices that (supposedly all) mothers make for their children, we must always be grateful to them and never criticise them, *no matter what*. Or the wonky thought that breaks one of the Patterns of Healthy Tribe, the notion that a child's love is something a mother can demand and expect, rather than it being something the mother needs to earn.

From mother to Mother

Think about a baby who is hungry. The baby knows that it needs *something*, but as yet it does not know what it is yearning for. If hugs do not satisfy it, nor toys, nor being sung to, but eating does, then it learns to associate that particular feeling with a need for food. It also begins to imprint on the kind of food it was given. If that is healthy food, then all well and good, but if the child is fed unhealthy food, then unhealthy food is what it will begin imprint on and seek out.

Like our hunger for food, we come into this world with an inbuilt yearning for Mother. We are born ready to seek a mother out and imprint on them when we find them. As with food, though, what we imprint on is not necessarily healthy for us. As children, because we are vulnerable and dependent, we have to make do with what is available.

In an ideal situation, our first experience of the Mother Archetype will come from a physical mother who is loving and welcoming. As Jasmin Lee Cori says in her book *"The Emotionally Absent Mother: A Guide to Self-Healing and Getting the Love You Missed"*, this is someone who provides a place of healthy attachment. Someone who is nurturing, a protector, a mentor and a cheerleader; who gives us the messages they are glad we are here, that they see us, love us, respect us, have time for us and enjoy us. If this happens, then this is what we imprint on and seek out. This then helps us to seek out and form healthy attachments as we grow and begin to take our place in the wider world. In this way, having had the initial experience of a loving relationship with mother, we can grow into a loving relationship with Mother Earth, and feel secure and welcome in the world.

However, if we have a wounded experience of mother, this can distort our picture of the Mother Archetype. This can follow through into our relationship with the wider world around us, and with Mother Earth herself. In other words, if we have a mother-wound, then, until we do something about it, this can become a Mother-Wound.

This happens not just on an individual level, but on a collective level, because our personal wounds feed into and create the collective. If the majority of people in a society have unhealthy stories about the Mother Archetype, then inevitably, the society they create will reflect that. They will create distorted collective stories about Mother Earth, such as the notion that the lower-world is hell and a place of evil. That the natural world is corruption and "lesser", and so we can do what we want with it, use it and abuse it. That humans are better than the other Peoples. That Masculine is better than Feminine, that men are better than women, and that the man should be the head of the household, and so on. These collective stories then *in turn* influence what happens on a personal level, affecting parenting and childhood. In this way, the personal and the collective become reflections of each other, and each affects the other. This is, of course, what has happened in the Taker cult, with its profoundly wounded relationship with Mother Earth.

People sometimes think that things like psychotherapy are self-indulgent and self-absorbed pastimes. In fact, though, the more people there are who heal their inner wounds, the more this heals the collective wound. Far from it being self-indulgent, we have a *responsibility* to the world around us to heal ourselves.

Facing the Truth

If you do have wounds from childhood, and most people do these days, then the first step in healing them (as is true with healing most things) is to face the truth. This means facing your wonky thoughts and letting them go. It includes stopping making excuses for your parents. If there were bad things in your childhood, then it means realising that even if there were good things, too, on a psychological level the good things *really do not* cancel the bad things out. It means seeing things as they *are*, not how you would like them to be or how you think they "should" be. It means stopping telling yourself the childhood stories you invented to help you cope. It means stopping being in avoidance and denial.

Many people tell themselves they had a good childhood even when, by any sane measure, this is not true. It is a common experience as a psychotherapist to hear clients who are new to therapy saying that their childhood was fine, and then see how, as they gradually explore the issue that brought them to therapy (their depression, anxiety, lack of self-esteem, relationship issues, or whatever else it was), the more it dawns on them that the origins of these issues go back to having a childhood that was, in fact, dysfunctional.

There are a number of reasons why people may say (and believe) their childhood was happy even when it was not. Sometimes it is because people do not have anything to compare it with. They literally do not know any better. In talking about their childhood, it often takes the shocked look on a therapist's face for clients to begin to realise that what happened to them really was not okay. Sometimes, too, people may profess to having had a happy childhood because they had to tell themselves that in order to cope, and they come to believe the story they made up: "my mum (or dad) loved me really". Sometimes they may have been told by their parents that their childhood was great, and they feel it is disloyal or ungrateful to think otherwise.

I am not saying that nobody in this culture has a happy childhood, of course! That would be absurd. Whilst I doubt that any childhood is perfect, some are obviously much happier than others. Some experiences are at the good end of the scale and others at the bad end. However, if we add hunter-gatherer cultures into the scale, then things look very different. Even our "good" childhood experiences seldom match what anthropologists usually report about hunter-gatherer childhoods. Like the frog in the saucepan, we accept things as normal these days that are in fact not normal at all.

This is something we need to be willing to see and face, because, as we have seen, what we experience in childhood shapes how we experience and treat the world around us. If we are to find our way back to being a healthy society, then being prepared to honestly look at our childrearing practices *must* be part of that process. As with most things, that means looking to our hunter-gatherer ancestors both as a healthy standard to measure things against, and a healthy template to remodel things on.

Neither Judging, nor Forgiving

If you *do* have issues that go back to the way you were parented, then stopping making excuses for your parents is not being judgemental. Nor is it being unkind, ungrateful, or disloyal. It is simply about seeing the truth, and making excuses just gets in the way of doing that. It is perfectly possible to know your parents may have been doing their best, *and* still acknowledge that you did not get the kind of parenting you needed.

Maybe because of their own damaged childhoods, your parents were simply not that great at being parents themselves. Often, though, people use things like this as an excuse for their parents, in a way that stops them seeing the truth of what happened to them and the consequences of it. For example, people may say their parents never hugged them, or were too strict with them, because that is how their parents themselves had been raised. That may be true, but the reasons why things happened, and the impact of them, are two different things. If you were not hugged as a child or brought up in a way that was overly strict, then that is damaging, *whatever* the reasons. Reasons do not cancel out impact.

Having said that, sometimes it is also fine to judge. After all, there are plenty of behaviours we do judge, and rightly so. Things like child sexual abuse, domestic violence, cruelty, neglect, and so on. Whatever the reasons may be, sometimes people choose to behave in ways that are simply not okay, and sometimes this goes for parents, too.

Another thing that can get in the way of facing the truth can be forgiveness. This might sound strange, as how can forgiveness be anything other than helpful? The answer is, when it is what the author and body-centred psychotherapist Jeff Brown calls "forgiveness bypassing". Just as spiritual bypassing is a way of avoiding dealing with unresolved emotional issues, forgiveness bypassing does the same thing. Rather than face and work through the anger, grief and pain, people choose to "forgive". The problem is that, as with spiritual bypassing, this does not actually resolve anything. It is, instead, another form of denial.

There is nothing necessarily wrong with forgiveness, of course! However, *healthy* forgiveness is a process, not a thought-form that we use to avoid dealing with our feelings. *Feelings need to be felt.* They need to be brought into consciousness and allowed to work their way through both the body and the psyche. If we try and bypass them, they do not go away, but instead become part of what Jung called the Shadow—something that haunts us and becomes stronger the more we deny it. When forgiveness is healthy, it is something that emerges in an organic way from working through the issues. And if forgiveness does not emerge, then that is absolutely fine too. When it comes to forgiveness, the damaging thing is not whether it emerges; the damaging thing is faking it, as that means we are still in denial and so cannot heal.

Your Lower-World Mother

Because Mother is the first relationship we seek in life, if the attachment formed is not a healthy one, then this is sometimes referred to as the "primary" or "base" wound, as everything else is built on these damaged foundations. When it comes to therapy, the problem with working on this wound is that it happened when we were a baby. This is before we have acquired language, and also usually a period of our life that, as adults, we have little or no conscious memory of. This means the wound is an embodied and somatic one, an unconscious one, and so not one that can easily be accessed through language. This makes it difficult to work with through talking-therapies alone. Working with pre-verbal material usually requires therapies that use imagery, such as art therapy, or therapies that focus more on sensations and movement, such as the various body-centred psychotherapies. Shamanic journeying can also be highly effective in working with pre-verbal material, given that it is largely non-verbal, and can be very somatic, visceral and embodied.

Interestingly, the work of Louis Tinnin and Linda Gantt, two researchers in trauma treatment and art therapy, may back up how effective shamanism can be in working with pre-verbal material. Their approach is based on cutting edge brain research, many years of clinical observations, the accounts of trauma survivors, and on understanding animal survival mechanisms. Tinnin and Gantt say that it is the right hemisphere of the brain that contains the memory of pre-verbal times. At the point when a child develops spoken language and verbal thinking, the left hemisphere then dominates and claims ownership of the whole self, suppressing the right hemisphere in doing so. The right hemisphere does maintain a strong connection with the rest of the physical body, though, including things like the digestive, immune, endocrine and autonomic nervous systems. The memories in the right hemisphere then get pushed into the unconscious and locked into the body. The left hemisphere thinks of itself as "I" and dismisses the right hemisphere and the body as "it". The right hemisphere can then only express itself, and be best accessed, through physical and symbolic expression. Given that shamanism draws so heavily on the right hemisphere and is largely non-verbal and symbolic, this makes it potentially ideally suited for healing pre-verbal trauma.

In a shamanic journey, you can go to the lower-world to have the experience of being nurtured as a baby. You can experience what it is like to feel a secure attachment to a Mother, to feel protected, cared for and loved. Because it is non-traumatic, somatic and sensory, doing this in journeys can begin to gently release the primary wounding patterns locked in the right hemisphere and the body. This allows them to relax and find healthier patterns; patterns that are based on feelings of secure attachment, and on knowing that Mother Earth loves you.

In doing this next exercise, sometimes people's history makes it difficult or impossible for them to imagine being nurtured by a loving Human Mother. Sometimes people even recoil at the very idea of doing this. If this is the case, people usually find that they can imagine receiving this nurturing from another Animal, instead. This could be any Animal that nurtures its young, but in order to help the most with the somatic element of the healing, it is best done with another Animal that suckles their young (i.e. another Mammal). So, Animals like She-Bear, She-Wolf, Lioness, and so on. Doing this usually allows people to move onto a Human Mother in their own time.

If and when you are comfortable with journeying to meet a Human, this could be an individual Human Mother in your lower-world Tribe. Or, you might experience what it is like to be a baby being looked after by all the Mothers in the Tribe.

Whether you are starting with an Animal or Human Mother, or Mothers, start off as a new-born baby. This is the heart of the journey. You may remain as a baby throughout the journey. Or, you may experience growing up in that environment of secure attachment, but in this case, make sure you are not rushing over (i.e. avoiding) spending time as a baby. Remember, the primary wound occurs early in life, and so that is the age where the most healing needs to be done.

Exercise 23: Journeying to Meet A Lower-World Mother

The intent of this journey is to go to the lower-world to experience bonding with a loving Mother.

Prepare yourself for doing a shamanic journey as usual.

Start the drumming.

Go to your Axis Mundi and deliberately and consciously hollow-out.

Tell your Guides that you wish to be taken to the lower-world to meet and bond with a healthy Mother.

Experience being a baby being cared for by the Mother. Relax and let go. Soak up the experience.

On the call-back, return to your adult, physical body.

This exercise usually benefits from being repeated several times.

Being your own Parent

I want to remind you of one of the things that was on the list of the qualities of a true Adult. An Adult:

"Can engage in healthy parenting when appropriate (including nurturing, setting healthy boundaries, teaching and protecting)."

You may not have children yourself, so you might feel this particular aspect of Adult does not apply to you. Except it does.

For example, as a therapist, in one of my workshops, a student might be talking about feeling anxious about an upcoming event, maybe about giving a presentation at work. They are worried about feeling judged, or about making a fool of themselves. In working with them, one thing I might do is to ask them to tune into the part of them that is feeling those things. I might then ask them how old they feel that part of them is. Not all of the time, but often, this will turn out to be a young part of them, a part that goes back to childhood. If this is the case, two things need to happen. One is that the child part needs to be listened to, shown love and gentleness, and then told that it does not need to do the presentation. It can stay at home that day. Really, it should not be going to work in the first place.

The second thing that needs to happen is that the person's Adult needs to turn up. So, if the student in question understands what a true Adult is, then I might suggest they take a moment to become their Adult self. Not just imagine being them, but to really bodily become them. For good measure, I might suggest that they sense their Power Animal by their side too, because, remember, a true Adult is not an independent being but an *interconnected* being. Now if I ask them to imagine doing the presentation from this place, the anxiety is usually considerably lessened, and often gone entirely.

So, what has happened here? The answer lies in shapeshifting, and in the child-part getting what it needed.

Taking the shapeshifting first, remember that as humans, shapeshifting is what we do. It is our nature. We have the ability to put our awareness into someone or something else and imagine what it is to be them. We do it all the time—when we are dreaming at night, or daydreaming during the day, when we become engrossed in a novel, are watching a film, are empathising with someone, and so on. This is, of course, what we do in shamanic journeys, too. In hollowing-out, we are stepping away from our familiar middle-world identity and becoming an "awareness" that can then travel the shamanic realms and which we can place into something else, becoming it and experiencing it.

If you think about it, without this ability to shapeshift, things like stories, plays, films, and even a lot of paintings, would simply be meaningless and not exist, and shamanism would be impossible.

As well as being able to think our way into things that are other-than-self, we can also shapeshift into different parts-of-self at different times. To understand this, it is important to realise that our middle-world self is made up of many sub-parts. Most of these are formed in childhood and, until we do the necessary healing, these childhood parts are the ones that we unconsciously and habitually inhabit (which is why, of course, given our lack of initiation into Adulthood and the prevalence of Mother-Wounds in our society, most people really are operating from a place of their childhood patterns).

It is also important to understand that any part of us that carries childhood wounds *is a child-part, not an Adult*. It is a child-part that is variously lonely, sad, feeling hurt, frightened, angry, lost or confused. A child that needs a loving, kind parent to comfort and support it. If your own parents could not be that parent, then it is time that somebody else steps up to that role. That person is you. Your wounded inner-child needs your Adult to arrive and parent it.

Someone else can temporarily help. In many ways, this is how psychotherapy works, with the therapist modelling Adult compassion and support to the wounded parts, so that the client's own Adult can develop and take over.

In fact, your wounded *inner*-child should really be an *outer*-child. Through things like psychotherapy, but also by doing the practices we looked at earlier in the book, in the section "Growing into What you Were Meant to Be", your awareness gradually becomes more habitually located in your *Adult* self, and not in your child-parts. Your child-part or parts then become parts-of-self that you can look after and care for, but parts who are no longer in charge. Remember one of the Patterns of Healthy Tribe:

"The Adults are the people in charge".

This applies not just to healthy outer Tribes, but to our inner-Tribe, too.

Life becomes much easier when this is the case.

CHAPTER EIGHT

Living a Soulful Life

Stories about the Meaning of Life

When teaching, students sometimes ask me what shamanism has to say about the meaning of life. So, one day I asked my main Human lower-world Guide. I was pretty sure I already knew the answer, but I thought I had better make sure. Her answer was, "Ask that rock". At first, I wondered if she meant that it was something to do with the Stone People. I asked her if that was true, and her response was, "Ask that tree". Then I wondered if it was something to do with the Stone People *and* the Plant People, because after all, shamans say they are the oldest and wisest of the Peoples. So, I asked her if that is what she meant. She pulled a face and said, "Ask your cat". Then I understood what she was saying.

With its myth of human supremacy, what passes for spirituality in the Taker cult is full of stories about how we humans are special. Stories that tell us we are more spiritually "evolved" than other animals, much more so than plants, and stones, of course, are not even alive at all. Things like that, amongst all animals, we humans are the ones closest to "God" and made in "his" image, and so we are unique in having the level of consciousness necessary to discover the meaning of life. This is, from a shamanic point of view, complete and utter nonsense.

What my Guide was pointing out was that we are literally surrounded by beings who know the meaning of life. The meaning of life is to be what Mother Earth intended you to be. Rocks, trees, and cats know that *exactly*. This is why shamans say the other Peoples are wiser than us Humans.

When we ask, "What is the meaning of life?", we are asking for a story to guide us and to live by. In that sense, what we are really asking is, "How shall I live my life?". In a sense, this is fair enough, as everything needs a Story to live by. What makes us unique as humans, though, is not that we are *better* than the other Peoples, but that we forget how we are meant to live.

We forget the Story of Human given to us by Mother Earth and invent human-made stories, instead. Some of these are good, in that they are close to Mother Earth's Story of Human. These are the ones that our hunter-gatherer ancestors knew; stories that told them how to live and kept them from losing their way. The Taker cult is full of stories about the meaning of life and how to live, too. Some of these are good ones, in that they are close to the ones our ancestors knew and can help us find our way again, and some of the Taker cult stories are just plain terrible. What follows is one of the good ones. Although it dates from the Taker cult and as such is full of Taker cult imagery, its message is still highly shamanic. It goes like this:

Indra, the Ants, and the Blue-Skinned Boy

In a titanic battle against the demons, the god Indra defeats the serpent Vritra and saves the world from drought. Elevated to the rank of King of the gods, Indra commissions Vishvakarma, the god of architecture and creativity, to build him a great palace. However, Indra's success in battle and elevation to King goes to his head. He becomes full of his own self-importance, and his plans for his palace become more and more demanding and extravagant. As a result, in desperation, Vishvakarma asks Brahma the Creator and Vishnu the Supreme Being to intervene.

Vishnu visits Indra's palace disguised as a blue-skinned boy. Indra welcomes him and Vishnu praises the palace, casually adding that it is the finest one he has ever seen an Indra build. Indra tells the boy not to be so ridiculous as there have never been other Indras and that he alone is the great Indra, the immortal King of the gods. The boy shakes his head and begins to tell Indra about the great cycles of creation and destruction, and the infinite number of universes, each with its own Indra.

As the boy is talking, the doors of the palace blow open. A never-ending procession of ants begin to march through the hall. Seeing the ants, the boy laughs. Feeling the hairs rise on the back of his neck, Indra asks the boy about the ants. The boy replies that each ant was once an Indra whose pride got the better of them.

Another visitor arrives. This is the god Shiva, disguised as a hermit. On his chest is a circle of hairs with a gap in the circumference. The hermit says that each hair represents the life of an Indra. When a hair falls off, an Indra dies.

His ego and self-importance thoroughly crushed, Indra abandons his palace and duties as King, and decides to become a hermit, devoting his life to spirituality. As word of this gets around, the demons begin to rise again, and threaten the world. The danger is such that Indra's wife, Shuchi, asks the priest Brihaspati to change her husband's mind. Brihaspati teaches Indra that, whilst in the greater scheme of things nothing really matters, on another level things do matter, and the importance of keeping a balance between those two truths. In understanding this, Indra accepts both the spiritual life and the worldly life. He takes his place in the world and defeats the demons again, but this time with humility. Balance is restored, and the world is saved.

Spirit *and* Soul

From a shamanic perspective, this story illustrates the need to keep the balance between Spirit and Soul. Rather than abandoning the world to live an ungrounded and unbalanced life devoted only to Spirit, in taking his place in the world, Indra is being true to his Soul, to what he was meant to be in the world. He learns to do this with the healthy detachment and perspective that Spirit brings. In doing this, he accepts and holds the right balance between Soul and Spirit. This is what shamanism teaches—that we must cultivate Soul and Spirit in *equal* measure. Our body and middle-world self can then become the means by which we express our Soul and Spirit and be of *service* in the world.

The More Down To Earth Version

Much as I love the Indra story, it is of course about gods. When it came to translating the story into more human and everyday terms, back in the late 1980s I watched something on television that helped me do that. It was in a series of programmes called The Power of Myth, where Joseph Campbell, author of books such as *"The Hero with a Thousand Faces"* and *"The Masks of God"*, is being interviewed by the American journalist Bill Moyers. Towards the end of the series, Campbell is asked what the peak moment of his life has been. His answer surprised me, as I had been expecting something more obviously "spiritual". Campbell's answer was that his main peak experiences had been as a young man doing athletics. In particular, he describes two races as being beautiful because he was immersed in doing something completely competently, times when everything flowed and came together. He described such times as being when "something has come through in your experience of your relationship to the harmony of being", and that such moments have a message. They can tell you how to live your life. In other words, when you are committed to doing something you are designed to do, when you are being what you are meant to be, then something greater comes through you. You become not just an individual but part of something bigger, and there is a harmony in this, a sense of rightness.

Campbell's answer really stayed with me. It helped me to understand the difference between Soul and Spirit, and that each is as important as the other (and how much we have lost in cutting off from Soul and elevating Spirit above it). A few years later I was watching some athletics on television. I remember watching a couple of the athletes being interviewed and being struck by how completely and fully alive they seemed. They were clearly having the same kind of experience that Campbell had talked about. Since then, I have heard mountaineers talk in the same way, and have had similar experiences myself when I took up sword-fencing—times when my mind disappeared and I became completely in the moment, and part of something bigger that was flowing through me.

Such peak experiences do not only come through physical activity, of course. Musicians, painters, mathematicians and philosophers also describe them. Sometimes they can happen when having sex, or through quiet contemplation. They have happened to me when sitting around a campfire, when dancing, and when listening to the ocean.

What Campbell is saying though is not that it is the point of life to seek out peak experiences. What he is saying is much more interesting. It is not the thrill of such experiences that matter, but the message of them. They are telling you that if you are true to your Soul, to what you are meant to be, then something comes through you. You experience an inter-connectedness, a knowing you are part of something bigger than you. With this comes a deep feeling of rightness, a "harmony of being".

The more you shape your life around your Soul (or allow your Soul to shape your life), the less important the peak experiences become. Because what grows in you is a quieter but more constant and grounded feeling of rightness. A harmony of being that comes from being the Human Being you are meant to be.

The next exercise is to help you to tune in more to the nature of your Soul.

Exercise 24: Knowing your Soul

You might want to make yourself a recording of the instructions in this exercise, to play back to yourself whilst doing it.

Sit quietly somewhere and close your eyes.

Take some time to tune into your breath. Just notice how your body moves as you breathe in and out.

After a while, become aware of any tension in your body. As you do so, with each outbreath, let the tension go. In doing this, let yourself become more relaxed and grounded.

Now, think about your lower-world self, the Human hunter-gatherer who you journeyed to meet earlier on in this book.

Take a moment to get a felt sense of them. A sense of their essence.

When ready, ask yourself the following questions:

1. If that essence was a place in nature, what would it be like? In other words, if your Soul was a place in the natural world, would it be a place high up in the mountains, or a glade in a forest, a wildflower meadow, a tropical beach, or so on?

2. If your soul was an Animal, what would it be? This may turn out to be the same Animal as your Power Animal, or something else instead. What Animal best describes your Soul?

3. If your Soul were a tree, what kind of tree would it be?

4. If your Soul were a time of day, what time would that be?

5. If it were a time of year, when would that be?

6. What colour would it be?

7. What smell would evoke the feeling of it?

8. If it were a shape, what would it look and feel like?

9. What kind of natural sound would it be?

10. What kind of music would it be?

11. If it were a painting, what style of painting would it be?

Activism

"Not to hurt our humble brethren is our first duty to them, but to stop there is not enough. We have a higher mission—to be of service to them wherever they require it." – St. Francis of Assisi

The author and activist Derrick Jensen says he is often asked why he does not run more workshops. His answer is that, as an extreme introvert, being a teacher is a nightmare for him. Instead, he does what he can do to help, which for him is to write. He also says that every morning when he wakes up, he asks himself whether he should write, or go and blow up a dam instead, because he knows that it is not a lack of words that is killing salmon in the northwest of America, but dams. He does then go on to make a strong case for the need for words, too. Personally, I am deeply grateful to him for choosing to write, because he writes powerful words, and we need better stories to live by.

As I said at the beginning of this book, it is nonsensical to ask for help and teaching from the other Peoples whilst ignoring their plight in the middle-world. Doing that is just wrong. If part of the stories of your Soul involve shamanism, if it is how you need to express yourself in the world, then that has to involve being of service, too. Jensen says we need to find the things in the natural world that we love, and fight for them. How we do this depends on what kind of a person we are, but whether it is through teaching or writing, supporting charities, campaigning and lobbying, or the choices we make in terms of what we eat, our environmental impact, and so on, we have to act in the world to help the things we love, and show them gratitude and support. Doing that is at the very heart of what it is to practice shamanism.

I would just add one thing to what Jensen says. I think that fighting for the things you love is best done from an Adult place. The answer to the question "How shall I live my life?" is, of course, up to you. Just as a suggestion, though, whatever else it involves, I would consider including this:

> *Find the true Stories of your Soul.*
>
> *Let your Human, Adult Soul shape your life.*
>
> *From that place, find ways to be of service in the world.*

A REQUEST

This book is the teaching of my shamanic Guides. I give gratitude to them for it, and to you for having read it.

If you have enjoyed the book and wish to help spread the word about Therapeutic Shamanism, then you really can help by writing a review for the book on sites such as Amazon, Waterstones, and Barnes and Noble. Positive reviews help enormously with book sales, and so in turn can help more people discover the shamanic path. A review does not need to be long—just a single sentence or a few words will still make a difference. So, if you could take a moment now to write a review, both my Guides and I would really appreciate it.

NEXT BOOKS IN THE SERIES

Most books on shamanism tend to be introductory guides, with a few others covering specialist areas. To the best of my knowledge, there has never been a coherent, step-by-step *series* of books written on shamanism, books that build on each other and form a modern-day shamanic apprenticeship. My intention is to try and do just that—write a series of books that can take people, one stage at a time, deep into the practice of Therapeutic Shamanism.

The Next Book in this Series is:

"Beyond the Self: Mindfulness, Meditation and Shamanic Spirituality". Volume 4 in the "Therapeutic Shamanism" series. This book goes deeper still into shamanic practice and is focused on the upper-world in particular. Topics covered include:

- The difference between Father Sky and Mother Earth.
- How the shamanic realms are formed.
- The nature of the upper-world and how it differs from the other realms.
- Why upper-world work is crucially important.
- The purpose of spiritual practice from a shamanic perspective.
- Spirituality as service.
- What meditation really is (it is not what most people think!).
- Cultivating the Aware Self.
- Types of meditation practices.
- Shamanic meditation practices.
- Making the vague solid and real.
- Meeting your upper-world Self.

- The upper-world as a place of ethics and spiritual perspective.
- Finding your Spiritual Lineage guides and teachers.
- The "Council of the Elders" and putting right unhealthy relationships and entanglements.
- "Curses" and contracts.
- Working with alchemists, potion-makers, artefact-makers, etc.
- Upper-world shamanic healings, including convalescence, disentanglements, colour and sound healings.
- Meeting and working with upper-world beings such as Angels, Gods and Goddesses.
- Meeting Father Sky (God).

The book is scheduled for publication sometime in the first half of 2020.

Further Volumes in the Series

These are in no decided order at the time of writing this.

- *"Shamanism and the Wheel of Life: A Guide to Seasons and Cycles, Both Inner and Outer"*.
- *Shamanism and the Energy Body: The Shamanic Guide to the Chakras and the Five Elements.*
- *"Soul Loss and the Fort-Holder: Shamanic Soul Retrieval for the Modern World"*.
- *"How to Live Here: Exploring the Shamanic Middle-World"*.
- *"Healing Ancestral and Family Wounds with Shamanism"*.
- *"Recapitulation: The Shamanic Guide to Releasing the Past and Choosing the Future"*.
- *"Head and Heart, Body and Soul: A Shamanic Perspective"*.
- *"How to Grow Up: The Shamanic Guide to Becoming an (actual) Adult"*.

- *"Healing the Mother Wound and the Father Wound"*.
- *"Healing the Lover Wound: Connecting to the Healthy Masculine and Feminine"*.
- *"Death and Dying: A Shamanic Perspective"*.
- *"Shamanic Healing: A Therapeutic Shamanism Guide"*.
- *"Good Boundaries, Bad Boundaries: A Shamanic Guide to Working with Boundaries and Protection"*.
- *"Critic Taming: A Shamanic Guide to Working with Troublesome Inner-Critics (and other Sub-Personalities)"*.
- *"Being a Shamanic Practitioner: Ethics, Power, and Practicalities"*.
- *"The Animal People: A Guide to Working with Power Animals and Other Animal Guides in Shamanism"*.
- *"Bird Medicine: Birds as Teachers and Healers in Shamanism"*.
- *"Plant Spirit Medicine: A Guide to Working with the Plant People in Shamanism"*.
- *"The Standing People: A Guide to Working with Trees in Shamanic Healing"*.
- *"The Stone People: A Guide to Working with Crystals in Shamanism"*.
- *"Sea Shamanism: Healing and Teaching from the Sea and the Shoreline"*.
- *"The Shamanic Lands: Exploring the Meaning and Healing Gifts of the Sea, Shore, Mountains, Forests, Deserts, Grasslands, Caves, Sky, and Other Realms in Shamanism"*.
- *"The Shadow and the Hero's Journey: A Shamanic Guide"*.
- *Shamanism, Counselling and Psychotherapy.*
- *"Shamanic Grokings"* – various books on working in detail and depth with specific Plants, Animals, and Stones.

COURSES, TRAINING AND RESOURCES

The Three Ravens College of Therapeutic Shamanism and Animism

I founded the college in 2008 to teach Therapeutic Shamanism. Originally the college was based in Lancaster in northwest England, before finally moving to its current home in Llandudno in North Wales in 2014.

Face-To-Face Courses

These are at all levels, from introductory days, through to a full practitioner training. Course topics include the Stone People, the Plant People, Soul Retrieval, Rewilding Your Life, and many more.

Online Courses

With the success of the books, I have had requests for people all over the world asking for online training. So, beginning sometime in 2020, the college will be offering online workshops and mentoring based on the books.

Course Information

To find out about the courses, visit the college's website:

www.therapeutic-shamanism.co.uk

FINDING A SHAMANIC PRACTITIONER

The Three Ravens College
Shamanic Practitioner Register

If you are looking for a trained and registered practitioner of Therapeutic Shamanism for one-to-one shamanic healing, there is a register of practitioners.

Although based in the UK, most of the practitioners offer distance work worldwide.

The practitioners all strive to work to high standards of ethics and professional responsibility. The code of ethics is on the website.

To Find a Practitioner

Visit www.shamanic-practitioners.co.uk

BIBLIOGRAPHY

There are hundreds of books that have helped me get to the point where I could write this book. This bibliography contains some of them. The influence of some may not seem that obvious, but they have all played a part in shaping my shamanic journey. Ones that I have particularly drawn on are underlined. Ones that I especially recommend are in bold type. Ones that I both especially recommend *and* drew on for this book are in both bold type and underlined. I have left out details of publishers, years etc., as these days, with the internet, books are so easy to find, and now come in so many different editions and formats.

Abram, David.

    <u>*Becoming Animal: An Earthly Cosmology.*</u>

    <u>*The Spell of the Sensuous: Perception and Language in a More-Than-Human World.*</u>

Almquist, Imelda.

    Natural Born Shamans: A Toolkit for Life.

Andrews, Ted.

    <u>*Animal-Speak.*</u>

    <u>*Animal-Wise.*</u>

Aron, Elaine N.

The Highly Sensitive Person: How to Thrive When the World Overwhelms You.

Baumann Brunke, Dawn.

Dreaming with Polar Bears: Spirit Journeys with Animal Guides.

Berne, Eric.

Games People Play.

Beyar, Blanca.

Soul Retrieval: Unveiling Your Wholeness.

Boehm, Christopher.

Hierarchy in the Forest.

Bohm, David.

Wholeness and the Implicate Order.

Bond, Tim.

Standards and Ethics for Counselling in Action.

Bran, Zoe.

Where Shamans Go: Journeys into Extra-ordinary Reality.

Bremner, Matthew.

How to Be Human: The Man Who Was Raised by Wolves.

Brink, Nicholas.

Trance Journeys of the Hunter-Gathers: Ecstatic Practices to Connect with the Great Mother and Heal the Earth.

Brow, Jeff.

Grounded Spirituality.

Carson, David.

How to Find Your Spirit Animal: Connect with Your Animal Helper for Guidance, Strength and Healing.

Campbell, Joseph.

The Hero's Journey.

Historical Atlas of World Mythology. Volume 1: The Way of the Animal Powers.

Historical Atlas of World Mythology. Volume 2: Mythologies of the Great Hunt.

Historical Atlas of World Mythology. Volume 3: The Way of the Seeded Earth.

The Power of Myth.

Conway, Deanna J.

By Oak, Ash, & Thorn: Modern Celtic Shamanism.

Cori, Jasmin Lee.

The Emotionally Absent Mother: A Guide to Self-Healing and Getting the Love You Missed.

Cowan, Eliot.

Plant Spirit Medicine: The Healing Power of Plants.

Cowan, Thomas.

Fire in the Head: Shamanism and the Celtic Spirit.

Shamanism as a Spiritual Practice for Daily Life.

Crockett, Tom.

Stone Age Wisdom: The Healing Principles of Shamanism.

Day, Kenn.

Post-Tribal Shamanism: A New Look at the Old Ways.

Deatsman, Colleen.

The Hollow Bone: A Field Guide to Shamanism.

de Waal, Frans.

<u>*Are We Smart Enough to Know How Smart Animals Are?*</u>

Diamond, Jared.

<u>*The World Until Yesterday: What Can We Learn from Traditional Societies?*</u>

Diamond, Julie, and Jones, Lee Spark.

A Path Made by Walking: Process Work in Practice.

Drake, Michael.

The Shamanic Drum: A Guide to Sacred Drumming.

Eisenstein, Charles.

The Ascent of Humanity: Civilization and the Human Sense of Self.

The More Beautiful World Our Hearts Know is Possible.

Eliade, Mircea.

Shamanism: Archaic Techniques of Ecstasy.

Forbes, Jack D.

Columbus and Other Cannibals: The Wetiko Disease of Exploitation, Imperialism, and Terrorism.

Fries, Jan.

Seidways: Shaking, Swaying and Serpent Mysteries.

Gendlin, Eugine.

Focusing: How to Gain Direct Access To Your Body's Knowledge: How to Open Up Your Deeper Feelings and Intuition.

Focusing-Oriented Psychotherapy: A Manual of the Experiential Method.

Germer, Christopher and Siegel, Ronald.

Wisdom and Compassion in Psychotherapy: Deepening Mindfulness in Clinical Practice.

Goswami, Amit and Reed, Richard.

Self-Aware Universe: How Consciousness Creates the Material World.

Gredig, Florian.

Finding New Cosmologies: Shamans in Contemporary Europe.

Gray, Peter.

How Hunter-Gatherers Maintained Their Egalitarian Ways. Psychology Today, May 2011.

The Play Theory of Hunter-Gatherer Egalitarianism.
Psychology Today, August 2019.

Halifax, Joan.

The Fruitful Darkness: A Journey Through Buddhist Practice and Tribal Wisdom.

Hanh, Thich Nhat.

Love Letter to the Earth.

Harari, Yuval Noah.

Sapiens: A Brief History of Humankind.

Harding, Stephan.

Animate Earth: Science, Intuition and Gaia.

Harner, Michael.

Cave and Cosmos.

The Way of the Shaman.

Harrell, S. Kelley.

Gift of the Dreamtime: Awakening to the Divinity of Trauma.

Teen Spirit Guide to Modern Shamanism: A Beginner's Map Charting an Ancient Path.

Hartmann, Thom.

The Last Hours of Ancient Sunlight: Waking up to personal and global transformation.

Heaven, Ross.

A Journey to You: A Shaman's Path to Empowerment.

Hinterkopf, Elfie.

Integrating Spirituality in Counselling.

Holmes, Peter

The Energetics of Western Herbs.

Horn, Mary Phyllis.

Transforming the Soul: Beyond Soul Retrieval and Integration.

Hughes, Jez,

The Heart of Life: shamanic initiation and healing in the modern world.

Hutton, Ronald.

Shamans: Siberian Spirituality and the Western Imagination.

Ingerman, Sandra.

Awakening to the Spirit World: The Shamanic Path of Direct Revelation.

Mending the Fragmented Self.

Shamanic Journeying: A Beginner's Guide.

Soul Retrieval.

Walking in Light: The Everyday Empowerment of a Shamanic Life.

Jensen, Derrick.

A Language Older Than Words.

As the World Burns: 50 Things You Can Do to Stay in Denial.

Endgame Vol.1: The Problem of Civilization.

How Shall I Live my Life.

The Culture of Make Believe.

The Myth of Human Supremacy.

Jones, Caroline.

Questions of Ethics in Counselling and Therapy.

Jung, Carl Gustav.

The Earth Has a Soul: C. G. Jung's Writings on Nature, Technology and Modern Life.

Man and His Symbols.

Memories, Dreams, Reflections.

Modern Man in Search of a Soul.

Kahili King, Serge.

Urban Shaman.

King, Juliet L. (Editor).

Art Therapy, Trauma, and Neuroscience.

Laloux, Frederic.

Reinventing Organizations.

Le Guin, Ursula.

The Dispossessed.

The Wizard of Earthsea.

Levy, Paul.

Dispelling Wetiko: Breaking the Curse of Evil.

Levy, Robert.

Shamanism for Teenagers, Young Adults, and the Young at Heart.

Lushwala, Arkan.

The Time of the Black Jaguar: An Offering of Indigenous Wisdom for the Continuity of Life on Earth.

Macy, Joanna, and Johnstone, Chris.

Active Hope: How to Face the Mess We're in without Going Crazy.

Macy, Joanna and Young Brown, Molly.

Coming Back to Life: Practices to Reconnect Our Lives, Our World.

Madden, Kristin.

The Book of Shamanic Healing.

Mancuso, Stefano and Viola, Alessandra

Brilliant Green: The Surprising History and Science of Plant Intelligence.

Masters, Robert Augustus.

Spiritual Bypassing: When Spirituality Disconnects Us from What Really Matters.

Matthews, Caitlin.

    Singing the Soul Back Home.

Matthews, John.

    The Celtic Shaman: A Practical Guide.

    The Shamanism Bible.

Macfarlane, Robert.

    The Wild Places.

Mindell, Arnold.

    Dance of the Ancient One.

    Dreambody: The Body's Role in Revealing the Self.

    Dreaming While Awake: Techniques for 24-Hour Lucid Dreaming.

    Earth-Based Psychology: Path Awareness from the Teachings of Don Juan, Richard Feynman, and Lao Tse.

    Quantum Mind: The Edge Between Physics and Psychology.

    Quantum Mind and Healing: How to Listen and Respond to Your Body's Symptoms.

    Riding the Horse Backwards: Process Work in Theory and Practice.

    Rivers Way.

    The Dreambody in Relationships.

    The Dreammaker's Apprentice: Using Heightened States of Consciousness to Interpret Dreams.

The Quantum Mind and Healing: How to Listen and Respond to Your Body's Symptoms.

The Shaman's Body: A New Shamanism for Transforming Health, Relationships, and the Community.

The Year One.

Working on Yourself Alone.

Working with the Dreaming Body.

Morgan, Jacob.

The Future of Work.

Narby, Jeremy.

The Cosmic Serpent: DNA and the Origins of Knowledge.

Natiello, Peggy.

The Person-Centred Approach: A passionate presence.

Nelson, Melissa K. (editor).

Original Instructions: Indigenous Teachings for a Sustainable Future.

Paver, Michelle.

Chronicles of Ancient Darkness Collection - (Spirit Walker, Wolf Brother, Outcast, Soul Eater, Ghost Hunter, Oath Breaker).

Penczak, Christopher.

Spirit Allies: Meet Your Team from the Other Side.

Phillips, Adam.

Winnicott.

Plotkin, Bill.

Soulcraft: Crossing into the Mysteries of Nature and Psyche.

Pratt, Christina.

An Encyclopaedia of Shamanism, Volumes One and Two.

Proctor, Gillian.

Values & Ethics in Counselling and Psychotherapy.

Pullman, Philip.

His Dark Materials trilogy (Northern Lights, The Subtle Knife, The Amber Spyglass).

Purton, Dr Campbell.

Person-Centred Therapy: The Focusing-Oriented Approach.

Quinn, Daniel.

Ishmael: An Adventure of the Mind and Spirit.

My Ishmael.

Providence.

Story of B.

Rebellion, Extinction.

This Is Not A Drill: An Extinction Rebellion Handbook.

Rebollot, Paul.

The Call to Adventure: Bringing the Hero's Journey to Daily Life.

Rinpoche, Tenzin Wangyal.

The True Source of Healing.

Roberts, Llyn.

Shamanic Reiki.

Rogers, Carl.

A Way of Being.

Client-centred Therapy.

On Becoming a Person.

On Personal Power: Inner Strength and Its Revolutionary Impact.

Scott, Gini Graham Ph.D.

Complete Idiot's Guide to Shamanism.

Scott Card, Orson.

Speaker for the Dead.

Xenocide.

Seed, John, Macy, Joanna, and Fleming, Pat.

Thinking Like a Mountain: Towards a Council of All Beings.

Selby, John.

Kundalini Awakening: Gentle Guide to Chakra Activation and Spiritual Growth.

Sentier, Elen.

Shaman Pathways - Elen of the Ways: British Shamanism - Following the Deer Trods.

Smil, Vaclav

Harvesting the Biosphere: What We Have Taken from Nature.

Smith, Kenneth.

Awakening the Energy Body: From Shamanism to Bioenergetics.

Steiger, Brad.

Totems: The Transformative Power of Your Personal Animal Totem.

Stevens, Jose and Stevens, Lena S.

Secrets of Shamanism: Tapping the Spirit Power Within You.

Talbot, Michael.

<u>The Holographic Universe.</u>

Mysticism and the New Physics.

Taylor, Steve.

<u>The Fall: The Insanity of the Ego in Human History and the Dawning of a New Era</u>.

Tedlock, Barbara.

The Woman in the Shaman's Body: Reclaiming the Feminine in Religion and Medicine.

Thomas, Elizabeth Marshall

    The Old Way: A Story of the First People.

Villoldo, Alberto.

    Shaman, Healer, Sage.

    Mending the Past and Healing the Future.

Von Petzinger, Genevieve.

    The First Signs: Unlocking the Mysteries of the World's Oldest Symbols.

Walsh, Roger.

    The World of Shamanism: New Views of an Ancient Tradition.

Walter, Mariko and Fridman, Eva.

    Shamanism: An Encyclopaedia of World Beliefs, Practices, and Culture, Volumes One and Two.

Weatherup, Katie.

    Practical Shamanism: A Guide for Walking in Both Worlds.

Webb, Hillary S.

    Traveling Between the Worlds: Conversations with Contemporary Shamans.

Weiser Cornell, Ann.

    The Radical Acceptance of Everything: Living a Focusing Life.

Wilber, Ken.

Grace and Grit: Spirituality and Healing in the Life of Treya Killam Wilber.

Williams, Mike.

Follow the Shaman's Call: An Ancient Path for Modern Lives.

Winnicott, Clare.

Home is Where We Start from: Essays by a Psychoanalyst.

Wohlleben, Peter.

<u>The Hidden Life of Trees: What They Feel, How They Communicate.</u>

GLOSSARY OF TERMS

A Guide to Terminology

Ancestral Kin. One's Human Guides from the lower-world.

Animism. The experience that everything is alive and has a soul.

Archetype. A perfect pattern of how something should be. Also, something we are programmed to seek out (Mother, Father, Lover, and so on).

Axis Mundi. a.k.a. The World Tree. The centre of the worlds. A place where all worlds connect, and so a place that can be used to travel between the worlds.

Call-back. A short period of fast and erratic drumming signalling the end of a journey.

Collective Unconscious. Repressed of unconscious material that goes beyond the personal. The unconscious and unintegrated material of society as a whole.

Convergence points. At the very top of the upper-world, and at the very bottom of the lower-world, points where everything merges back into oneness (into Father Sky at the upper point, and into Mother Earth at the lower point).

De-possession. The removal of a living entity.

Domestication, Human. The period starting around 11,000 years ago, where we abandon our wild, hunter-gatherer lifestyle and take up totalitarian agriculture, domesticating not just other animals and plants, but ourselves in the process.

Entity/Intrusion. Something inside someone or attached to them, but which does not belong to them. Can be various things, including an introject, a thought form, an entity, and so on. May be an "inanimate" thing (i.e. "a knife in one's back", "a thorn in one's side"), or a "living thing".

Extraction. The removal of a non-living entity.

Fall, The. The period from around 4,000 BC that sees the emergence of city-based societies, kingdoms, nations, empires, patriarchy, hierarchy, mass inequality and organised religions.

Four Parts of Self, The. The body, the middle-world self, the lower-world Soul, and the upper-world Spirit.

Great Forgetting, The. The idea that civilisation only started around 4,000 BC. The ignoring of the tens of thousands of years of successful hunter-gatherer culture that proceeded it. The notion that we have always been agriculturalists, that this is natural to us, and just who we are.

Great Remembering, The. Remembering how we used to live before the Fall and our domestication. Remembering the wisdom of our hunter-gatherer ancestors. The antidote to the Great Forgetting.

Great Spirit. What everything is made of, including Father Sun and Mother Earth. The aliveness in everything.

Grok. To get inside something and know it deeply, from the inside out. Deep empathy.

Hollowing-out. The ability to put aside one's middle-world concerns, agendas, perceptions, and identity, and become a hollow vessel for Spirit to work through.

Introject. A "should" or "shouldn't", a "must" or "must not".

Intrusion. See "Entity".

Leaver culture (see: Taker society/cult). Hunter-gatherer cultures, where people only took what they needed, and left the rest.

Lower-world. The shamanic realm that is the origin of nature. Characterised by an abundance of animals, plants, geology, and people living close to nature. The realm of Mother Earth. A realm of safety and healing.

Medicine Wheel. A sacred space to do shamanic work in. Usually aligned to the four directions (north, south, east, and west), and made with an understanding of their significance, affinities, and power.

Middle-world. This physical world, and the energies "behind" it. Everyday reality, both seen and unseen.

Ordinary Reality. This world. a.k.a. the Tonal, the Explicate Order, Surface Reality, Consensual Reality, etc.

Neolithic. The "New Stone Age". The time from the adoption of totalitarian agriculture, to the beginning of the Bronze Age and city state cultures—from around 11,000 BC to around 4,000 BC. A time when farming replaced hunter-gathering in many parts of the world.

Palaeolithic. The Stone Age era before the adoption of totalitarian agriculture. From around 2,500,000 BC to around 11,000 BC. A time when all humans lived as hunter-gatherers.

Peoples, The. In shamanism, everything is alive. So, shamans recognise, in the material world ...

- **The Stone People** – the living rocks, minerals, crystals and chemical elements. The first of the People. Next came the ...
- **The Plant People.** Then came ...
- **The Standing People** – the trees. Then ...

- **The Animal People.** Lastly came ...
- **The Human People.**

In the energy world ...

- **The Elementals.** This includes nature spirits (fairies, elves etc.), archetypal beings (angels, dragons etc.), etc.

Personal unconscious. Repressed and unintegrated personal material that needs to be brought into consciousness.

Possession. When a living intrusion takes over somebody ("I don't know what came over me"). Some shamanic traditions will deliberately invite possession by a helpful spirit, for instance, in healing or for divination.

Power-loss. Being cut off from nature and from Mother Earth. Symptoms are the same as those of soul-loss, but with the addition of a disconnection from nature (urban lifestyle, no connection with other animals, plants etc., spending no time in nature etc.). Not the same thing as the loss of personal power.

Power retrieval. To reconnect with nature, the other Peoples and Mother Earth. Can take many forms, but in particular involves a "Power Animal retrieval" – finding one's Power Animal and developing a strong relationship with it.

Power objects. Objects used in shamanic journeying or healing for their properties: crystals, feathers, shields, etc. May be in this reality (corporeal), or not (non-corporeal).

Psychopomp. A shamanic practice to help lost or stuck souls of the dead move on and return to the light/Spirit.

Recapitulation. The process of letting go of the past and of gathering back energy that has been left in past events and interactions, and the reclaiming of one's wholeness and personal power.

Shape-shifting. The ability to shift one's form and appearance in a journey, and experience being something else, such as another animal or a tree.

Shaman cf. Shamanic Practitioner. We are shamanic practitioners. Shaman is a term conferred by one's community, not on one's self.

Shamanka. A term sometimes used to describe a female shaman.

Shamanic Reality/Realms. The realms behind this ordinary, surface reality. Also known as NOR (Non-Ordinary Reality), the Nagual, or the Implicate Order, etc.

Soul cf. Spirit. Soul is of the lower-world and the unique individual that Mother Earth wants us to be, the template for our life. Spirit is of the upper-world and a part of Father Sky.

SSC. "Shamanic State of Consciousness" – the trance state shamanic practitioners enter (as opposed to OSC – "Ordinary State of Consciousness"). Characterised by high levels of theta brainwaves—the brainwaves associated with creativity and spirituality. Can be a very light trance, or very deep. Usually entered through the use of the drum (or rattle) at around four beats a second.

Soul-loss. The idea that we lose a soul, or part of our soul, usually through things such as trauma, abuse, bereavement, co-dependency etc. Symptoms include things like depression, fatigue, feeling stuck, lack of enthusiasm, addictions, a sense of something missing.

Soul retrieval. The act of bringing back a lost soul or soul part.

Spirit. See: "Soul cf. Spirit".

Spiritual Bypassing. The attempt to avoid unresolved mental and emotional issues through ungrounded "spirituality".

Spiritual Lineage. One's group of regular helpers from the upper-world.

Taker society/cult. The Taker cult arose at the beginning of the Neolithic age and the adoption of totalitarian agriculture. The Taker cult wants to take everything and leave nothing. It replaced the Leaver cultures, the hunter-gatherer cultures whose people only took as much as they needed and left the rest. Compare to Leaver Culture.

Thought-form. A thought that persists and can take on a life of its own. May be a personal thought (such as "I am not good enough") or collective, such as "Blame the immigrants", "original sin" etc. Thought-forms may be positive, too ("I am good enough", "It is good to be tolerant and welcoming", and so on).

Totalitarian agriculture. Agriculture based on the belief in the supremacy of human beings and the idea of ownership of land. It is characterised by the wholesale change of the land (clearing forests to make way for fields, for example) and drastically reduced biodiversity as complex ecosystems are replaced by monocultures.

Transmutations. Being taken apart and then reformed in a journey, as a process of healing and transformation. Includes: dissolving into the lower or upper Convergence Points; dismemberment (being eaten by an Animal in the lower or upper-worlds, digested, reformed and then either regurgitated or defecated out); burial (earth); burning (fire); dissolving (water); dissipating (air), cocooning (being wrapped in a cocoon, dissolving to liquid, and then reforming).

Tutelary Spirits. Collective term for one's lower, middle and upper-world helpers.

Under-world. Not the same as the lower-world, but part of the middle-world. The realm of repressed and disowned psychic energies and parts of self, both personal and collective (the personal unconscious and collective unconscious).

Unquiet Dead. The souls of the dead who have not passed over, but who still wander the middle-world.

Upper-world. The "spiritual" world. Home of "aware" human or human-like beings—spiritual teachers, angels, etc. Also, the home of upper-world Gods and Goddesses, and the realm of Father Sky.

Upper-world Spirit. The part of us that is a part of Father Sky.

Made in the USA
Las Vegas, NV
19 July 2023